Get the eBook FREE!

(PDF, ePub, Kindle, and liveBook all included)

We believe that once you buy a book from us, you should be able to read it in any format we have available. To get electronic versions of this book at no additional cost to you, purchase and then register this book at the Manning website.

Go to https://www.manning.com/freebook and follow the instructions to complete your pBook registration.

That's it!
Thanks from Manning!

Tika in Action

Tika in Action

CHRIS A. MATTMANN
JUKKA L. ZITTING

MANNING
SHELTER ISLAND

Manning Publications Co.   Development editor: Cynthia Kane
20 Baldwin Road   Copyeditor: Benjamin Berg
PO Box 261   Proofreader: Katie Tennant
Shelter Island, NY 11964   Typesetter: Dottie Marsico
                          Cover designer: Marija Tudor

ISBN 9781935182856
Printed in the United States of America

To my lovely wife Lisa and my son Christian

—CM

To my lovely wife Kirsi-Marja and our happy cats

—JZ

brief contents

contents

foreword

I'm a big fan of search engines and Java, so early in the year 2004 I was looking for a good Java-based open source project on search engines. I quickly discovered Nutch. Nutch is an open source search engine project from the Apache Software Foundation. It was initiated by Doug Cutting, the well-known father of Lucene.

With my new toy on my laptop, I tested and tried to evaluate it. Even if Nutch was in its early stages, it was a promising project—exactly what I was looking for. I proposed my first patches to Nutch relating to language identification in early 2005. Then, in the middle of 2005 I become a Nutch committer and increased my number of contributions relating to language identification, content-type guessing, and document analysis. Looking more deeply at Lucene, I discovered a wide set of projects around it: Nutch, Solr, and what would eventually become Mahout. Lucene provides its own analysis tools, as do Nutch and Solr, and each one employs some "proprietary" interfaces to deal with analysis engines.

So I consulted with Chris Mattmann, another Nutch committer with whom I had worked, about the potential for refactoring all these disparate tools in a common and standardized project. The concept of Tika was born.

Chris began to advocate for Tika as a standalone project in 2006. Then Jukka Zitting came into the picture and took the lead on the Tika project; after a lot of refactoring and enhancements, Tika became a Lucene top-level project.

At that point in time, Tika was being used in Nutch, Droids (an Incubator project that you'll hear about in chapter 10), and many non-Lucene projects—the activity on Tika mailing lists was indicative of this. The next promising steps for the project involved plugging Tika into top-level Lucene projects, such as Lucene itself or Solr.

That amounted to a big challenge, as it required Tika to provide a flexible and robust set of interfaces that could be used in any programming context where metadata analysis was needed.

Luckily, Tika got there. With this book, written by Tika's two main creators and maintainers, Chris and Jukka, you'll understand the problems of document analysis and document information extraction. They first explain to the reader why developers have such a need for Tika. Today, content handling and analysis are basic building blocks of all major modern services: search engines, content management systems, data mining, and other areas.

If you're a software developer, you've no doubt needed, on many occasions, to guess the encoding, formatting, and language of a file, and then to extract its metadata (title, author, and so on) and content. And you've probably noticed that this is a pain. *That's what Tika does for you.* It provides a robust toolkit to easily handle any data format and to simplify this painful process.

Chris and Jukka explain many details and examples of the Tika API and toolkit, including the Tika command-line interface and its graphical user interface (GUI) that you can use to extract information about any type of file handled by Tika. They show how you can use the Tika Application Programming Interface (API) to integrate Tika commodities directly with your own projects. You'll discover that Tika is both simple to use and powerful. Tika has been carefully designed by Chris and Jukka and, despite the internal complexity of this type of library, Tika's API and tools are simple and easy to understand and to use.

Finally, Chris and Jukka show many real-life uses cases of Tika. The most noticeable real-life projects are Tika powering the NASA Science Data Systems, Tika curating cancer research data at the National Cancer Institute's Early Detection Research Network, and the use of Tika for content management within the Apache Jackrabbit project. Tika is already used in many projects.

I'm proud to have helped launch Tika. And I'm extremely grateful to Chris and Jukka for bringing Tika to this level and knowing that the long nights I spent writing code for automatic language identification for the MIME type repository weren't in vain. To now make (even) a small contribution, for example, to assist in research in the fight against cancer, goes straight to my heart.

Thank you both for all your work, and thank you for this book.

JÉRÔME CHARRON
CHIEF TECHNICAL OFFICER
WEBPULSE

preface

While studying information retrieval and search engines at the University of Southern California in the summer of 2005, I became interested in the Apache Nutch project. My professor, Dr. Ellis Horowitz, had recently discovered Nutch and thought it a good platform for the students in the course to get real-world experience during the final project phase of his "CS599: Seminar on Search Engines" course.

After poking around Nutch and digging into its innards, I decided on a final project. It was a Really Simple Syndication (RSS) plugin described in detail in NUTCH-30.[1] The plugin read an RSS file, extracted its outgoing web links and text, and fed that information back into the Nutch crawler for later indexing and retrieval.

Seemingly innocuous, the class taught me a great detail about search engines, and helped pinpoint the area of search I was interested in—content detection and extraction.

Fast forward to 2007: after I eventually became a Nutch committer, and focused in on more parsing-related issues (updates to the Nutch parser factory, metadata representation updates, and so on), my Nutch mentor Jérôme Charron and I decided that there was enough critical mass of code in Nutch related to parsing (parsing, language identification, extraction, and representation) that it warranted its own project. Other projects were doing it—rumblings of what would eventually become Hadoop were afoot—which led us to believe that the time was ripe for our own project. Since naming projects after children's stuffed animals was popular at the time, we felt we could do the same, and Tika was born (named after Jérôme's daughter's stuffed animal).

---

[1] https://issues.apache.org/jira/browse/NUTCH-30

It wasn't as simple as we thought. After getting little interest from the broader Lucene community (Nutch was a Lucene subproject and thus the project we were proposing had to go through the Lucene PMC), and with Jérôme and I both taking on further responsibility that took time away from direct Nutch development, what would eventually be known as *Tika* began to fizzle away.

That's where the other author of this book comes in. Jukka Zitting, bless him, was keenly interested in a technology, separate from the behemoth Nutch codebase, that would perform the types of things that we had carved off as Tika core capabilities: parsing, text extraction, metadata extraction, MIME detection, and more. Jukka was a seasoned Apache veteran, so he knew what to do. Jukka became a real leader of the original Tika proposal, took it to the Apache Incubator, and helped turn Tika into a real Apache project.

After working with Jukka for a year or so in the Incubator community, we took our show on the road back to Lucene as a subproject when Tika graduated. Over a period of two years, we made seven Tika releases, infected several popular Apache projects (including Lucene, Solr, Nutch, and Jackrabbit), and gained enough critical mass to grow into a full-fledged Apache Top Level Project (TLP).

But we weren't done there. I don't remember the exact time during the Christmas season in 2009 when I decided it was time to write a book, but it matters little. When I get an idea in my head, it's hard to get it out. This book was happening. *Tika in Action* was happening. I approached Jukka and asked him how he felt. In characteristic fashion, he was up for the challenge.

We sure didn't know what we were getting ourselves into! We didn't know that the rabbit hole went this deep. That said, I can safely say I don't think we could've taken any other path that would've been as fulfilling, exciting, and rewarding. We really put our hearts and souls into creating this book. We sincerely hope you enjoy it. I think I speak for both of us in saying, I know *we* did!

CHRIS MATTMANN

acknowledgments

No book is born without great sacrifice by many people. The team who worked on this book means a lot to both of us. We'll enumerate them here.

Together, we'd like to thank our development editor at Manning, Cynthia Kane, for spending tireless hours working with us to make this book the best possible, and the clearest book to date on Apache Tika. Furthermore, her help with simplifying difficult concepts, creating direct and meaningful illustrations, and with conveying complex information to the reader is something that both of us will leverage and use well beyond this book and into the future.

Of course, the entire team at Manning, from Marjan Bace on down, was a tremendous help in the book's development and publication. We'd like to thank Nicholas Chase specifically for his help navigating the infrastructure and tools to put this book together. Christina Rudloff was a tremendous help in getting the initial book deal set up and we are very appreciative. The production team of Benjamin Berg, Katie Tennant, Dottie Marsico, and Mary Piergies worked hard to turn our manuscript into the book you are now reading, and Alex Ott did a thorough technical review of the final manuscript during production and helped clarify numerous code issues and details.

We'd also like to thank the following reviewers who went through three time-crunched review cycles and significantly improved the quality of this book with their thoughtful comments: Deepak Vohra, John Griffin, Dean Farrell, Ken Krugler, John Guthrie, Richard Johannesson, Andreas Kemkes, Julien Nioche, Rick Wagner, Andrew F. Hart, Nick Burch, and Sean Kelly.

Finally, we'd like to acknowledge and thank Ken Krugler and Chris Schneider of Bixo Labs, for contributing the bulk of chapter 15 and for showing us a real-world example of where Tika shines. Thanks, guys!

CHRIS—I would like to thank my wife Lisa for her tremendous support. I originally promised her that my PhD dissertation would be the last book that I wrote, and after four years of sleepless nights (and many sleepless nights before that trying to make ends meet), that I would make time to enjoy life and slow down. That worked for about two years, until this opportunity came along. Thanks for the support again, honey: I couldn't have made it here without you. I can promise a few more years of slowdown now that the book is done!

JUKKA—I would like to thank my wife Kirsi-Marja for the encouragement to take on new challenges and for understanding the long evenings that meeting these challenges sometimes requires. Our two cats, Juuso and Nöpö, also deserve special thanks for their insistence on taking over the keyboard whenever a break from writing was needed.

about this book

We wrote *Tika in Action* to be a hands-on guide for developers working with search engines, content management systems, and other similar applications who want to exploit the information locked in digital documents. The book introduces you to the world of mining text and binary documents and other information sources like internet media types and Dublin Core metadata. Then it shows where Tika fits within this landscape and how you can use Tika to build and extend applications. Case studies present real-world experience from domains ranging from search engines to digital asset management and scientific data processing.

In addition to the architectural overviews, you will find more detailed information in the later chapters that focus on advanced features like XMP metadata processing, automatic language detection, and custom parser extensions. The book also describes common file formats like MS Word, PDF, HTML, and Zip, and open source libraries used to process files in these formats. The included code examples are designed to support hands-on experimentation.

No previous knowledge of Tika or text mining techniques is required. The book will be most valuable to readers with a working knowledge of Java.

Roadmap

Chapter 1 gives the reader a contextual overview of Tika, including its history, its core capabilities, and some basic use cases where Tika is most helpful. Tika includes abilities for file type identification, text extraction, integration of existing parsing libraries, and language identification.

Chapter 2 jumps right into using Tika, including instructions for downloading it, building it as a software library, and using Tika in a downstream Maven or Ant project. Quick tips for getting Tika up and running rapidly are present throughout the chapter.

Chapter 3 introduces the reader to the information landscape and identifies where and how information is fed into the Tika framework. The reader will be introduced to the principles of the World Wide Web (WWW), its architecture, and how the web and Tika synergistically complement one another.

Chapter 4 takes the reader on a deep dive into MIME type identification, covering topics ranging from the MIME hierarchy of the web, to identifying of unique byte pattern signatures present in every file, to other means (such as regular expressions and file extensions) of identifying files.

Chapter 5 introduces the reader to content extraction with Tika. It starts with a simple full-text extraction and indexing example using the `Tika` facade, and continues with a tour of the core `Parser` interface and how Tika uses it for content extraction. The reader will learn useful techniques for things such as extracting all links from a document or processing Zip archives and other composite documents.

Chapter 6 covers metadata. The chapter begins with a discussion of what metadata means in the context of Tika, along with a short classification of the existing metadata models that Tika supports. Tika's metadata API is discussed in detail, including how it helps to normalize and validate metadata instances. The chapter describes how to supercharge the `LuceneIndexer` from chapter 5 and turn it into an RSS-based file notification service in a few simple lines of code.

Chapter 7 introduces the topic of language identification. The language a document is written in is a highly useful piece of metadata, and the chapter describes mechanisms for automatically identifying written languages. The reader will encounter the most translated document in the world and see how Tika can correctly identify the language used in many of the translations.

Chapter 8 gives the reader an in-depth overview of how files represent information, in terms of their content organization, their storage representation, and the way that metadata is codified, all the while showing how Tika hides this complexity and pulls information from these files. The reader takes an in-depth look at Tika's RSS and HDF5 parser classes, and learns how Tika's parsers codify the heterogeneity of files, and how you can develop your own parsers using similar methodologies.

Chapter 9 reviews the best places to leverage Tika in your information management software, including pointing out key use cases where Tika can solely (or with a little glue code) implement many of the high-end features of the system. Document record archives, text mining, and search engines are all topics covered.

Chapter 10 educates the reader in the vocabulary of the Lucene ecosystem. Mahout, ManifoldCF, Lucene, Solr, Nutch, Droids—all of these will roll off the tongue by the time you're done surveying Lucene's rich and vibrant community. Lucene was the birthplace of Tika, specifically within the Apache Nutch project, and this chapter takes the opportunity to show you how Tika has grown up over the years into the load-bearing walls of the entire Lucene ecosystem.

Chapter 11 explains what to do when stock Tika out of the box doesn't handle your file type identification, extraction, and representation needs. Read: you don't have to pick another whiz-bang technology—you simply extend Tika. We show you how in this chapter, taking you start-to-end through an example of a prescription file type that you may exchange with a doctor.

Chapter 12 is the first case study of the book, and it's high-visibility. We show you how NASA and its planetary and Earth science communities are using Tika to search planetary images, to extract data and metadata from Earth science files, and to identify content for dissemination and acquisition.

Chapter 13 shows you how the Apache Jackrabbit content repository, a key component in many content and document management systems, uses Tika to implement full-text search and WebDAV integration.

Chapter 14 presents how Tika is used at the National Cancer Institute, helping to power data systems for the Early Detection Research Network (EDRN). We show you how Tika is an integral component of another Apache technology, OODT, the data system infrastructure used to power many national-scale data systems. Tika helps to detect file types, and helps to organize cancer information as it's catalogued, archived, and made available to the broader scientific community.

For chapter 15, we interviewed Ken Krugler and Chris Schneider of Bixo Labs about how they used Tika to classify and identify content from the Public Terabyte Dataset project, an ambitious endeavor to make available a traditional web-scale dataset for public use. Using Tika, Ken and his team demonstrate a classic search engine example, and identify several areas of improvement and future work in Tika including language identification and charset detection.

The book contains two appendixes. The first is a Tika quick reference. Think of it as a cheat-sheet for using Tika, its commands, and a compact form of some of Tika's documentation. The second appendix is a description of Tika's relevant metadata keys, giving the reader an idea of how and when to use them in a custom parser, in any of the existing `Parser` classes that ship with Tika, or in any downstream program or analysis desired.

Code conventions and downloads

All source code in the book is in a `fixed-width font like this`, which sets it off from the surrounding text. In many listings, the code is annotated to point out key concepts, and numbered bullets are sometimes used in the text to provide additional information about the code.

The source code for the examples in the book is available for download from the publisher's website at www.manning.com/TikainAction. The code is organized by chapter and contains special markers that link individual code snippets to specific sections in the book. See the respective chapters for details about the dependencies required to compile and run the examples.

All the example source code has been written for and tested with Tika version 1.0 and should work with any future Tika 1.x release. Visit http://tika.apache.org/ to download the latest Tika release. See chapter 2 for more details on how to get started.

Author Online

The purchase of *Tika in Action* includes free access to a public forum run by Manning Publications. The *Tika in Action* Author Online forum allows readers of the book to log on, write comments, interact with the authors, and discuss the book. Please feel free to jump on and share your thoughts!

You will find the Author Online link on the publisher's website at www .manning.com/TikainAction.

about the authors

CHRIS MATTMANN has a wealth of experience in software design and in the construction of large-scale data-intensive systems. His work has infected a broad set of communities, ranging from helping NASA unlock data from its next generation of Earth science system satellites, to assisting graduate students at the University of Southern California (his alma mater) in the study of software architecture, all the way to helping industry and open source as a member of the Apache Software Foundation. When he's not busy being busy, he's spending time with his lovely wife and son braving the mean streets of Southern California.

JUKKA ZITTING is a core Tika developer with more than a decade of experience with open source content management. Jukka works as a senior developer for Adobe Systems in Basel, Switzerland. His work involves building systems for managing ever-larger and more-complex volumes of digital content. Much of this work is contributed as open source to the Apache Software Foundation.

about the cover illustration

The figure on the cover of *Tika in Action* is captioned "Habit of Turkish Courtesan in 1568" and is taken from the four-volume *Collection of the Dresses of Different Nations* by Thomas Jefferys, published in London between 1757 and 1772. The collection, which includes beautiful hand-colored copperplate engravings of costumes from around the world, has influenced theatrical costume design since its publication.

The diversity of the drawings in the *Collection of the Dresses of Different Nations* speaks vividly of the richness of the costumes presented on the London stage over 200 years ago. The costumes, both historical and contemporaneous, offered a glimpse into the dress customs of people living in different times and in different countries, making them come alive for London theater audiences.

Dress codes have changed in the last century and the diversity by region, so rich in the past, has faded away. It's now often hard to tell the inhabitant of one continent from another. Perhaps, trying to view it optimistically, we've traded a cultural and visual diversity for a more varied personal life. Or a more varied and interesting intellectual and technical life.

We at Manning celebrate the inventiveness, the initiative, and the fun of the computer business with book covers based on the rich diversity of regional and theatrical life of two centuries ago, brought back to life by the pictures from this collection.

Part 1

Getting started

"The Babel fish," said The Hitchhiker's Guide to the Galaxy quietly, "is small, yellow and leech-like, and probably the oddest thing in the Universe. It feeds on brainwave energy not from its carrier but from those around it. It absorbs all unconscious mental frequencies from this brainwave energy to nourish itself with. It then excretes into the mind of its carrier a telepathic matrix formed by combining the conscious thought frequencies with nerve signals picked up from the speech centers of the brain which has supplied them. The practical upshot of all this is that if you stick a Babel fish in your ear you can instantly understand anything said to you in any form of language."

—Douglas Adams, *The Hitchhiker's Guide to the Galaxy*

This first part of the book will familiarize you with the necessity of being able to rapidly process, integrate, compare, and most importantly *understand* the variety of content available in the digital world. Likely you've encountered only a subset of the thousands of media types that exist (PDF, Word, Excel, HTML, just to name a few), and you likely need dozens of applications to read each type, edit and add text to it, view the text, copy and paste between documents, and include that information in your software programs (if you're a programmer geek like us).

We'll try to help you tackle this problem by introducing you to Apache Tika—a software framework focused on automatic media type identification, text extraction, and metadata extraction. Our goal for this part of the book is to equip you with historical knowledge (Tika's motivation, history, and inception), practical knowledge (how to download and install it and leverage Tika in your application), and the steps required to start using Tika to deal with the proliferation of files available at your fingertips.

The case for the digital Babel fish

This chapter covers

- Understanding documents
- Parsing documents
- Introducing Apache Tika

The Babel fish in Douglas Adams' book *The Hitchhiker's Guide to the Galaxy* is a universal translator that allows you to understand all the languages in the world. It feeds on data that would otherwise be incomprehensible, and produces an understandable translation. This is essentially what Apache Tika, a nascent technology available from the Apache Software Foundation, does for digital documents. Just like the protagonist Arthur Dent, who after inserting a Babel fish in his ear could understand Vogon poetry, a computer program that uses Tika can extract text and objects from Microsoft Word documents and all sorts of other files. Our goal in this book is to equip you with enough understanding of Tika's architecture, implementation, extension points, and philosophy that the process of making your programs file-agnostic is equally simple.

In the remainder of this chapter, we'll familiarize you with the importance of understanding the vast array of content that has sprung up as a result of the information age. PDF files, Microsoft Office files (including Word, Excel, PowerPoint, and so on), images, text, binary formats, and more are a part of today's digital lingua franca, as are the applications tasked to handle such formats. We'll discuss this issue and modern attempts to classify and understand these file formats (such as those from the Internet Assigned Numbers Authority, IANA) and the relationships of those frameworks to Tika. After motivating Tika, we'll discuss its core `Parser` interface and its use in obtaining text for processing. Beyond the nuts and bolts of this discussion, we'll provide a brief history of Tika, along with an overview of its architecture, when and where to use Tika, and a brief example of Tika's utility.

In the next section, we'll introduce you to the existing work by IANA on classifying all the file formats out there and how Tika makes use of this classification to easily understand those formats.

1.1 Understanding digital documents

The world of digital documents and their file formats is like a universe where everyone speaks a different language. Most programs only understand their own file formats or a small set of related formats, as depicted in figure 1.1. Translators such as import modules or display plugins are usually required when one program needs to understand documents produced by another program.

There are literally thousands of different file formats in use, and most of those formats come in various different versions and dialects. For example, the widely used PDF format has evolved through eight incremental versions and various extensions over the past 18 years. Even the adoption of generic file formats such as XML has done little to unify the world of data. Both the Office Open XML format used by recent versions of Microsoft Office and the OpenDocument format used by OpenOffice.org are XML-based formats for office documents, but programs written to work with one of these formats still need special converters to understand the other format.

Luckily most programs never need to worry about this proliferation of file formats. Just like you only need to understand the language used by the people you speak with, a program only needs to understand the formats of the files it works with. The trouble begins when you're trying to build an application that's supposed to understand most of the widely used file formats.

For example, suppose you've been asked to implement a search engine that can find any document on a shared network drive based on the file contents. You browse around and find Excel sheets, PDF and Word documents, text files, images and audio in a dozen different formats, PowerPoint presentations, some OpenOffice files, HTML and Flash videos, and a bunch of Zip archives that contain more documents inside them. You probably have all the programs you need for accessing each one of these file formats, but when there are thousands or perhaps millions of files, it's not feasible for you to manually open them all and copy-paste the contained text to the search engine for indexing. You need a program that can do this for you, but how would you write such a program?

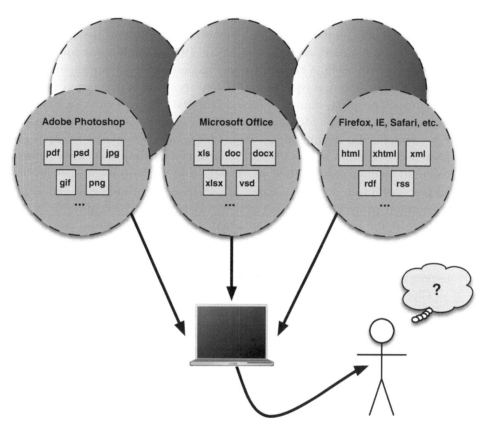

Figure 1.1 Computer programs usually specialize in reading and interpreting only one file format (or family of formats). To deal with .pdf files, .psd files, and the like, you'd purchase Adobe products. If you needed to deal with Microsoft Office files (.doc, .xls, and so on), you'd turn to Microsoft products or other office programs that support these Microsoft formats. Few programs can understand all of these formats.

The first step in developing such a program is to understand the properties of the proliferation of file formats that exist. To do this we'll leverage the taxonomy of file formats specified in the Multipurpose Internet Mail Extensions (MIME) standard and maintained by the IANA.

1.1.1 A taxonomy of file formats

In order to write the aforementioned search engine, you must understand the various file formats and the methodologies that they employ for storing text and information. The first step is being able to identify and differentiate between the various file types. Most of us understand commonly used terms like *spreadsheet* or *web page*, but such terms aren't accurate enough for use by computer programs. Traditionally extra information in the form of filename suffixes such as .xls or .html, resource forks in Mac OS, and other mechanisms have been used to identify the format of a file. Unfortunately these mechanisms are often tied to specific operating systems or installed applications, which makes them difficult to use reliably in network environments such as the internet.

The MIME standard was published in late 1996 as the Request for Comment (RFC) documents 2045–2049. A key concept of this standard is the notion of *media types*[1] that uniquely name different types of data so that receiving applications can "deal with the data in an appropriate manner." Section 5 of RFC 2045 specifies that a media type consists of a `type/subtype` identifier and a set of optional `attribute=value` parameters. For example, the default media type `text/plain; charset=us-ascii` identifies a plain-text document in the US-ASCII character encoding. RFC 2046 defines a set of common media types and their parameters, and since no single specification can list all past and future document types, RFC 2048 and the update in RFC 4288 specify a registration procedure by which new media types can be registered at IANA. As of early 2010, the official registry[2] contained more than a thousand media types such as `text/html`, `image/jpeg`, and `application/msword`, organized under the eight top-level types shown in figure 1.2. Thousands of unregistered media types such as `image/x-icon` and `application/vnd.amazon.ebook` are also being used.

Given that thousands of media types have already been classified by IANA and others, programmers need the ability to automatically incorporate this knowledge into their software applications (imagine building a collection of utensils in your kitchen without knowing that pots were used to cook sauces, or that kettles brewed tea, or that knives cut meat!). Luckily Tika provides state-of-the-art facilities in automatic media type detection. Tika takes a multipronged approach to automatic detection of media types as shown in table 1.1.

We're only scratching the surface of Tika's MIME detection patterns here. For more information on automatic media type detection, jump to chapter 4.

Now that you're familiar with differentiating between different file types, how do you make use of a file once you've identified it? In the next section, we'll describe parser libraries, used to extract information from the underlying file types. There are a number of these parser libraries, and as it turns out, Tika excels (no pun intended) at abstracting away their heterogeneity, making them easy to incorporate and use in your application.

1.1.2 Parser libraries

To be able to extract information from a digital document, you need to understand the document format. Such understanding is built into the applications designed to

---

[1] Though often referred to as MIME type, the MIME standard in reality was focused on extending email to support different extensions, including non-text attachments and multipart requests. The use of MIME has since grown to cover the array of media types, including PDF, Office, and non-email-centric extensions. Although the use of MIME type is ubiquitous, in this book, we use *MIME type* and the more historically correct *media type* interchangeably.

[2] The official MIME media type registry is available at http://www.iana.org/assignments/media-types/.

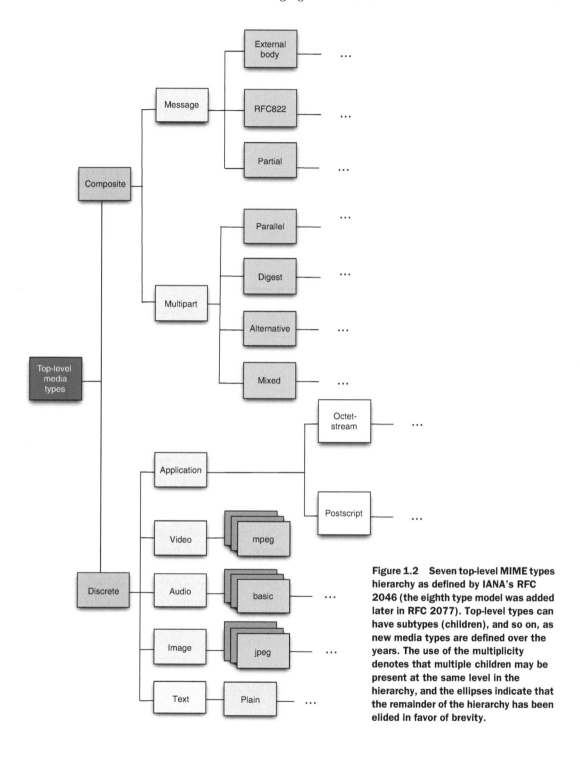

Figure 1.2 **Seven top-level MIME types hierarchy as defined by IANA's RFC 2046 (the eighth type model was added later in RFC 2077). Top-level types can have subtypes (children), and so on, as new media types are defined over the years. The use of the multiplicity denotes that multiple children may be present at the same level in the hierarchy, and the ellipses indicate that the remainder of the hierarchy has been elided in favor of brevity.**

Table 1.1 Tika's main methods of media type detection. These techniques can be performed in isolation or combined together to formulate a powerful and comprehensive automatic file detection mechanism.

Detection mechanism	Description
File extension, filename, or alias	Each media type in Tika has a *glob* pattern associated with it, which can be a Java regular expression or a simple file extension, such as *.pdf or *.doc (see http://mng.bz/pNgw).
Magic bytes	Most files belonging to a media type family have a unique signature associated with them in the form of a set of control bytes in the file header. Each media type in Tika defines different sequences of these control bytes, as well as offsets used to define scanning patterns to locate these bytes within the file.
XML root characters	XML files, unique as they are, include hints that suggest their true media type. Outer XML tags (called *root elements*), namespaces, and referenced schemas are some of the clues that Tika uses to determine an XML file's real type (RDF, RSS, and so on).
Parent and children media types	By leveraging the hierarchy shown in figure 1.2, Tika can determine the most accurate and precise media type for a piece of content, and fall back on parent types if the precise child isn't detectable.

work with specific kinds of documents. For example, the Microsoft Office suite is used for reading and writing Word documents, whereas Adobe Acrobat and Acrobat Reader do the same for PDF documents. These applications are normally designed for human interaction and usually don't allow other programs to easily access document content. And even if programmatic access is possible, these applications typically can't be run in server environments.

An alternative approach is to implement or use a parser library for the document format. A *parser library* is a reusable piece of software designed to enable applications to read and often also write documents in a specific format (as will be shown in figure 1.3, it's the software that allows text and other information to be extracted from files). The library abstracts the document format to an API that's easier to understand and use than raw byte patterns. For example, instead of having to deal with things such as CRC checksums, compression methods, and various other details, an application that uses the java.util.zip parser library package included in the standard Java class library can simply use concepts such as ZipFile and ZipEntry, as shown in the following example that outputs the names of all of the entries within a Zip file:

```
public static void listZipEntries(String path) throws IOException {
    ZipFile zip = new ZipFile(path);
    for (ZipEntry entry : Collections.list(zip.entries())) {
        System.out.println(entry.getName());
    }
}
```

In addition to Zip file support, the standard Java class library and official extensions include support for many file formats, ranging from plain text and XML to various image, audio, video, and message formats. Other advanced programming languages and platforms have similar built-in capabilities. But most document formats aren't supported, and even APIs for the supported formats are often designed for specific use cases and fail to cover the full range of features required by many applications. Many open source and commercial libraries are available to address the needs of such applications. For example, the widely used Apache PDFBox (http://pdfbox .apache.org/) and POI (http://poi.apache.org/) libraries implement comprehensive support for PDF and Microsoft Office documents.

> **THE WONDERFUL WORLD OF APIS** *APIs,* or *application programming interfaces,* are interfaces that applications use to communicate with each other. In object-oriented frameworks and libraries, APIs are typically the recommended means of providing functionality that clients of those frameworks can consume. For example, if you're writing code in Java to read and/or process a file, you're likely using `java.io.*` and its set of objects (such as `java.io .File`) and its associated sets of methods (`canWrite`, for example), that together make up Java's IO API.

Thanks to parser libraries, building an application that can understand multiple different file formats is no longer an insurmountable task. But lots of complexity is still to be covered, starting with understanding the variety of licensing and patent constraints on the use of different libraries and document formats. The other big problem with the myriad available parser libraries is that they all have their own APIs designed for each individual document format. Writing an application that uses more than a few such libraries requires a lot of effort learning how to best use each library. What's needed is a unified parsing API to which all the various parser APIs could be adapted. Such an API would essentially be a universal language of digital documents.

In the ensuing section, we'll make a case for that universal language of digital documents, describing the lowest common denominator in that vocabulary: structured text.

1.1.3 *Structured text as the universal language*

Though the number of multimedia documents is rising, most of the interesting information in digital documents is still numeric or textual. These are also the forms of data that current computers and computing algorithms are best equipped to handle. The known search, classification, analysis, and many other automated processing tools for numeric and textual data are far beyond our current best understanding of how to process audio, image, or video data. Since numbers are also easy to express as text, being able to access any document as a stream of text is probably the most useful abstraction that a unified parser API could offer. Though plain text is obviously close to a least common denominator as a document abstraction, it still enables a lot of useful applications to be built on top of it. For example, a search engine or a semantic classification tool only needs access to the text content of a document.

A plain text stream, as useful as it is, falls short of satisfying the requirements of many use cases that would benefit from a bit of extra information. For example, all the modern internet search engines leverage not only the text content of the documents they find on the net but also the links between those documents. Many modern document formats express such information as hyperlinks that connect a specific word, phrase, image or other part of a document to another document. It'd be useful to be able to accurately express such information in a uniform way for all documents. Other useful pieces of information are things such as paragraph boundaries, headings, and emphasized words and sentences in a document.

Most document formats express such structural information in one way or another (an example is shown in figure 1.3), even if it's only encoded as instructions like "insert extra vertical space between these pieces of text" or "use a larger font for that sentence." When such information is available, being able to annotate the plain text stream with semantically meaningful structure would be a clear improvement. For example, a web page such as ESPN.com typically codifies its major news categories using instructions encoded via HTML list (`<li>`) tags, along with Cascading Style Sheets (CSS) classes to indicate their importance as top-level news categories.

Such structural annotations should ideally be well known and easy to understand, and it should be easy for applications that don't need or care about the extra information to focus on just the unstructured stream of text. XML and HTML are the best-known and most widely used document formats that satisfy all these requirements. Both support annotating plain text with structural information, and whereas XML offers a well-defined and easy-to-automate processing model, HTML defines a set of semantic document elements that almost everyone in the computing industry knows and understands. The XHTML standard combines these advantages, and thus provides an ideal basis for a universal document language that can express most of the interesting information from a majority of the currently used document formats. XHTML is what Tika leverages to represent structured text extracted from documents.

1.1.4 Universal metadata

Metadata, or "data about data," as it's commonly defined, provides information that can aid in understanding documents independent of their media type. Metadata includes information that's often pre-extracted, and stored either together with the particular file, or stored in some registry available externally to it (when the file has an entry associated with it in some external registry). Since metadata is almost always less voluminous than the data itself (by orders of magnitude in most cases), it's a preferable asset in making decisions about what to do with files during analysis. The actionable information in metadata can range from the mundane (file size, location, checksum, data provider, original location, version) to the sophisticated (start/end data range, start/end time boundaries, algorithm used to process the data, and so forth) and the richness of the metadata is typically dictated by the media type and its choice of *metadata model(s)* that it employs.

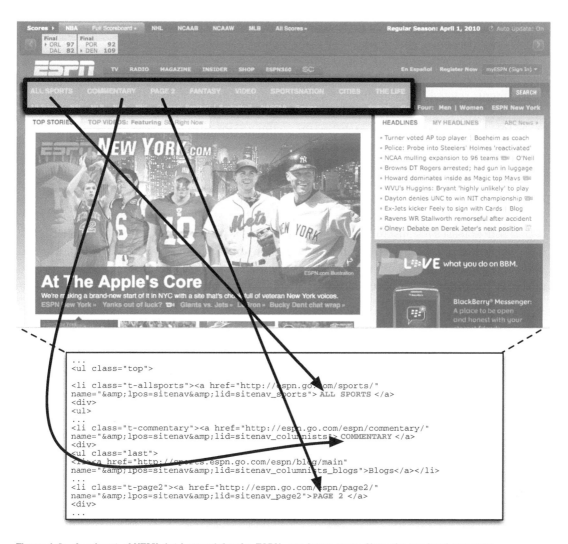

Figure 1.3   A snippet of HTML (at bottom) for the ESPN.com home page. Note the top-level category headings for sports (All Sports, Commentary, Page 2) are all surrounded by `<li>` HTML tags that are styled by a particular CSS class. This type of structural information about a content type can be exploited and codified using the notion of structured text.

One widely accepted metadata model is the Dublin Core standard (http://dublin-core.org/) for the description of electronic resources. Dublin Core defines a set of 15 data elements (read *attributes*) that are said to sufficiently describe any electronic resource. These elements include attributes for data format (HDF, PDF, netCDF, Word 2003, and so on), title, subject, publisher language, and other elements. Though a sound option, many users have felt that Dublin Core (which grew out of the digital library/library science community) is too broad and open to interpretation to be as expressive as it purports.

Metadata models can be broad (as is the case for Dublin Core), or narrow, focused on a particular community—or some hybrid combination of the two. The *Extensible Metadata Platform (XMP)* defined by Adobe is a combined metadata model that contains core elements (including those defined by Dublin Core), domain-specific elements related to Photoshop files, images, and more, as well as the ability for users to use their own metadata schemas. As another example, the recently developed *Climate Forecast (CF)* metadata model describes climate models and observational data in the Earth science community. CF, though providing limited extensibility, is primarily focused on a single community (climate researchers and modelers) and is narrowly focused when compared with the likes of Dublin Core or XMP.

Most times, the metadata for a particular file format will be influenced by existing metadata models, likely starting with basic file metadata and then getting more specific, with at least a few instances of metadata pertaining to that type (Photoshop-specific, CF-specific, and so on). This is illustrated in figure 1.4, where three example sets of metadata driven by three metadata models are used to describe an image of Mars.

In order to support the heterogeneity of metadata models, their different attributes, and different foci, Tika has evolved to allow users to either accept default metadata elements conforming to a set of core models (Dublin Core, models focused on document types such as Microsoft Word models, and so forth) supported out of the box, or to define their own metadata schema and integrate them into Tika seamlessly. In addition, Tika doesn't dictate how or where metadata is extracted within the overall

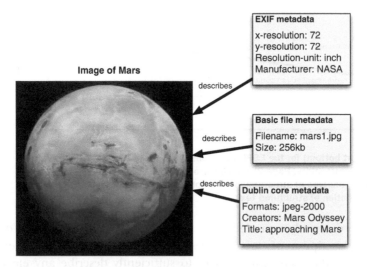

Figure 1.4 An image of Mars (the data), and the metadata (data about data) that describes it. Three sets of metadata are shown, and each set of metadata is influenced by metadata models that prescribe what vocabularies are possible, what the valid values are, what the definitions of the names are, and so on. In this example, the metadata ranges from basic (file metadata like filename) to image-specific (EXIF metadata like resolution-unit).

content understanding process, as this decision is typically closely tied to both the metadata model(s) employed and the overall analysis workflow, and is thus best left up to the user.

Coupled with the ability to flexibly extract metadata comes the realization that not all content on the web, or in a particular software application, is of the same language. Consider a software application that integrates planetary rock image data sets from NASA's Mars Exploration Rover (MER) mission with data from the European Space Agency's Mars Express orbiter and its High Resolution Stereo Camera (HRSC) instrument, which captures full maps of the entire planet at 10m resolution. Consider that some of the earliest full planet data sets are directly available from HRSC's principal investigator—a center in Berlin—and contain information encoded in the German language. On the other hand, data available from MER is captured in plain English. To even determine that these two data sets are related, and that they can be correlated, requires reading lengthy abstracts describing the science that each instrument and mission is capturing, and ultimately understanding the languages in which each data set is recorded. Tika again comes to the rescue in this situation, as it provides a language identification component that implements sophisticated techniques including N-grams that assist in language detection.

More information on structured text, metadata extraction, and language identification is given in chapter 6. Now that we've covered the complexity of dealing with the abundance of file formats, identifying them, and doing something with them (such as parsing them and extracting their metadata), it's time to bring Tika to the forefront and show you how it can alleviate much or all of the complexity induced by the modern information landscape.

1.1.5 *The program that understands everything*

Armed with the knowledge that Tika can help us navigate the modern information ecosystem, let's revisit the search engine example we considered earlier, depicted graphically in figure 1.5. Imagine that you're tasked with the construction of a local search application whose responsibility is to identify PDF, Word, Excel, and audio documents available via a shared network drive, and to index those documents' locations and metadata for use in a web-based company intranet search appliance.

Knowing what you know now about Tika, the steps required to construct this search engine may go something like the following. First, you leverage a crawling application that gathers the pointers to the available documents on the shared network drive (depending on your operating system, this may be as simple as a fancy call to `ls` or `find`). Second, after collecting the set of pointers to files of interest, you iterate over that set and then determine each file's media type using Tika (as shown in the middle-right portion of figure 1.5). Once the file's media type is identified, a suitable parser can be selected (in the case of PDF files, Apache's PDFBox), and then used by Tika to provide both the extracted textual content (useful for keyword search, summarizing and ranking, and potentially other search functions such as highlighting), as

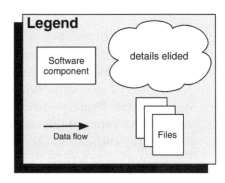

Figure 1.5 **Revisiting the search engine example armed with Tika in tow. Tika provides the four canonical functions (labeled as software components in the figure) necessary for content detection and analysis in the search engine component. The remainder of the search engine's functions (crawling, fetching, link analysis, scoring) are elided in order to show the data flow between the search engine proper, the files it crawls from the shared network drive, and Tika.**

well as extracted metadata from the underlying file (as shown in the upper-middle portion of figure 1.5). Metadata can be used to provide additional information on a per-media-type basis—for example, for PDF files, display a lock icon if a metadata field for locked is set, or for Excel files, listing the number of cells in the document or the number of rows and columns in a sheet. From there, you'd decide whether to display additional icons that link to services that can further process the file pointed to by each search result returned from a query. The final step is language identification. Language identification is a process that discerns what language a document is codified in. Search engines can use this information to decide whether a link to an associated translation service should be provided along with the original document. This process is summarized in figure 1.5.

As can be gleaned from the discussion thus far, Tika strives to offer the necessary functionality required for dealing with the heterogeneity of modern information content. Search is only one application domain where Tika provides necessary services. Chapters 12 through 15 describe other domain examples, including content management, data processing at NASA, and grid systems at the National Cancer Institute.

Before getting any further down the rabbit hole, it's worth providing a bit of history on Tika's inception, discussing its design goals, and describing its relationship to its parent project, Apache Lucene, and other related technologies.

1.2 What is Apache Tika?

We've talked a lot about Tika already, but much like a new friend at school, you probably are still lacking a bit of context, and some of the background details (what city was that friend from; how many brothers does she have, or sisters?) that would make you feel better about continuing the relationship. We'll begin with some details on Tika's grandparents and parents: technologies originating in parts from the world of search engines at Apache, from work in XML parsing at Sourceforge.net, and from origins in document management. After an introduction to Tika's predecessors, you'll want some information on Tika's key philosophies, its goals, and where it wants to be in five years. Is Tika your friend for life, or simply filling a hole until you meet the next great technology? Read on and we'll give you that information on your new pal Tika.

1.2.1 A bit of history

Figure 1.6 shows a timeline of Tika's development, from proposal to top-level project.

As the figure depicts, the idea for Tika was originally proposed in the Apache Nutch project. Nutch is best described as an open source framework for large-scale web search. The project commenced as the brainchild of Doug Cutting (the father of the Lucene and Hadoop projects, a general wizard of open source search), who was frustrated with commercial search companies and the proprietary nature of their ranking algorithms and features. As the original Nutch website at Sourceforge.net stated:

> *Nutch provides a transparent alternative to commercial web search engines. Only open source search results can be fully trusted to be without bias. (Or at least their bias is public.) All existing major search engines have proprietary ranking formulas, and will not explain why a given page ranks as it does. Additionally, some search engines determine which sites to index based on payments, rather than on the merits of the sites themselves. Nutch, on the other hand, has nothing to hide and no motive to bias its results or its crawler in any way other than to try to give each user the best results possible.*

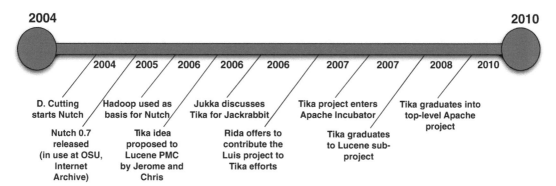

Figure 1.6   A visual timeline of Tika's history. Its early beginnings formed from the Apache Nutch project, which itself spawned several children and grandchildren, including Apache Hadoop and its subprojects. After some steps along the way, as well as the work of a few individuals who kept the fire lit, Tika eventually moved into its current form as a top-level Apache project.

Nutch rapidly grew from a nascent effort into an established framework, with community involvement spanning academia (the Central Web Services department at Oregon State); industry, for example, at the Internet Archive (a nonprofit focused on digitally archiving the web); government (with some of the search efforts in planetary science and cancer research performed by yours truly at NASA); and dozens of other commercial entities and efforts. Eventually, Nutch reached its upper limits in scalability, around 100 million web pages, a factor of 40 less than that of the commercial search engines such as Google. Around the same time, the grid computing team at Yahoo! came into the picture and began to evaluate Nutch, but the scalability limitation was a problem that needed to be solved.

The most promising approach for obviating the scalability problem came when Google published its seminal papers describing its MapReduce and Google File System (GFS) technologies, and when Doug Cutting ran across these papers. Doug, along with Mike Cafarella, decided to implement the software and algorithms described therein in the open source community at Apache. Nutch quickly moved from a technology that ran on a single node, and maxed out around 100 million web pages, to a technology that could run on 20 nodes and scale to billions of web pages. Once the initial prototype was demonstrated, Yahoo! jumped in with engineers and resources, and eventually the Apache Hadoop project was born. Apache Hadoop was the result of an effort to generalize the MapReduce and Distributed File System portions of Nutch implemented by Cutting and Cafarella, and to port them to a standalone project, making it easier to inherit their capabilities in isolation, without pulling all of Nutch in.

Around the same time, we and others (including Jerome Charron) saw the value in doing *the exact same thing* for the parsing code in Nutch, and for its MIME detection capabilities. Jerome and Chris sent a proposal to the Apache Lucene Project Management Committee (PMC), but despite positive feedback, the idea gained little momentum until later in the year when Jukka came along with the parsing and content-detection needs of the Apache Jackrabbit community, and others, including Rida Benjelloun, offered to donate the Lius framework Rida developed at Sourceforge (a set of parsers and utilities for indexing various content types in Lucene). Critical mass was achieved, and the Tika idea and project were brought into the Apache Incubator. After a successful incubating release, and a growing community, Tika graduated as a full-fledged Lucene subproject, well on its way to becoming the framework that you're reading about today.

WHAT'S A TIKA?   Tika's name followed the open source baby-naming technique du jour circa 2005—naming the project after your child's stuffed toy. No, we're not kidding. Doug Cutting, the progenitor of Apache Lucene, Apache Nutch, and Apache Hadoop, had a penchant for naming open source projects after his children's favorite stuffed animals. So, when Jerome and Chris were discussing what to call their proposed text analysis project, *Tika* seemed a perfect choice—it was Jerome's son's stuffed animal!

Now that you've heard about Tika's ancestors and heritage, let's familiarize you with Tika's current state of mind and discuss its design goals, now and going forward.

1.2.2 *Key design goals*

A summary of Tika's overall architecture is provided in figure 1.7. Throughout this section, we'll describe the key design goals that influenced Tika's architecture and its key components: a parser framework (middle portion of the diagram), a MIME detection mechanism (right side of the diagram), language detection (left side of the diagram), and a facade component (middle portion of the diagram) that ties all of the components together. External interfaces, including the command line (upper-left portion of the diagram) and a graphical user interface (discussed in chapter 2 and shown in the upper-right portion of the diagram), allow users to integrate Tika into their scripts and applications and to interact with Tika visually. Throughout its architecture, Tika leverages the notion of repositories: areas of extensibility in the architecture. New parsers can be easily added and removed from the framework, as can new MIME types and language detection mechanisms, using the repository interface. Hopefully, this terminology has become second nature to you by now!

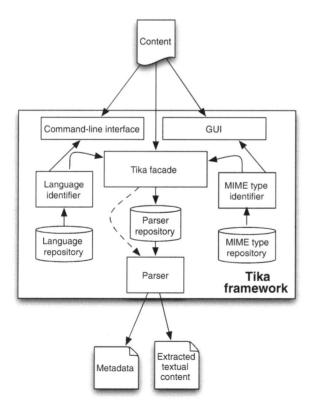

Figure 1.7 High-level Tika architecture. Note explicit components exist that deal with MIME detection (understanding how to identify the different file formats that exist), language analysis, parsing, and structured text and metadata extraction. The Tika facade (center of the diagram) is a simple, easy-to-use frontend to all of Tika's capabilities.

Strong early interest in Tika paved the way for discussions on the mailing lists, for birds-of-a-feather (BOF) meetings at ApacheCon (Apache's flagship conference), and for other public forums where much of the original design and architecture for Tika were fleshed out. Several of the concepts we've already discussed—providing a means to extract text in XHTML format; allowing for flexible metadata models, and explicit interfaces for its extraction; and support for MIME-type detection—were all identified as necessary first-order features and input accordingly into Tika's JIRA issue tracking system. The key design goals are summarized in table 1.2, and further discussed in the remainder of this section.

UNIFIED PARSING INTERFACE

One of the main early discussions was regarding the creation of the `org.apache.tika.parser.Parser` interface. The choices were many: Parse content in one fell swoop or parse the content incrementally? How should the parsed text be provided—via the return of the method signature or via reference? What was the relationship of the parsers to media types?

Table 1.2 Tika's key design goals, numbered and described briefly for reference. Each design goal is elaborated upon in detail in this section, and ties back to the overall necessity for Tika.

Design goal	Description
G1: Unified parsing	Provide a single uniform set of functions and a single Java interface to wrap around heterogeneous third-party parsing libraries.
G2: Low memory footprint	Tika should be embeddable within Java applications at low memory cost so that it's as easy to use Tika in a desktop-class environment with capacious network and memory as it is within a mobile PDA with limited resources on which to operate.
G3: Fast processing	The necessity of detecting file formats and understanding them is pervasive within software, and thus we expect Tika to be called all the time, so it should respond quickly when called upon.
G4: Flexible metadata	There are many existing metadata models to commonly describe files, and Tika has the burden of understanding all of the file formats that exist, so it should in turn understand the formats' associated metadata models.
G5: Parser integration	Just as there are many metadata models per file format, there are also many parsing libraries. Tika should make it easy to use these within an application.
G6: MIME database	MIME types provide an easy-to-use, understandable classification of file formats and Tika should leverage these classifications.
G7: MIME detection	There are numerous ways to detect MIME types based on their existing IANA classifications (recall table 1.1), and Tika should provide a means for leveraging all or some combination of these mechanisms.
G8: Language detection	Understanding what language a document's content is in is one of the cornerstones of extracting metadata from it and its textual information, so Tika should make language identification a snap.

LOW MEMORY FOOTPRINT AND FAST PROCESSING

After lengthy discussions, the decision was made to parse text incrementally and output it as SAX-based XHTML events. SAX, the Simple API for XML processing, is *the* primary alternative to parsing XML using the Document Object Model (DOM), which loads the entire XML document into memory and then makes it available via an API. SAX, on the other hand, parses tags incrementally, causing a low memory footprint, allowing for rapid processing times, and ultimately providing the functionality required by the Tika architecture. After that, you may be wondering, why does DOM even exist? DOM exists because it provides a more conceptually understandable API than SAX, where you have to be cognizant of state (if you're parsing a complex XML model with many tags) as you iterate over the XML document. SAX parsers by their nature attach "handler" code to callback functions (agglomerated as `org.xml.sax.ContentHandler` implementations) that implement the workflow of processing an XML document. SAX callback functions include `startDocument` (called when the SAX parser begins parsing), `endDocument` (called when the SAX parser is finished), `startElement` (called when an XML open tag is encountered for a tag with a given name, such as <book>), and `endElement` (called when the SAX parser encounters an end XML tag, such as </book>), to name a few. Developers fill in the body of these functions to tell the SAX parser what to do as it parses the XML document piecemeal. In DOM, these details are obfuscated from the user and handled by the DOM implementation provider, at the cost of memory footprint and overall speed.

By adopting the SAX model, Tika allows developers and those wishing to customize how Tika's `Parser` deals with extracted information to define custom `org.xml.sax` `.ContentHandlers` that describe what to do: pass along a subset of the extracted XHTML tags; pass along all of the tags, discard others, and so on.

FLEXIBLE METADATA

The next major question to answer in Tika's `Parser` was determining how extracted metadata should be provided. Earlier versions of Tika focused on modifying a passed-in `org.apache.tika.metadata.Metadata` object instance, and adding the extracted metadata to that object. Modern and future versions of Tika have moved in the direction of an `org.apache.tika.parser.ParseContext` object, containing the returned state from the parser, including the extracted text and metadata. The decision of how to deal with extracted metadata boils down to the metadata's lifecycle. Questions include, what should Tika do with existing metadata keys (overwrite or keep)? Should Tika return a completely new `Metadata` object instance during each parse? There are benefits of allowing each scenario. For example, MIME detection can benefit from a provided metadata "hint"—whereas creating a new `Metadata` object and returning it per parse simplifies the key management and merge issues during metadata extraction.

EASY-TO-INTEGRATE NEW PARSER LIBRARIES

Some other early design considerations in Tika's parsing framework were focused on exactly how third-party parsing libraries should be provided. Should Tika developers become experts in the underlying parsing libraries, and as such, should Tika be in the business of providing parser library implementations? The resounding community consensus was *no*, and fittingly so, as each parsing library can be the result of many years of work from hundreds of developers and users. The consensus from a design perspective was that Tika should look to virtualize underlying parser libraries, and ensure their conformance to Tika's `org.apache.tika.parser.Parser` interface. But much complexity is hidden in that simple sentence. Dealing with underlying parser exceptions, threads of control, delegation, and nuances in each of these libraries has been a large effort in its own right. But this effort is a cost well spent, as it opens the door to cross-document comparison, uniformity, standardized metadata and extracted text, and other benefits we're hopefully starting to ingrain in your mind.

MIME DATABASE

Several design considerations in Tika's MIME framework pervade its current reification in the Tika library. First and foremost, we wanted Tika to support a flexible mechanism to define media types, per the discussion on IANA and its rich repository and media type model discussed earlier. Because the IANA MIME specification and the aforementioned RFCs were forward-looking, they defined a mechanism procedurally for adding additional media types as they're created—we desired this same flexibility for Tika's MIME repository. In addition, we wanted Tika to provide an easy, XML-based mechanism (similar to Freedesktop.org, Apache Nutch, and other projects) for adding media types, their magic character patterns, regular expressions, and glob patterns (such as *.txt) for identifying filename patterns and extensions.

Besides ensuring that the definition of media types in Tika is user-friendly and easy, we also wanted to support as many of the existing IANA types as possible. One of our design considerations was the creation of the *comprehensive* media type repository, akin to the MIME information used by Apache's HTTPD web server, or by Freedesktop.org's shared MIME-info database. With more than 1,276 defined MIME types and relationships captured, Tika is well on its way in this regard.

PROVIDE FLEXIBLE MIME DETECTION

To expose the MIME information programmatically, we decided to expose as many MIME detection mechanisms (via `byte[]` arrays, `java.io.Files`, filenames and `java.net.URLs` pointing to the files, and so forth) as possible to end users of the Tika API. Tika's `org.apache.tika.mime.MimeTypes` class was designed to act as this honest broker of functionality. The class loads up a Tika XML MIME repository file, and then provides programmatic access to detection mechanisms and allows users to obtain `org.apache.tika.mime.MimeTypes` (encapsulating not only the name, but other MIME information such as the parents, magic characters, patterns, and more), or simply the names of the detected type for the provided file.

Another important consideration for Tika's MIME repository was tying the MIME information to that of `org.apache.tika.parser.Parsers` that deal with extracting text content and metadata. The main details to flush out in this arena were whether Tika `Parsers` should deal with only single media types, or handle many per `Parser`.

This issue dictates whether specific `Parser` implementations are allowed to be complex (dealing with multiple media types), or whether each supported Tika `Parser` should be more canonical, dealing with a single media type, and increasing the number of parsers in the Tika framework. Beyond that detail (Tika opted to allow one to many types per `Parser`, achieving the greatest flexibility and decreasing the overall number of parsers), the exchange of MIME information between `Parser` and `Metadata` object was another important consideration, as the detected media type can be useful information to return as extracted metadata along with the parsing operation.

PROVIDE LANGUAGE DETECTION

Language identification, though a newer feature in Tika, fits into the overall Tika framework, because it's simply another piece of information that can be fed into the `Parser` and leveraged (similar to the media type information) during the parsing process. Much of the design discussion to date in this area is centered on mechanisms to improve language-specific charset detection, and to inject that information into the overall Tika lifecycle (for example, make it present in the `Metadata` object, make it available during parsing, and so on).

In the following section, we'll detail more on the best places to use Tika, provide some example domains, and set the stage for advanced discussion of Tika features in the forthcoming chapters.

1.2.3 *When and where to use Tika*

Now that you have an idea of what Tika is and what it does, the next question is where and when it's best used, and more importantly, is it of any use to you? This section covers some of the more prominent use cases and domains where Tika is now being used.

SEARCH ENGINES AND CONTENT REPOSITORIES

The main use case for which Tika was originally conceived is supporting a search engine to index the full-text contents of various kinds of digital documents. A search engine typically includes a crawler component that repeatedly traverses a set of documents and adds them to a search index. Since the search index normally only understands plain text, a parser is needed to extract the text contents from the documents. Tika fits this need perfectly, and we'll cover this use case in more detail in chapter 10 where we discuss integration with the various search engine components of the Apache Lucene project. The case study in chapter 15 takes a more practical view on how Tika fits into such a search engine.

A related use case includes different kinds of document and content repositories that make all contained documents searchable. Whenever a document is added to or modified in the repository, its content is extracted and indexed. A generic and extensible parsing tool such as Tika allows the repository to support virtually any kind of documents, and Tika's metadata extraction capabilities can be used to automatically classify or annotate the documents stored in the repository. The case study in chapter 13 shows how the Apache Jackrabbit project uses Tika for such purposes.

DOCUMENT ANALYSIS

The field of artificial intelligence is often associated with large promises and poor results, but the decades of research *have* produced some impressive tools for automatically analyzing documents on a semantic level and extracting all sorts of interesting information. Some of the simpler practical applications, are the ability to extract key terms, such as people and places and their relationships, from normal written text, and the ability to automatically classify documents based on the key topics covered. Projects such as Apache UIMA and Mahout provide open source tools for such applications, and Tika can be used to easily extend the scope of the applications from plain text to any kind of digital documents.

DIGITAL ASSET MANAGEMENT

The key assets of many organizations are increasingly digital. CAD drawings, book manuscripts, photographs, music, and video are just some examples of digital assets with high value. Instead of storing such documents on a disk or backup tape somewhere, organizations are increasingly using more sophisticated digital asset management (DAM) applications to keep track of these assets and to guide related processes. A DAM system often categorizes tracked documents by type, annotates them with rich metadata, and makes them easily searchable, all of which can easily be implemented with support from Tika.

1.3 *Summary*

We've introduced you to Apache Tika, an extensible Java-based framework for content analysis and detection. First, we explained the motivation for Tika by describing the proliferation of content types such as PDFs, Word, Excel, and HTML, and tools associated with performing functions on those types. The sad fact is that the typical pattern involves specializing knowledge of these types to particular applications, and needing to maintain a set of applications to deal with each type of file (the Microsoft Office suite, Adobe Photoshop, XML editors, and so forth). Beyond applications, many application programming interfaces (APIs) exist that handle these document types, but they're highly heterogeneous—they make different assumptions, provide different interfaces, and support varying qualities of service. Enter Apache Tika, a mechanism to bridge the content type diversity and to deal with file types in a uniform way.

The nuances and complexity in writing an application (such as a search engine) that must deal with all of these content types at once quickly grow to be untenable without a technology like Tika. Clearly, the problem of obtaining information from these file types is centered around the ability to identify the type of file automatically (especially when dealing with large numbers of such files), extract the textual information, and extract common metadata (such as Dublin Core) useful for quickly comparing and understanding the file types. Language detection is also a needed feature (similar to MIME detection) to determine means for extracting out the textual information from each file type. As it turns out, Apache Tika (big surprise!) provides simple mechanisms to address these functions in modern software.

To familiarize you more with Tika, we provided some history, explaining how and why certain design decisions and goals were arrived upon. Tika's modular design and its assumptions were detailed, hopefully providing more intimate understanding of the existing framework and its high-level benefits, strengths, and weaknesses.

We gave you some tips and high-level advice on where to leverage Tika in your applications: where it works, and where you shouldn't even think of putting it. (Hint: it doesn't cook your breakfast for you!) We wrapped up the chapter by grounding our discussion in some real-world domains, using the discussion to describe Tika's utility clearly and concisely.

In the next chapter, we'll get you familiar with how to obtain Tika from the Apache Software Foundation (ASF), how to construct your application (including Tika's code, its distribution JAR files, and so on), and we'll travel further down the path of automatic content detection and analysis engendered by the Tika technology.

Getting started with Tika

This chapter covers

- Working with the Tika source code
- The Tika application
- Tika as an embedded library

Equipped with sufficient background on Apache Tika, you're probably thinking to yourself: how do I start leveraging Tika in my own application? Tika is a modern Java application, and its development has undergone the natural evolution that most Java applications do: beginning as a set of Java classes exported as an API, followed by a basic command-line interface, and culminating with a graphical user interface (GUI) for the command-line neophyte (or those with a preference for visual interfaces).

Executing Tika at runtime is a separate step from building Tika from source code. Because Tika is an open source project at the Apache Software Foundation and provided under the Apache License version 2.0 (ALv2),[1] many of its users (you may be one of them) will be perfectly comfortable grabbing the Tika source code

---

[1] The Apache Software Foundation is a community of open source projects characterized by a collaborative and consensus-based development process. The Apache License used by Apache projects is a permissive open source license that allows software with the license to be used and redistributed as a part of proprietary software. See the Apache website at http://www.apache.org/ for more details.

and building/integrating it into their applications. To do so, you'll need some basic knowledge of the primary Tika build tool, Apache Maven, along with some basic knowledge of JUnit tests in order to make sure the Tika software will execute correctly in your environment.

In this chapter, we'll cover the basics of integrating Tika into your environment, whether you prefer executing Tika via command line, API, GUI form, or starting from the source code. We'll start by introducing you to building Tika using Apache Maven or Apache Ant, a world you'll need to familiarize yourself with (albeit briefly) to get working with the Tika source code.

2.1 Working with Tika source code

Before we get too deep into building Tika, we'll briefly describe how to obtain the Tika source code, the starting point for building Tika and for integrating Tika into your Java application. You can skip this section if you're only interested in using released Tika binaries, but as with any open source project, having access to and being able to modify and build the source code gives you a lot of extra opportunities.

2.1.1 Getting the source code

The first step in building Tika, obviously, is getting the source code. You download the source code of all Tika releases from the download section of the Tika website (http://tika.apache.org), but often the most interesting stuff is in the latest development tree that you can find in the version control system.

All Apache projects manage their source code in a big Subversion repository at http://svn.apache.org/, and Tika is no exception. Assuming you have a Subversion client installed, you can check out the latest Tika development tree with the following command:

```
svn checkout http://svn.apache.org/repos/asf/tika/trunk tika-trunk
```

> **GIT MIRRORS**   If you prefer the Git version control system over Subversion, you'll want to check out the Git mirrors that Apache makes available at http://git.apache.org/. The Git clone URL for Tika is git://git.apache.org/tika.git and you can find Tika also on Github at http://github.com/apache/tika.

To keep up with the latest developments, run `svn update` (or `git pull` if you use Git) in the checked-out directory. This updates your copy with the latest changes committed to the Subversion repository. And if you want to submit a bug fix or a new feature to Tika, you can use `svn diff` to get a nicely formatted patch that includes all the changes you've made to your local copy of the source tree. But let's not get ahead of ourselves—first we need to get the source code to build!

2.1.2   *The Maven build*

The Tika build is based on Apache Maven. If you don't already have Maven installed on your computer, you can grab the latest version from the Maven website at http://maven.apache.org/. Once you've done that, you can start the Tika build by executing the following command in the project directory that you just checked out:

```
mvn clean install
```

That's it. You can do a lot with Maven, but the preceding command will automatically clean up the build environment, download all the external dependencies, compile and package all the Tika source code, run the included unit and integration tests, and finally install the tested Tika libraries to your local Maven repository. You can, for example, find the freshly built standalone tika-app JAR file in the tika-app/target directory.

> **MAVEN RUNNING OUT OF MEMORY?**   Running into memory issues when trying to compile Tika? Recent versions of Tika build several deliverable JAR files, some of which pull in many dependencies. If you're getting Java or Maven OutOfMemory exceptions when running mvn install, try setting environment variable MAVEN_OPTS="-Xmx512m". This will allocate 512 megabytes of memory to Java and Maven; most times, this will get you through the build.

All of the major integrated development environment (IDE) tools such as Eclipse, IDEA, and NetBeans have good support for Maven builds, so you can easily import Tika to your IDE workspace for easy access to this functionality and more. See the relevant documentation of your favorite IDE for details on how to work with Maven projects.

2.1.3   *Including Tika in Ant projects*

Though Tika's build is optimized for Maven, it's fairly easy to use Tika with Apache Ant, another popular build tool. Ant is commonly included with many modern *nix distributions, but if you need to install Ant for any reason, you can grab it from the Ant website at http://ant.apache.org/. We'll assume that you've created a build.xml file to begin working with Ant in your project. Including Tika in that Ant project is as simple as finding the existing <classpath> entry in your build.xml file (or adding a new <classpath> entry) and then including the Tika JARs in your <classpath> block.

It's worth noting that version numbers could change by the time you read this, so to discern the actual dependencies, it's better to use the mvn dependency:list or mvn dependency:tree commands to determine the latest versions of dependent libraries:

```
<classpath>
    ... <!-- your other classpath entries -->
  <pathelement location="path/to/tika-core-1.0.jar"/>
  <pathelement location="path/to/tika-parsers-1.0.jar"/>
  <pathelement location="path/to/slf4j-api-1.5.6.jar"/>
  <pathelement location="path/to/slf4j-log4j12-1.5.6.jar"/>
  <pathelement location="path/to/log4j-1.2.14.jar"/>
  <pathelement location="path/to/commons-logging-1.1.1.jar"/>
  <pathelement location="path/to/commons-codec-1.4.jar"/>
```

```
    <pathelement location="path/to/commons-compress-1.1.jar"/>
    <pathelement location="path/to/netcdf-4.2-min.jar"/>
    <pathelement location="path/to/pdfbox-1.5.0.jar"/>
    <pathelement location="path/to/fontbox-1.5.0.jar"/>
    <pathelement location="path/to/jempbox-1.5.0.jar"/>
    <pathelement location="path/to/poi-3.8-beta2.jar"/>
    <pathelement location="path/to/poi-scratchpad-3.8-beta2.jar"/>
    <pathelement location="path/to/poi-ooxml-3.8-beta2.jar"/>
    <pathelement location="path/to/poi-ooxml-schemas-3.8-beta2.jar"/>
    <pathelement location="path/to/xmlbeans-2.3.0.jar"/>
    <pathelement location="path/to/dom4j-1.6.1.jar"/>
    <pathelement location="path/to/geronimo-stax-api_1.0_spec-1.0.1.jar"/>
    <pathelement location="path/to/tagsoup-1.2.jar"/>
    <pathelement location="path/to/asm-3.1.jar"/>
    <pathelement location="path/to/metadata-extractor-2.4.0-beta-1.jar"/>
    <pathelement location="path/to/apache-mime4j-0.6.jar"/>
    <pathelement location="path/to/bcmail-jdk15-1.45.jar"/>
    <pathelement location="path/to/bcprov-jdk15-1.45.jar"/>
    <pathelement location="path/to/boilerpipe-1.1.0.jar"/>
    <pathelement location="path/to/rome-0.9.jar"/>
    <pathelement location="path/to/jdom-1.0.jar"/>
</classpath>
```

Alternatively, you may include just the tika-app-1.0.jar file as a classpath element in your build.xml:

```
<classpath>
    ... <!-- your other classpath entries -->
    <pathelement location="path/to/tika-app-1.0.jar"/>
</classpath>
```

Once you've integrated Tika into your classpath using one of these methods, to get going with your build, run

```
ant -f build.xml
```

... and you're set!

Now that you've built Tika and learned how to integrate it into your Ant project, it's time to learn how to interact with its two primary external interfaces: the command line and Tika's graphical user interface (GUI).

2.2 The Tika application

The first step in revving up your new Babel Fish is deciding between two simple external interfaces that are part of the Tika application: a graphical user interface (GUI) that provides drag-and-drop functionality, and a command-line interface for folks comfortable with scripting environments. In this section we'll first show you how to download Tika, and then walk you through each of these interfaces.

The quick-and-easy way to get started with Tika is to use the Tika application, a standalone JAR archive that contains everything you need to access the key Tika features. The application is available for download from the Tika website at http://tika.apache.org/. The current version of Tika is 1.0 at the time of writing this book, so we'll use that in our examples, but any recent Tika version should work equally well if not better. It's worth noting that you'll need Java 5 or higher to run the standalone JAR archive, called tika-app-1.0.jar. The archive is available after you compile Tika inside of the tika-app/target directory.

To start up the standalone JAR, use the java command's -jar option: java -jar tika-app-1.0.jar. The --help option displays a summary of the available command-line options and a brief description of the application, as shown next.

Listing 2.1   Built-in documentation of the Tika application

```
$ java -jar tika-app-1.0.jar --help
usage: java -jar tika-app.jar [option...] [file|port...]

Options:
    -? or --help          Print this usage message
    -v or --verbose       Print debug level messages

    -g or --gui           Start the Apache Tika GUI
    -s or --server        Start the Apache Tika server

    -x or --xml           Output XHTML content (default)
    -h or --html          Output HTML content
    -j or --json          Output JSON content
    -t or --text          Output plain text content
    -T or --text-main     Output plain text content (main content only)
    -m or --metadata      Output only metadata
    -l or --language      Output only language
    -d or --detect        Detect document type
    -eX or --encoding=X   Use output encoding X
    -z or --extract       Extract all attachments into current directory

    --list-parsers
        List the available document parsers
    --list-parser-details
        List the available document parsers, and their supported mime types
    --list-met-models
        List the available metadata models, and their supported keys
    --list-supported-types
        List all known media types and related information

Description:
    Apache Tika will parse the file(s) specified on the
    command line and output the extracted text content
    or metadata to standard output.

    Instead of a file name you can also specify the URL
    of a document to be parsed.

    If no file name or URL is specified (or the special
    name "-" is used), then the standard input stream
    is parsed. If no arguments were given and no input
    data is available, the GUI is started instead.

  - GUI mode

    Use the "--gui" (or "-g") option to start the
```

```
    Apache Tika GUI. You can drag and drop files from
    a normal file explorer to the GUI window to extract
    text content and metadata from the files.

- Server mode

    Use the "-server" (or "-s") option to start the
    Apache Tika server. The server will listen to the
    ports you specify as one or more arguments.
```

As you can see, the graphical user interface (GUI) mode is invoked with the `--gui` option or if you run tika-app.jar without any arguments. The GUI provides a visual means of navigating Tika's features, along with a simple drag-and-drop interface for exploring a document's extracted textual content and metadata, as well as for determining whether the document was parsed correctly. Let's take a look at the GUI first before discussing the other methods of interacting with Tika.

2.2.1 Drag-and-drop text extraction: the Tika GUI

The Tika GUI mode is especially useful when you're sitting in front of your computer interactively trying to figure out how well Tika understands some specific documents. By "how well," we mean the information that Tika is able to identify about the document, such as its MIME type, its language, the structured text, and the extracted metadata. In particular, it's important to interactively explore Tika's understanding of your document types, as you may be dealing with files that Tika has never seen before, or that contain content for which Tika needs tuning to better understand. In this regard, first interactively exploring the document using the Tika GUI is a viable solution before turning your deployed Tika app into a lights-out solution that you can run in batch mode automatically (we'll see more of that in the command-line section).

At its core, the Tika GUI is a simple tool that allows you to try out the canonical Tika features (text extraction, metadata extraction, and so on) on all sorts of files. To start the GUI, use the `--gui` option like this: `java -jar tika-app-1.0.jar --gui`. This starts up a simple Apache Tika GUI window as shown in figure 2.1.

Figure 2.1   Tika GUI window

You can drag and drop files or URL links from a file explorer or a web browser into this window, and Tika will automatically extract all the content and metadata it can from the given document. The various forms of extracted information are shown in separate views as described in table 2.1. Any parsing errors or other problems are reported in a separate window that shows the relevant error message and related stack trace.

Table 2.1 Information included in views of the Tika GUI window

View	Description
Formatted text	Extracted text content as formatted XHTML. You can use this view to see how well Tika understands the structure of the document that was parsed. Ideally you should see all content in correct order with details such as links and headings in place.
Plain text	Extracted text content as plain text. This view is most useful for understanding how (for example) a simple search index that doesn't care about text structure sees your document.
Structured text	Extracted text content as raw XHTML. Shows the exact XHTML output produced by the Tika parser. See chapter 5 for more details on this and the other two text views.
Metadata	Extracted document metadata. This view will tell you the exact document type and any other information, such as title or author of the document, that Tika was able to extract. See chapter 6 for more details about document metadata.

The Tika GUI is great for interaction-driven exploration of your files and documents, but what if you want to automatically process large batches of documents or to integrate Tika with other (existing) applications automatically, without human intervention? This is where the other command-line options come in.

2.2.2 *Tika on the command line*

When you don't specify the `--gui` option, the standalone JAR will act as any normal command-line application would. It reads a document from standard input and writes the extracted content to standard output. The default command-line behavior is highly relevant, especially after exploring your Tika deployment and its understanding of your document types interactively via the GUI. In most cases, once you're comfortable parsing your documents via the GUI, you'll move into a mode of batch processing the documents with Tika, leveraging that default command-line behavior.

You can customize the command-line behavior with various command-line options, but by default the output consists of the extracted text in XHTML format. In the following example, we first call Tika and provide (via a Unix input pipe, the < symbol) the contents of the document.doc file, then take the output results of the Tika command (extracted XHTML text) and write that output (via the Unix output pipe, the > symbol) to the file extracted-text.xhtml:

```
java -jar tika-app-1.0.jar < document.doc > extracted-text.xhtml
```

You can use this command-line mode to integrate Tika with non-Java environments, such as shell scripts or other scripting languages. For example, it's easy to use Tika as a part of a Unix pipeline either directly on the command line, or as part of a more complex script. In the following example, a document is printed to Unix standard output (via `cat`), then piped into a call to Tika (the `java -jar..` command), and then specific text is identified in the extracted text output using the Unix `grep` command:

```
cat document.doc | java -jar tika-app-1.0.jar | grep some-text
```

> **SAVE SOME TYPING** If you're using the bash shell on a Unix-like computer, you can avoid some extra typing by defining the following alias: `alias tika="java -jar /path/to/tika-app-1.0.jar"`. Then you can run the Tika application by typing just `tika` on the command line. The syntax of the alias command may differ slightly if you use another shell such as `tcsh`. See the relevant `man` page for details.

If the input document is available as a normal file or can be downloaded from a URL, then you can pass the filename or the URL as a command-line argument. Tika will read the document from the given file or URL instead of from the standard input, and will also use the filename or a possible content type setting returned by a web server as additional information when processing the document:

```
java -jar tika-app-1.0.jar http://www.example.com/document.doc
```

Instead of XHTML output, you can also request traditional HTML or plain text by specifying the `--html` or `--text` command-line option:

```
java -jar tika-app-1.0.jar --text document.doc
```

Note that Tika will by default output text using the normal character encoding used on your computer. This is great if you're using Tika with tools such as your command-line console window that expect this default character encoding, but may cause trouble otherwise. To avoid unexpected encoding problems, you can explicitly set the output encoding with the `--encoding` option:

```
java -jar tika-app-1.0.jar --encoding=UTF-8 --text document.doc
```

If you're more interested in the document metadata than in the contents of the document, you can ask for a metadata printout with the `--metadata` option. This will output the extracted document metadata in the Java properties file format:

```
java -jar tika-app-1.0.jar --metadata document.doc
```

The GUI and command-line modes are useful tools, but as Java developers likely already understand, leveraging Tika as an embedded library within Java is where the full power of Tika *really* lies. Tika's GUI and command-line interface are powered under the hood by a set of Java classes and APIs that the GUI and command-line interface expose to Tika's users. From a GUI perspective, interaction with visual aids and via clicks and drag-and-drop actions are a means to codify user intent—to turn that intent into a series of method calls to Tika's Java API, grab the results from Tika, and present those findings to the user. The same goes for the command-line API. It grabs user interaction in the form of command-line arguments and switches, then sends that information to the Tika Java classes. It gets the results and finally presents those results to the user by printing the results to the terminal output. Because both the GUI and command-line interface ultimately restrict interaction to their mode of choice and simplify the underlying complexity of the Tika library (which is a good thing because it lowers the entry barrier to using Tika), a lot of "advanced user" expressiveness and flexibility are limited to what's provided in those interaction modes. Using Tika in native Java affords you all of the necessary language-level and build-level tools to overcome those interaction limitations and unlock the power and features of Tika.

So, now that we've covered most of Tika's GUI and command-line functionality, we'll switch gears and start writing some Java code to help you unlock Tika's true flexibility and expressiveness!

2.3 *Tika as an embedded library*

Though GUIs and command-line integration are rapid ways of exploring what Tika has to offer, the real power of Tika is unveiled when you leverage Tika Java classes and APIs in your application. We'll start with the simplest and most direct way of calling Tika from Java: the `Tika` facade. After the facade discussion, you'll be introduced to Tika's modules and source code organization, a necessary primer for building and running Tika code and ultimately for integrating Tika into your Java project.

2.3.1 *Using the Tika facade*

As we'll see in later chapters, Tika provides powerful and detailed APIs for many content detection and analysis tasks. This power comes with a price of some complexity, which is why Tika also contains a facade class that implements many basic use cases while hiding most of the underlying complexity. This facade class, `org.apache` `.tika.Tika`, is what we'll be using in this section.

Think of the facade as you would a financial broker that manages your investments. You provide your broker investment capital and that broker works behind the scenes to invest your money in different bonds and stocks that meet your desired level of risk. To do so, the broker must understand what companies suit your risk profile and are a sound investment; where to find those companies; how to purchase stock in your name; what's been going on in the market—navigating the complex financial landscape on your behalf. Your interface to this broker is the simple exchange of money, along with some high-level specifications for your investment strategy.

In the same vein, the `Tika` facade is an honest broker of the information landscape. Its goal is to simplify the complexity behind all of the unique aspects of the underlying Tika library: its MIME detection mechanism, used to quickly and accurately identify files; its parsing interface, used to quickly summarize a document by extracting its text and metadata; its language detection mechanism; and so on. As we'll see in later chapters, the use of each one of these features within Tika deserves a chapter's worth of material in its own right. But the Tika facade's job is to obfuscate this complexity for you (just like the financial broker) and to provide simple, clear methods for making document file analysis and understanding a snap.

The SimpleTextExtractor class shown next uses the Tika facade for basic text extraction. A Tika object is first created with the default configuration and then used to extract the text content of all files listed on the command line.

Listing 2.2   Simple text extractor example

```java
import java.io.File;
import org.apache.tika.Tika;

public class SimpleTextExtractor {

    public static void main(String[] args) throws Exception {
        // Create a Tika instance with the default configuration
        Tika tika = new Tika();

        // Parse all given files and print out the extracted text content
        for (String file : args) {
            String text = tika.parseToString(new File(file));
            System.out.print(text);
        }
    }

}
```

The standalone JAR archive discussed earlier contains everything that this SimpleTextExtractor class needs, so you can compile and run it with the javac and java commands included in the standard Java Development Kit (JDK):

```
$ javac -cp tika-app-1.0.jar SimpleTextExtractor.java
$ java -cp tika-app-1.0.jar:. SimpleTextExtractor document.doc
```

Or, if you're a Maven guru, you can compile and run the SimpleTextExtractor from the book's source code using your favorite document.doc file by issuing the below command:

```
$ mvn exec:java -
    Dexec.mainClass="tikainaction.chapter2.SimpleTextExtractor" \
-Dexec.args="document.doc"
```

As you can see from this simple text extractor example, the Tika facade is a powerful tool. In a few lines of code, we've created an application that can understand and process dozens of different file formats. Let's see what else you can do with the facade. The class diagram in figure 2.2 summarizes the key features.

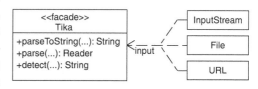

Figure 2.2   Overview of the Tika **facade**

Each of these three key methods takes an input document as an argument and returns information extracted from it. The document can be passed in as a generic `java.io.InputStream` instance or a more specific `java.io.File` or `java.net.URL` instance. The key methods are described in more detail in table 2.2.

Table 2.2 Key methods of the `Tika` facade

Method name	Description
`parseToString()`	The `parseToString()` method used in the preceding example parses the given input document and returns the extracted plain-text content as a simple string. The length of the returned string is limited by default, so you don't need to worry about running out of memory even when parsing huge documents. You can set a custom string length limit with the `setMaxStringLength()` method.
`parse()`	To conserve memory or to avoid the size limit, you can use the `parse()` method that returns a `java.io.Reader` instance for incrementally reading the text content of the input document. This method starts a background thread that parses the given document on demand as your application consumes the returned reader.
`detect()`	You can use the `detect()` method to detect the internet media type of a document. As discussed in more detail in chapter 4, Tika uses heuristics like known file extensions and magic byte patterns to detect file types. This method hides the details of all those mechanisms and returns the media type that most likely matches the given document.

Despite its simplicity, the `Tika` facade covers many of the basic text extraction and detection use cases. For example, the "program that understands everything" that we set out to create in section 1.1 can easily be implemented using the functionality of the `Tika` facade.

We've spent most of the chapter thus far discussing various means of interacting with Tika: calling it from the command line or via a GUI, and ultimately integrating Tika's classes and APIs into Java code for maximum flexibility. Now, we're going to open up the hood and learn about how Tika's modules and code are organized. This should help you understand how to extend Tika, compile its sources, and begin to integrate Tika into your existing Java applications as an external dependency.

2.3.2 *Managing dependencies*

Tika's facade interface exposes functionality provided by Tika's canonical Java classes, relationships, and APIs. As you begin to use the facade, or even the other aspects of Tika's API that will be discussed in later chapters, you'll probably wonder why certain class imports (such as `org.apache.tika.Tika`) are organized in particular packages, and why those packages are part of separate projects, such as `tika-core` versus `tika-parsers`. In short, you'll need to understand the organization of the Tika code, shown in figure 2.3.

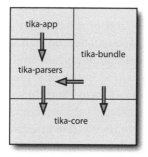

Figure 2.3 **The Tika component stack. The bottom layer, `tika-core`, provides the canonical building blocks of Tika: its Parser interface, MIME detection layer, language detector, and the plumbing to tie it all together. `tika-parsers` insulates the rest of Tika from the complexity and dependencies of the third-party parser libraries that Tika integrates. `tika-app` exposes `tika-parsers` graphically, and from the command line to external users for rapid exploration of content using Tika. Finally, `tika-bundle` provides an Open Services Gateway Initiative (OGSI)-compatible bundle of `tika-core` and `tika-parsers` for using Tika in an OGSI environment.**

Tika is separated into four concrete components—tika-core, tika-parsers, tika-app, and tika-bundle—as shown in the bottom, middle left, top left, and top right of figure 2.3, respectively. Each of the four components is organized as a Maven project, all referencing a tika-parent Maven project which stores project defaults such as common dependencies, mailing lists, developer contact, information, and other goodies that are fairly independent of the source code and the four aforementioned components.

TIKA-CORE

The tika-core component is the base component on which the other three package components are built. The component provides the Tika facade, the classes for MIME type detection (the org.apache.tika.mime package); the core parser interface (the org.apache.tika.parser package that Parsers in tika-parsers extend and implement the interface from); the language identifier interface (the org.apache.tika.language package); the core metadata structure (from the org.apache.tika.metadata package) output from Tika; and the methods for outputting structured text (the org.apache.tika.sax package). The tika-core component is also home to the Tika configuration (which configures the overall framework with properties, sets defaults, allows for extensibility, and so forth) and other utilities useful for other Tika components to leverage.

TIKA-PARSERS

The tika-parsers component represents the Tika wrappers around different parsing libraries, providing implementations of the generic org.apache.tika.parser.Parser interface specified by the tika-core component. Each package within tika-parsers provides all the necessary classes and functionality to wrap the underlying parser library, and insulates the dependencies and uniqueness of those classes from the rest of the Tika core framework components. In this manner, users wanting to take advantage of MIME detection or language identification independent of actually parsing the extracted text and metadata can do so without pulling in the vast array of (downstream) dependencies induced by integrating many parsing libraries into a single framework.

TIKA-APP

The tika-app component provides the command line and graphical user interface aspects of Tika, and is built on top of tika-parsers. Ultimately, the GUI and command-line interface expose the underlying parsing functionality, and through this elements of MIME detection and language identification are eventually plumbed as metadata output from a Tika Parser after its execution. In providing these external interfaces through tika-app, users are given a single packaged solution containing all of Tika (it's what we showed you earlier in terms of the command-line interface), without having to worry about the underlying APIs and classes used to provide that external interface. This package also ensures fairly automatic interaction with Tika, as opposed to manually building and constructing Tika core classes (say, via tika-core and/or tika-parsers), and then calling their functionality as a series of methods that we'll see later in the book. The trade-off here is automatically serving and exposing functionality for higher-level batch processing use cases within Tika.

TIKA-BUNDLE

The tika-bundle component rounds out the Tika stack: it's used to provide an Open Services Gateway Initiative (OGSI) bundle so that Tika can be included in an OGSI environment. OGSI is essentially a software component model and middleware framework for allowing component-based software development in Java. This means that OGSI is highly similar to Java Beans, a model for describing and implementing Java classes that deal with data as plain old Java objects (POJOs), and for operating both computationally and in a data-intensive matter on those POJOs. The goal of Java Beans was to pave the way for a component marketplace, separation of concerns, and ultimately for modular software to be written in Java so that systems and components could be extended, ported to a number of platforms, and evolved with as little direct code modifications as possible. OGSI encourages this mode of development, and defines on top of it explicit lifecycle phases for bundles; a security mechanism for those bundles; a means for registering and discovering bundles; and finally a way to make use of those bundles (call them, deploy them, and so on). The tika-bundle package was created because of a need in recent Tika deployments to include the full Tika stack (ideally, tika-app), but without pulling in all of tika-app's transitive dependencies.

 We've covered some basic Tika code, its use in Java, as well as its organization, and you're hopefully familiar enough with Tika to start leveraging it via the command line, Tika's GUI, or including its classes in your application.

2.4   *Summary*

Our goal in this chapter was to highlight the power of Tika, be it from a command-line shell, GUI, or by integrating Tika into your existing Java code. Along the way we covered the ancillary steps (tips for using Tika from a command shell, downloading Maven or Subversion) as well, but didn't spend much time since most of those topics are the subjects of books in their own right.

The simplest and most visual method of using Tika is via its GUI, a thin wrapper around the `tika-parsers` module which exposes the ability to extract structured text, metadata, and plain text from any type of content through drag and drop. A lot of power with little barrier to entry.

If you're a command-line hacker, or are looking to run Tika in batch mode, the command-line interface is your tool of choice. We covered the basics of Tika's command-line help system, inputting files into Tika via pipes, writing out extracted text from Tika to files, and piping data into or out of Tika into the next application.

Tika is written in Java, which is where it gets most of its flexibility and expressiveness. We covered Tika's facade, an interface to the underlying MIME detector, parsing framework, and language detection framework, and showed how in a few lines of Java code you too can quickly extract text and metadata from all of your documents.

In the next chapter, we'll take a step back and reflect on the information landscape. Where are documents and other forms of content housed, and how do we unlock that information so we can send it to Tika? What are some advanced technologies to simplify getting and analyzing information, and how can Tika work with those technologies to improve how computers automatically comprehend information? Read on, and you'll find out!

The information landscape 3

This chapter covers

- The information landscape
- Using Tika in search engines
- Machine learning

Now that you've gotten started with Tika, you probably feel ready to attack the information content that's out there. The interfaces that you know so far will allow you to grab content from the command line, GUI, or from Java, and feed that content into Tika for further analysis. In upcoming chapters, you'll learn advanced techniques for performing those analyses and extending the powerful Java API on which Tika is constructed to classify your content, parse it, and represent its metadata.

Before diving too deep into Tika's guts, as we'll do in the next few chapters, we'd like you to collectively take a step back and consider this: where does all of the information that you feed to your Babel Fish come from? How is it stored? What's the information's ultimate utility, and where can Tika help to deliver that utility in the way that you (or others) expect?

For example, take movies from a movie content provider, as shown in figure 3.1. You can probably think of a few existing ones that either ship movies to you on DVD or Blu-ray, or that stream movies over the internet to one of a number of powerful computing devices such as a computer, video game system, or specialized hardware

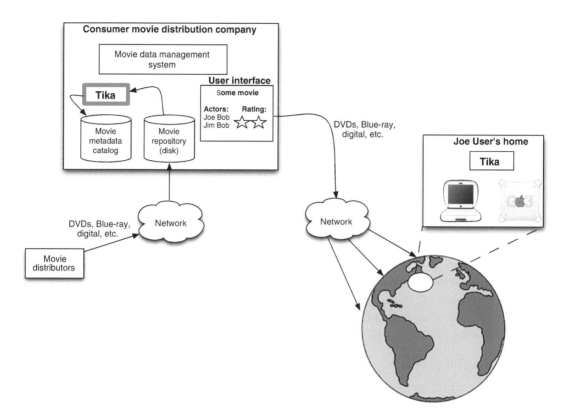

Figure 3.1 A postulated movie distribution system. Movies are sent via the network (or hard media) to a consumer movie distribution company. The company stores the electronic media on their hard disk (the movie repository), and then metadata and information is extracted (using Tika) from the movie files and stored in a movie metadata catalog. The metadata and movie files are made available electronically to consumers from the company's user interface. An average user, Joe User, accesses the movie files, and, potentially, to save bandwidth across the wire, Tika can be called on the server to extract summaries, provide ratings, and so on from the streamed movie to the end user's console systems.

unit. Though the ability to extract text such as speech from these movie files is more of a research task than a turnkey practice, the extraction of metadata isn't. All sorts of metadata is useful in these situations! A movie title, its production company, a series of lead actors and actresses—these are just the set of metadata that you may search on. Beyond these attributes, you may be interested in textual summaries of the movie (which unlike speech *are* easily extractable), your ratings of the movies, your friends' ratings, and so on.

As we've learned by now, making this type of metadata and text available to Tika unlocks the ability to differentiate and categorize those movie files (based on their MIME type); to identify the relevant language of the movie, the representation of ratings, and other user-defined metadata; and much more. In reality, Tika is useful in a number of areas—the question is *how* the content is provided to Tika. Is Tika called on the client side of this application, living inside your computer, video game system, or custom hardware? Or is Tika present in some server-side functionality, leveraged to categorize and classify movie content which is then presented back to you as a user of the system?

The goal of this chapter is to paint a picture of where and how information is stored out there and what kind of information-processing mechanisms could benefit from using Tika. In doing so, we'll characterize that landscape in terms of scale, growth, and heterogeneity, and suggest how and where Tika can be used to incrementally and efficiently navigate the space.

3.1 *Measuring information overload*

In this section, we'll give you a feel for the scale and growth rate of the internet by exploring some real data. We'll discuss why the internet is growing at the rate that it is, and explore its underlying architecture from first principles. What follows is a discussion of the growing complexity of the internet in terms of the types of information available (PDF files, Word documents, JPEG images, QuickTime files), and in terms of the number of languages and encoding schemes that this information is provided in. Aren't you glad that frameworks such as Tika exist to help you weed through this electronic haystack?

3.1.1 *Scale and growth*

The internet has grown tremendously over the years—by some estimates nowadays (see figures 3.2 and 3.3) well into the hundreds of millions of websites, and into the tens of billions of web pages. According to one published report (http://mng.bz/qvry), as of 2007 the amount of digital information available had reached well into the 281 *exabyte* range, which is somewhere near 281 billion gigabytes.

Much of this information is courtesy of the World Wide Web (WWW). The collective knowledge of the world is made available through technologies such as HTML (a language for authoring web documents), components called *web servers* that respond to user requests for HTML documents, and client browsers (Firefox, Safari, Internet Explorer, and so on) that request those HTML documents (and other forms of content) from those web servers. A wealth of content is also available from File Transfer Protocol (FTP) servers, especially science data sets.

Each element can be thought of as a *component* in the overall WWW's *architecture*. In the traditional sense, architecture is the blueprint that guides how software systems are designed. It consists of the logical components of the architecture, their interactions, and the principles that enforce a particular methodology for arranging the components and guiding their interactions. The WWW's architecture is called *REST*. The REST architecture and its foundational principles have a direct causal relationship on the WWW's inherent scalability and growth properties.

The web's architecture was first comprehensively documented in 2000 by Roy Fielding in his Ph.D. dissertation, *Architectural Styles and the Design of Network-based Software Architectures*, where he described the *Representational State Transfer (REST)*

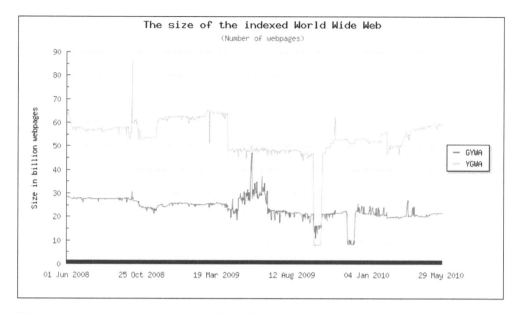

Figure 3.2   An estimate of the size of the World Wide Web from http://www.worldwidewebsize.com/. The graph is estimated and generated dynamically by inspecting results from Google, Yahoo!, Bing, and Ask.com from 2008–2010. The size of the web has remained relatively constant, with a large gap between those results that are weighted using Google's estimate (GYWA) and those weighted using Yahoo!'s estimate (YGWA) (a +20–30 *billion* page difference, with Google having the more conservative estimate). Still, the scale is representative of both the amount of information out there, as well as the difficulty in understanding it (your home library likely nowhere near approaches 10 billion pages in size!).

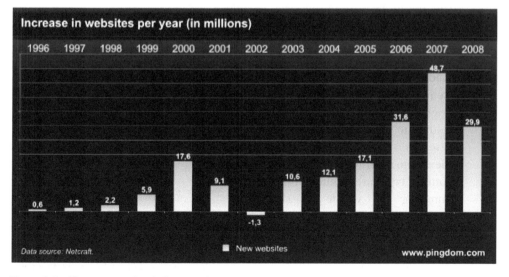

Figure 3.3   The amount of website growth per year (in millions of websites) over the last decade, estimated by http://pingdom.com with data provided by Netcraft. There was steady growth (tens of millions of sites per year) for the later part of the 1990s and into the early 2000s, but between 2005–2008 there has been three orders of magnitude growth (from 10 million to ~30 million) in new websites per year.

architecture. REST prescribes the methodology by which the internet has grown to its current scale, including promotion of intermediaries to reduce single points of failure and enhance scalability, enforcing that all interactions are context-free, and promoting the use of metadata in interactions, to name a few. These principles (and others) have helped to grow the web's scale and ultimate availability of information, as shown in table 3.1.

Table 3.1 Some underlying principles of the REST architecture and their influence on the web's scalability. These are only a cross-section of the full description of REST from Fielding's dissertation.

REST principle	Influence
Promotion of intermediaries	This principle promotes scalability and reliability by increasing the number of replicas of data, and replicas of software and components in the form of gateways, proxies, and other providers.
Context-free interaction	Not requiring state means that actions and histories of actions required to produce a result need not be maintained, which lessens memory requirements and increases scalability.
Use of metadata	Interaction and resources within the REST architecture are both described using rich metadata. The use of this metadata directly enables technologies that understand metadata, like Tika, to have a good shot at understanding not just the ultimate content (web pages, PDFs, and so on) out there, but also the interactions which obtain the content.

3.1.2   *Complexity*

You might be wondering: *why is scale important?* or *how does this relate to Tika?* Scale influences the web's overall complexity in that the more content that's made available (which is growing at a tremendous rate), the greater the likelihood of the content's non-uniformity. And, true to form, this is certainly the case. By some accounts (see http://filext.com), between 15,000 and 51,000 content types are available out there (a sampling of which is shown in figure 3.4), and despite efforts to classify those types, the number is growing at a rate faster than any standards body can keep up with.

Content types typically vary along several dimensions such as size, scale, format, and encoding, all of which

Figure 3.4   A sampling of well-known content types of the up to 51,000 in existence. As a user of the modern internet, you'll likely see some of these documents and files while navigating and searching for your topic of interest. What's even more likely is that custom applications are required to view, modify, or leverage these documents and files in your particular task.

make it difficult to bring the data together and "mash it up" for the purposes of study and exploration. As a further illustration of this, consider some of the recent discussion within the Tika community regarding *character sets* (often abbreviated *charsets*), which are (sometimes numerical) encodings of characters from a particular alphabet, language, or dialect used to ensure interoperability and proper representation of heterogeneous electronic textual formats. Examples of charsets include the American Standard Code for Information Interchange (ASCII) and Unicode.

The charset discussion centered on results (shown in figure 3.5) from a topical test run wherein which a large public internet dataset called the Public Terabyte Dataset (PTD: see http://mng.bz/gYOt) was used along with Tika to determine what types of charsets were in use on the internet. PTD contains somewhere between 50–250 million pages from the top million US domains, and is a sufficiently rich, representative example of the internet.

The results were informative. Besides demonstrating that character detection at internet scale is tricky (Tika ranged anywhere from 60% accuracy in terms of correctly identifying charsets from an average number of pages in the dataset to a low of 30% in

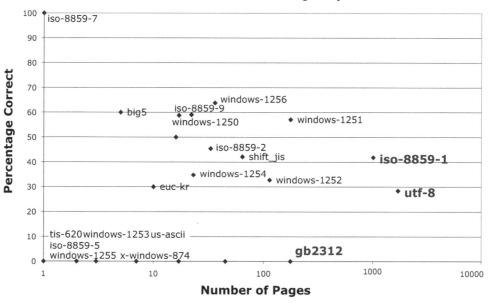

Figure 3.5   Results from a test run by Bixolabs and its Public Terabyte Dataset (PTD) project. The dataset contains 50–250 million representative pages crawled from the top million US-traffic domains. The test involved running a large-scale crawl job programmed in Cascading (a concurrent workflow construct and API for running jobs on a Hadoop cluster) on Amazon EC2. One part of the crawl job used Tika to evaluate the charset of the document being crawled. The Y axis demonstrates accuracy in detection, and the points show the particular charset and its frequency within documents in the dataset. The results of the test demonstrate decent (60%) accuracy on charsets that were in the median frequency of the dataset, and mixed results (30%) on some common charsets such as UTF-8.

accuracy on some of the more common charsets, such as UTF-8), the test highlighted the proliferation of charsets in use today, and the strong need to improve on software's ability to interpret and understand these encodings (we're working on it in Tika!). See chapter 15 for a more detailed case study of this PTD experiment.

By understanding the rationale behind the internet's growth, we're better equipped in Tika to exploit that information in developing novel solutions to navigating the internet's vast information landscape. As an example, understanding the scale and growth of the internet helped inform the importance of having a sound MIME classification framework as part of Tika. Additionally, in understanding the principles of REST such as context-free interactions, we can leverage the existing metadata provided in each HTTP request to obtain more information (such as the provided content type, content length, and content encoding) about the files we feed into Tika to classify and analyze.

Luckily, as information and content has accumulated, so has our collective skill in searching through the information rapidly and accurately. Modern search engines can deal with the internet's scale and still provide results in a few milliseconds. In the next section, we'll examine how search engines have dealt with the information overload, and point to areas where Tika fits in and helps reduce the work that the search engine must perform to sift through the information.

3.2   *I'm feeling lucky—searching the information landscape*

The digital world is vast, but thankfully we're not flying blind. More than 15 years ago, the first modern search engines arrived on the scene (anyone remember Hotbot?), spawned by the desire to enter a few keywords and quickly sift through the results. Though the first search engines weren't as quick as we'd expect in modern days, they did inspire the development of improvements in speed, scalability, and quality of results that gave us the eventual search engine architecture, described by Sergey Brin and Lawrence Page in their seminal Ph.D. research project on Google (see http:// ilpubs.stanford.edu:8090/361/). We'll cover the search engine architecture in this section, providing information about its techniques for helping to accurately and rapidly allow users to sift through information. Then, we'll tell you where Tika fits into that overall search engine architecture and how it enables many of its features.

3.2.1   *Just click it: the modern search engine*

Search engines are a big part of how we cope with the information overload nowadays. Though search has been in the mainstream for the past 15–20 years, only since the early '90s and the advent of the G word (yes we're talking about Google) has search solidified its place in the technology stack.

Modern search engines are complex, distributed software systems that must deal with all of the aforementioned heterogeneity of the internet. They must decide what content is the most appropriate to crawl and make available in the system, how to obtain that content, what to do with it (parse out the relevant text and metadata), and then how to index the content at scale so that it can be made available for search to the system's end users. Even with all of those responsibilities, we've still significantly simplified what the search engine system is actually doing; for example, the problem of determining what content is worth crawling is extremely complex.

See the example search engine architecture shown in figure 3.6. The crawler (denoted by the bold label C) navigates different website nodes on the internet, guided by its internal architecture shown in the upper-right portion of the figure. Two core components of that architecture are *URL filtering* and *deduplication*. URL filtering is the process of selecting URLs from the internet to crawl based on some criteria, such as a set of accepted sites (white list), sets of unacceptable sites (black list), acceptable file types (PDF, Word, but not XLS, for example), domain-based URL filtering (all .edu domain pages, all .com pages), and so forth.

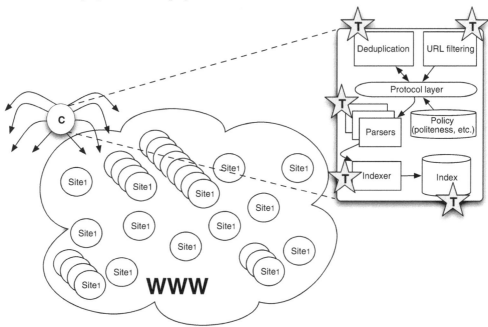

Figure 3.6 **The architecture of a web search engine. The circular structures in the middle of the diagram are websites that the crawler (the eight-legged creature labeled with a bold C) visits during a full web crawl. The crawler is itself made up of several functional components, shown magnified in the upper-right corner of the figure. The components include URL filtering (for narrowing down lists of URLs to sites that the crawler must visit); deduplication (for detecting exact or near-exact copies of content, so the crawler doesn't need to fetch the content); a protocol layer (for negotiating different URL protocols such as http://, ftp://, scp://); a set of parsers (to extract text and metadata from the fetched content); and finally an indexer component (for taking the parsed text and metadata, and ingesting them into the search index, making them available for end users). The crawler is driven by configurable policy containing rules and semantics for politeness, for identification of the crawler, and for controlling the behavior of the crawler's underlying functional components. The stars labeled with T indicate areas where Tika is a critical aspect of the crawler's functionality.**

Deduplication is the process of determining similarity of fetched content to that of existing content in the index, or to-be-fetched URLs later on in the fetch list. This is performed to weed out the indexing and fetching of duplicate content, which saves resources such as disk space, and helps the overall politeness rating of the crawler by not wasting resources on web content providers and their already overloaded web servers. Deduplication can feed into URL filtering, and vice versa.

Deduplication can be classified into a few areas. The first area is concerned with URL detection and virtual hosting, such as noting that two different URLs point at the same content (such as http://www.espn.com and http://espn.go.com, which both point to ESPN's main website). Beyond URL detection, deduplication can also involve content-matching techniques, which boil down to either exacting similarity (such as examining the bytes of two fetched URLs and hashing them using the MD5 or SHA1 hashing algorithms, and then comparing the resultant hash values) or near-similarity (two pages that have the same content, but that differ in ads present on the page, timestamps, counters, or some other form of dynamic content). Deduplication can also be concerned with the link structure of pages, looking and filtering out sets of pages that link to one another in similar ways, or the physical properties of the network such as node structures, ISPs, and content available only in certain countries or in certain languages.

3.2.2   *Tika's role in search*

The preceding is a simple illustration that even a subset of the functional components in a search codify complex processes that make the end user experience more fulfilling and do much to alleviate the complexity of navigating the information landscape. What's more, Tika provides many of the capabilities that *directly* enable both the simple and more complex capabilities required by the search engine. For example, many of the mechanisms for URL filtering discussed earlier can be provided through Tika's MIME detector, which provides classification based on URL or file extension. The process of deduplication? In many cases, it's a snap with Tika's parsing framework, which extracts structured text that can be used for feature comparison and for hashing to determine exact and near-exact similarity matching, as well as page link structure. This pervasiveness is noted in figure 3.6 everywhere you see a star—these indicate places where Tika's capabilities provide significant functionality leveraged by the search engine and the crawler. You'll hear more about this when we cover Nutch and Tika in chapter 10.

Once the search engine and its crawler decide which URLs to visit and which URLs are duplicates of one another, the content must be obtained somehow. Crawlers typically have robust protocol handlers and a *protocol layer* that understands how to interpret a URL and map it to a mechanism to obtain the content (if it's an HTTP URL, a HTTP request must be made, and so forth). The protocol layer obtains the bits of the remote files referenced by the URLs, and once those bits are obtained, they must be analyzed and summarized, two steps that are regularly handled by a set of *parsers* that are available to the crawler. As we've seen, Tika provides a fairly generalized and robust interface for normalizing the heterogeneity of parsing libraries. In addition, the process by which the crawler decides which parser (or set of parsers) to call for a particular fetched content item is another area where Tika shines—its MIME detection framework and its `AutoDetectParser` perform this mapping automatically. Once the content is parsed by the crawler, the extracted text and metadata are sent to a search index by the indexer component, which is interested in metadata to make available for search. This is another area where Tika shines: in reducing the overall complexity of the activity through its rich support for metadata, which we'll learn more about in chapter 6.

If we've whetted your appetite for thinking about the overall search engine stack, its use in providing a roadmap for the information landscape, and Tika's relationship to the search engine's success, then we direct you to chapter 10 for a more detailed breakdown of Tika's involvement in Apache Lucene. Lucene is a family of search-related projects at the Apache Software Foundation, including a RESTful search web service called Solr; Lucene-java, the core indexing and searching library; and formerly including Mahout, a classification, clustering, and analysis platform which we'll briefly discuss in the next section.

We've focused at length on dealing with information discovery as a means of navigating information, but once you've found the information, you need to do something with it. Cluster it. Make a hypothesis. Leverage it to determine what types of books you may be interested in buying. You can do a lot with the data that you find and retrieve with a search engine. We'll discuss some neat things you can do with your data in the next section, and pinpoint the utilities of Tika in these activities along the way.

3.3   *Beyond lucky: machine learning*

Cruising around the internet with a powerful search engine is great, but after awhile, you may develop a set of favorite websites that you regularly visit and no longer require a search engine to get you there. What's more, as you frequent these sites, you begin to notice that they *remember* certain things about you: products that you like to purchase, other users of the sites with similar interests, and so forth. How do they do this? The sites exploit modern approaches to machine learning, which you'll learn about in this section. Techniques for machine learning help reduce the complexity of the information landscape by using information that sites remember about you to make highly accurate recommendations for content you'll be interested in, obviating the need to search any further for it. We'll discuss some common uses of machine learning, and then discuss two real-world implementations of machine learning algorithms from the open source community at Apache—we're pleased to say that Tika is a part of both of them! Read on to find out the how and the where.

3.3.1   *Your likes and dislikes*

So far, we've discussed finding your way around the information landscape with a search engine, whose main goal is data reduction, and navigating the landscape via exploration. Another common approach is to have software suggest what information would be relevant to you, based on indicated preferences—movie genres you've declared that you like, your past purchase history, and so on. These are all types of *machine learning*, or *ML*. Some of the more popular ML techniques that are relevant to our discussion are *collaborative filtering* for providing item- and user-based recommendations, *clustering* (of seen content) based on similarities deduced, and *categorization* (of unseen content and users) for the purposes of shoe-horning that content and those users into existing clusters. These techniques are often combined to make recommendations to users about what items to buy, other users who are similar to them, and so on. A good example of collaborative filtering in action is the recommendations that you regularly get from e-commerce sites like Amazon.com when you log in, as shown in figure 3.7.

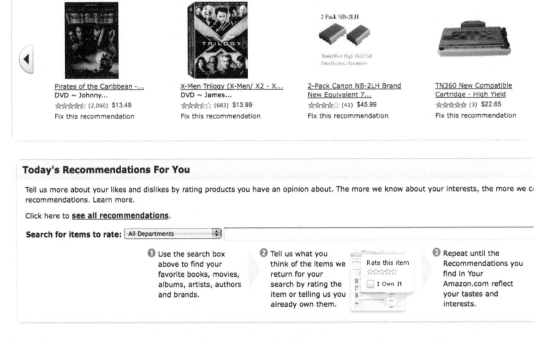

Figure 3.7   An example of collaborative filtering as provided by Amazon.com. Recommendations are automatically suggested on entering the site through collection and processing of past purchases and user preferences. In the bottom portion of the figure, Amazon explicitly solicits feedback and ratings for items in a category from the user to use in future recommendations.

E-commerce websites have recently taken up ML techniques so that they can take advantage of the data that they have been collecting for years. The collected information falls into a few basic categories, a representative cross-section of which is shown in table 3.2.

Table 3.2 Information representative of the type collected about users of e-commerce sites. This would then be fed into a collaborative filtering, clustering, or categorization technique to provide recommendations, find similarities between your purchasing history with that of other users, and so on.

Information category	ML utility
Item rating	By explicitly requesting that a user rate an item (as shown in the bottom portion of figure 3.7) websites can obviate the need to sense your mental model of popularity. Ratings are typically on some numerical scale, such as 1–5, or 1–10, and visually depicted as "tagging" an item with gold stars. Ratings can be fed into algorithms such as Slope One, an approach for collaborative filtering which uses your ratings and those of other users to determine future recommendations tailored to your tastes.
User purchase history	Purchase history typically includes information such as item bought, category, number of times purchased, date purchased, cost, and other information that can be fed into clustering techniques to relate your purchase history to that of like users. If the websites can determine the appropriate cluster for you and your fellow users, and map that to the items you and others in that cluster have purchased, it has a good sense of what future items you and your cluster mates may be interested in purchasing.
User characteristics	Includes information such as location, gender, credit card type, and other demographics that can be used to relate you to users of similar characteristics. Tying this information with existing user-to-item mappings deduced from purchase history or ratings can allow websites to provide recommendations immediately to users as soon as they enter the site.

As the internet has grown, and with the advent of social media such as Facebook and Twitter, more and more information is being gathered, even outside of the realm of the traditional e-commerce sites. Imagine all of the information that you as a user include in your Facebook profile that would be useful for Amazon.com to relate to the items that it would like to sell you. For example, Facebook user profiles have a Likes and Interests section, which users create by clicking the Like button on pages belonging to rock bands, political parties, types of food, all sorts of different things. Imagine that Amazon.com is promoting a new book on Southern-style cooking. Ideally, Amazon.com would only want to recommend this book to those interested in buying it, because recommending it to someone who isn't interested weakens the belief of users that Amazon.com really understands their likes and dislikes. On the other hand, recommending the book to a user who enjoys Southern food is an instant recipe for increasing Amazon.com's profits.

Amazon.com doesn't collect information about your likes and dislikes. But Facebook and Twitter do, and provide open APIs for other companies to access your information based on your declared privacy ratings. So the clear goal of a company like

Amazon.com would be to leverage the social media information about you to increase its chances of targeting the right users for sales. That said, *accessing* your social information is only one part of the battle, as we've seen by now! Once the information is acquired, it's likely in a form that requires further processing, including text and metadata extraction, exactly like the processing provided by Tika! Likes and dislikes as provided by social media APIs might not be in the format that Amazon.com expects, and may be annotated with HTML tags (for emphasis and structure), as well as relevant metadata that could be useful as well.

3.3.2 *Real-world machine learning*

Three recent open source software projects that directly implement many of the ML techniques we've discussed are Apache Mahout (http://mahout.apache.org/), Apache UIMA (Unstructured Information Management Architecture: see http://uima.apache.org/), and the Behemoth project (https://github.com/jnioche/behemoth). All three have extensions built in that leverage Tika in a fashion similar to our Amazon.com example.

Apache Mahout is a framework for providing ML algorithms on top of a scalable cloud computing platform called *Apache Hadoop*. Mahout implements collaborative filtering, clustering, and categorization techniques, and provides an extension mechanism and architecture called *Taste*. With Taste, users can write their own ML algorithms, provide them vector data from a variety of different sources, and then produce user recommendations. Common mechanisms for providing data via Taste include CSV files, Java programs that extract and translate internet data sources, approaches involving databases, and so forth. A recent extension to Mahout involved integrating Tika to assist in taking arbitrary binary content, extracting its text and metadata, and then using the combination of text and metadata to form vector input to Mahout's ML algorithms. This process is depicted in the upper portion of figure 3.8.[1]

Apache UIMA is an open source implementation of the UIMA standard actively being worked on by the OASIS standards organization. UIMA was originally donated to the Apache Software Foundation by IBM, and has since grown into an Apache Top Level Project (TLP), in a fashion similar to Mahout. UIMA's goal is to make sense of unstructured information by providing explicit support for modeling, analyzing, and processing it in a number of programming languages, including Java and C++. One use case of UIMA is taking in content and running several analyzers on it to produce what UIMA calls *annotations*, which are content features extracted by the UIMA annotators. A recent contribution to UIMA is the *Tika Annotator*, which uses Tika to extract document text and metadata as a means of feature extraction. Features are grouped into a common analysis structure (CAS), which can then be fed into further information analysis and visualizations. This interaction is depicted in the bottom portion of figure 3.8.

---

[1] For more detail, have a look at another recent Manning book, *Mahout in Action* (http://manning.com/owen/).

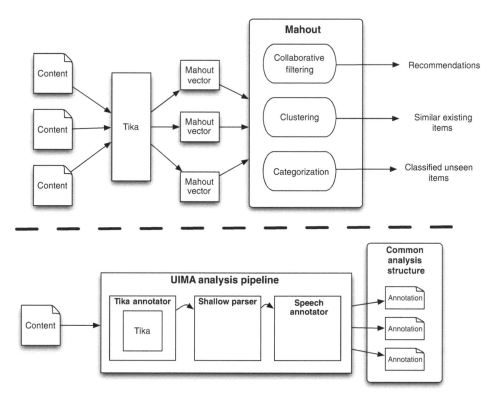

Figure 3.8 Tika's utility in machine learning (ML) applications. The dashed line in the middle of the figure delineates two use cases. The first is within the Apache Mahout project, whose goal is to use ML to provide collaborative filtering, clustering, and categorization. Mahout algorithms usually take vectors as input—descriptions of the clustering, user or item preferences, or categorizations of incoming content, where content can be arbitrary electronic documents. An emerging use case is to take files and use Tika to extract their textual contents and metadata, which can be translated into Mahout vectors to feed into its ML algorithms. In the bottom of the figure is a use case for Apache UIMA, a reference implementation of the UIMA standard being developed by OASIS. In this use case, Tika is used to implement a UIMA annotator that extracts features from incoming content, and then classifies those features in a UIMA Common Analysis Structure (CAS) model.

Another example of open source machine learning and analysis is the Behemoth framework. Behemoth brings together UIMA and the General Architecture for Text Engineering (GATE: see http://gate.ac.uk/) software toolkits, as well as Tika for providing textual analysis software that runs on top of the Hadoop framework. Behemoth allows users to rapidly go between GATE annotations and heterogeneous document formats using Hadoop as the underlying substrate. In a nutshell, Behemoth focuses on linking together various information extraction components which operate on documents. Many folks use Behemoth as "glue" to ease large-scale processing of documents and to help combine various open source projects such as Nutch, Tika, UIMA, Mahout, and Solr. For instance, Behemoth can take the output of a Nutch crawl, process it with Tika, get extra information using UIMA, and then convert it all into vectors for Mahout or send the data to index in Solr.

Tika's recent use with Mahout, UIMA, and Behemoth is likely only the tip of the iceberg as more ML technologies and techniques emerge and as more user information is made available on the internet with the advent of social media. E-commerce sites and other for-profit corporations are increasingly interested in collecting as much of the disparate information out there as possible and correlating it using machine learning techniques. Technologies such as Tika can insulate the ML techniques from having to deal with the heterogeneity of the information landscape, allowing them to focus on improving the way computers understand our documents, and ultimately increasing our collective ability to leverage the power of the information that's out there.

3.4   Summary

The focus of this chapter was to navigate the information landscape and reflect on the breadth of information out there in the form of HTML pages, PDF files, Word documents, and other goodies that you'll want Tika to automatically understand for you.

We started out examining the scale, growth, and complexity of the information that's available via the internet. Its distributed nature, its resiliency to failures, and its ultimate scalability have engendered its role in modern society, and at the same time increased the available information by orders of magnitude, well into the tens of billions of web pages. That includes much more than just HTML pages, which is why technologies such as search engines and content management systems must easily extract information from numerous types of documents available out there.

Search engines came about to help tame the complexity of the web by allowing users to type keywords into a text box to rapidly and accurately find documents that matched their interest. Dealing with the scale, complexity, and growth of the internet (or even a corporate intranet) required search engines to have a fairly detailed modular architecture, involving determining what links on the WWW to crawl, fetching the content pointed to by the links, parsing the content, indexing its metadata and text, and ultimately making the information available for query. We saw where Tika came into play in the overall search engine architecture, as well as its utility in understanding content at scale.

Once content is identified and obtained via the search engine process, most often it needs to be analyzed or processed in some way. We saw how technologies such as UIMA and Mahout make it easier to cluster and analyze data, and what role Tika can play in assisting those technologies even beyond the point of identifying the content and files that feed into them.

We're pretty far down the rabbit hole at this point in terms of looking at Tika, understanding its architecture, and integrating it into software. But we've only scratched the surface of what Tika can do. In the next few chapters, we'll get up close and personal with Tika and its Java codebase, looking first at its typical initial utility in your application: MIME type identification!

Part 2

Tika in detail

By now you should have a fairly good understanding of what Tika is, what it can do, and where it fits in the bigger picture of information-processing systems. If you read through chapter 2 and tried out the examples, you've seen Tika in action and written your first Tika-based application. But if you're anything like us, you're wondering how this toolkit is put together and what programming APIs it provides. Wait no more, because that's what we'll be covering in this part of the book!

We'll start in chapter 4 by describing the internet media type system and how Tika can detect the type of virtually any kind of document. Once the type is known, Tika can parse the document to extract its content and any associated metadata. Content extraction with Tika is covered in chapter 5, and metadata handling in chapter 6. In chapter 7, we'll show how Tika can help deduce information like the natural language in which a document is written. Finally, chapter 8 looks at some of the more popular file formats and the details that you should know when dealing with such files.

That's a lot of ground to cover, so let's get started!

Document type detection

This chapter covers

- Introduction to MIME types
- Working with MIME types in Tika
- Identifying file formats

Let's talk about *taxonomy*. Taxonomy is the science of classification. Taxonomies are used to identify and classify concepts in order to better understand them and to have a shared vocabulary for describing things. For example, the Linnaean taxonomy[1] is the classical system of naming all biological organisms using two-part Latin names that identify both the *genus* or category and the specific *species* within that category. The term *Homo sapiens* identifies the modern human species as a part of the family of earlier human-like species, along with the extinct *Homo neanderthalensis*. A similar taxonomy, called the internet media type system, is used to identify digital document formats.

---

[1] Carl Linnaeus, a famous Swedish scientist, wrote *Systema Naturae* in 1735, in which he describes and categorizes plants, animals, and minerals. The seminal work was one of the first widely known uses of *rank*-based classification, in which certain categories can be ranked higher or lower than others. In Linnaeus's taxonomy, plants, animals, and minerals are first ranked by class, then by order, and then by species. Relating back to this chapter, the IANA's (Internet Assigned Number Authority's) classification of internet media types mentioned in section 1.1.1 is a modern example of a rank-based classification system. MIME types are broken down into top-level categories, then specialized as subtypes within those categories.

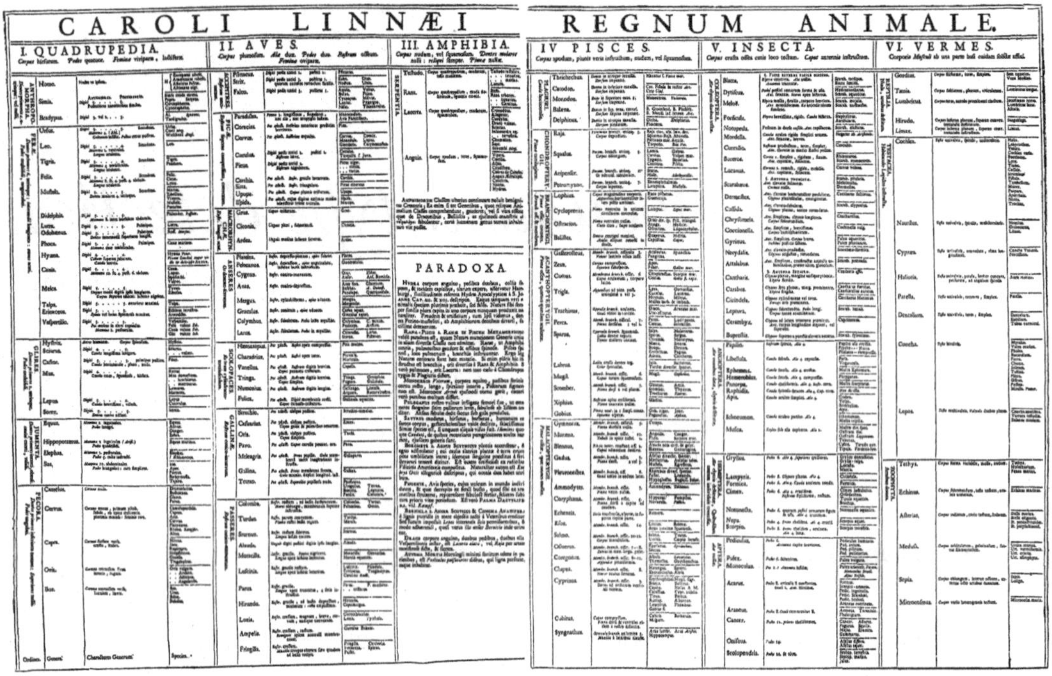

Figure 4.1   Table of the Animal Kingdom (Regnum Animale) from an early 1735 edition of Carolus Linnaeus's *Systema Naturae.* **This and Linnaeus's other seminal book,** *Species Plantarum,* **laid the groundwork for most of the biological nomenclature in use today. A similar classification of types can also be found in the internet media type system.**

Taxonomies are often associated with ways of identifying or detecting specific things. For example, biological taxonomies come with details such as descriptions of the appearance of species, their behavior or growth patterns, or ultimately their DNA structure as ways to identify the species of any single animal or plant. Similar mechanisms exist for detecting formats of digital documents.

In this chapter, we'll dive deep into the taxonomy of document formats and explain how to use the taxonomy and other mechanisms to determine a document's true classification. The first stop on our journey is an introduction to the internet media type system and how media types are handled by Tika. Then, we'll look at the different type detection mechanisms that are included in Tika. Finally, we'll put these things together in a simple example application to give you a feel for using Tika's document type detection system.

4.1   Internet media types

As you may remember from section 1.1.1, the internet media type system documented in RFC 2046 is the best available standard for identifying document types. Media types (or *MIME types,* as they're often called based on the Multipurpose Internet Mail

Extensions (MIME) standard that defined the concept) play a crucial role in the underlying interactions whenever you browse the web or read your email. In short, MIME types make the right applications run on your computer whenever you interact with a particular file. For example, have you ever wondered how your browser knows that when it encounters a QuickTime movie, rather than displaying the movie as binary or text content in your browser, it should load up your QuickTime player and start playing the file?

Most browsers either explicitly (as shown in figure 4.2 demonstrating Firefox's media type to application mapping) or implicitly have to understand the underlying media type of a file, and then know what to do with it. Without an understanding of media types on the internet and their associated applications, your internet browsing experience would still be composed mostly of plain ASCII text, which wouldn't be much fun at all.

We're ready to dive into the naming scheme for internet media types. After that, you'll be introduced to the eight top-level internet media types, as defined by the seminal Internet Assigned Number Authority (IANA) media type registry (http://www.iana.org/assignments/media-types/index.html). We'll briefly describe the IANA

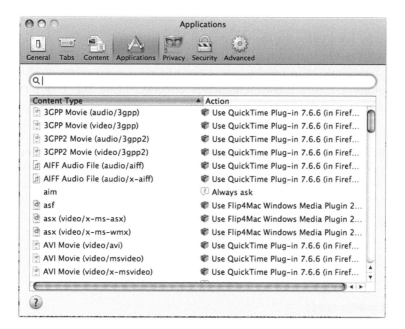

Figure 4.2   The document media type to application mapping from Mozilla Firefox. This panel can be brought up on a Mac by clicking on the Firefox menu, then selecting Preferences, then clicking on the Applications tab (note: this sequence depends on the operating system used, but is likely similar for platforms other than Mac). Each listed media type is mapped to one or more handler applications, which Firefox tries to send the content to when it encounters the document on the internet.

registry as well as a few other ones, and how Tika leverages the information present in any media type registry to accurately and reliably detect media types.

4.1.1   *The parlance of media type names*

The name of a media type consists of a *type/subtype* type definition and an optional set of *name=value* parameters as shown in figure 4.3, following the Linnaean (and more generally rank-based) taxonomy development approach. The type/subtype part and the parameter names are restricted to a subset of printable US-ASCII strings and are always treated case-insensitively.

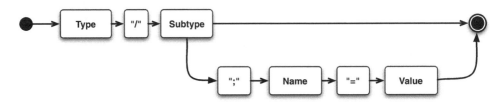

Figure 4.3   Railroad diagram of the syntax of media type names. See section 5.1 of RFC 2045 for the full details of the format.

The type/subtype part tells you the document format you're dealing with, and the optional parameters add format-specific information needed to properly process the document. For example, the media type `text/plain; charset=UTF-8` identifies a plain text document with Unicode characters encoded using the UTF-8 character encoding. Similarly, the `image/jpeg` type identifies an image stored in the JPEG/JFIF image format.

> **THE ODD BOX**   When dealing with lots of documents and media types, you're bound to encounter some abnormal cases sooner or later. A common mistake is to reverse the order of the parts in a media type name, for example, `charset=utf-8; text/html`. A toolkit such as Tika shields your application from having to deal with the complexities of such anomalies.

Now that we know what a media type looks like, it's natural to ask what kinds of types are being used out there and how the set of known media types is managed. Read on to find out.

4.1.2   *Categories of media types*

There are currently eight official top-level types as shown in table 4.1, and thousands of registered or otherwise known subtypes. Similar to Linnaeus's animal taxonomy, these top-level types form the basis for classifying and organizing a taxonomy of internet media types.

Table 4.1 Officially specified top-level media types by IANA. These types form the basis for a detailed classification framework of available document types. Children are allowed for each top-level type, indicating some specialization of the parent (a more specific schema, a slightly different encoding format, and so on).

Top-level type	Description
`text/*`	Text-based documents such as HTML (`text/html`) and Cascading Style Sheets (CSS, `text/css`) files, comma-separated values data (CSV, `text/csv`), and unformatted plain text (`text/plain`). All text documents are processed primarily as characters instead of as bytes, so a text media type is often accompanied with a `charset` parameter that identifies the character encoding used in a specific document.
`image/*`	Image formats such as JPEG (`image/jpeg`) and Portable Network Graphics (PNG, `image/png`). Most image documents share some basic characteristics like image size and resolution, color space and depth, and compression ratio (including whether the used image compression is lossy). All of this information is normally embedded within the image document in a format-specific way, so media type parameters are usually not used or needed for image types.
`audio/*`	Music and other audio formats such as MP3 (`audio/mpeg`) and Ogg audio (`audio/ogg`). There are also many audio formats designed for things like internet telephony and are usually used for transmitting instead of storing audio.
`video/*`	Video formats such as QuickTime (`video/quicktime`) and Ogg video (`video/ogg`). Typical characteristics of video formats are frame rate and size, and the possible inclusion of synchronized audio and text tracks.
`model/*`	File formats for expressing physical or behavioral models in various domains. The best-known example is the Virtual Reality Modeling Language (VRML, `model/vrml`) format used to express 3D models.
`application/*`	Application-specific document formats that don't necessarily fit any of the other top-level categories. Well-known examples include PDF (`application/pdf`) and Microsoft Word (`application/msword`) documents. The generic `application/octet-stream` type is used as a fallback for any documents whose exact type is unknown (the document can only be processed as a stream of bytes).
`message/*`	Email and other message types sent over the internet and other networks.
`multipart/*`	Container formats for multiple consecutive, alternative, or otherwise related component documents. Like `message/*` types, `multipart/*` documents are normally used for messages transmitted over the network, whereas packaging formats like Zip archives (`application/zip`) are categorized as application types.

In addition to the official top-level types, there's a reserved `example/*` category for use only in examples. Some experimental applications may also use unregistered top-level types of the format `x-*/*`, though more frequently you see applications using unregistered subtypes with names that match formats like `application/x-*` or `image/x-*`.

As media types are identified, they need to be persisted in some manner so that others can look up their definitions and understand their relationships. Media types are stored in a *media type registry* for this purpose. There are a few canonical media type registries, so before you go out and try creating your own, it's worth understanding some of the existing registries of media types, including the largest, most comprehensive source, the IANA registry.

4.1.3   *IANA and other type registries*

Among its other responsibilities, the Internet Assigned Numbers Authority maintains a list of officially registered media types. This list is publicly available on the web at http://www.iana.org/assignments/media-types/, and anyone may register new types by following the procedure described in RFCs 4288 and 4289.

There are hundreds of officially registered types, and more are constantly being added. Besides being one of the largest and most well-maintained media type registries in existence, the IANA registry is significant because the media types defined in it are of high quality, both in terms of the sheer amount of relationships captured (parent and child types), and because of the peer-reviewed nature of the attributes that are captured for each type (MAGIC byte patterns, file extensions, and so forth). IANA is a well-respected internet standards body, with many data curators and folks responsible for ensuring that the information captured in its registries isn't junk, but actually useful to consumers of the information held within.

There are also many widely adopted types that haven't been officially registered and thus haven't been as extensively vetted by the broader community. Information about such types may at times be hard to come by, may require searching through both online and offline resources, and may also require vetting of misleading or even incorrect information. A few websites, such as http://filext.com, http://file-extension.net/, and TrID (http://mark0.net/onlinetrid.aspx), maintain huge file format databases that often provide the best hints about some unknown media types that you may encounter, or at least have information that may not be present in the higher-quality, harder-to-get-into registries (like IANA). Unfortunately such information is often incomplete or contradictory, but luckily Tika solves some of these problems in a number of different ways, such as combining information from multiple existing media type registries, easily allowing for the addition and curation of those media types in a well-known format like XML (which in itself provides excellent tool support for managing media types), and finally by adopting a comprehensive specification for representing media types, allowing for their easy comparison, extension, and management. Now that we've covered the basics, let's take a deep dive into Tika's techniques for taming the complexity of media types.

4.2   *Media types in Tika*

Media types are the basic atomic building blocks of interaction with files and your computer's software—they tell your computer what applications to associate with what files. Detecting media types accurately and reliably is of the utmost importance, and something Tika happens to excel at (no pun intended).

Now that you know a bit about the hassle of dealing with media types, such as the eight top-level media types and their countless children, how to name the media types and classify them, and where they're stored (in registries, some high-quality and others not), it's time we told you how Tika simplifies the complexity of dealing with media types.

First, Tika maintains a rich, easy-to-update, easy-to-understand MIME database internal to the project, reducing external dependencies to existing registries. Second, Tika provides Java API and class-level support for interacting with the Tika MIME database, exposing management APIs for the database but also exposing all sorts of methods of media type detection (by magic byte patterns, file extensions, and so on) that we'll cover later in the chapter. The methods for media type detection are entirely driven by the richness of the underlying Tika MIME database that we'll explain in this section ad nauseam. Read on!

> **ALERT: SOURCE CODE AHEAD** Before getting too deep into the source code examples and MIME-info database in this chapter, we'd like to remind you to refresh your memory regarding working with the Tika source code and building the Tika codebase by reviewing section 2.1.

The Tika project maintains its own media type registry that contains both official IANA-registered types and other known types that are being used in practice. The Tika type registry also keeps track of associated information such as type relationships and key characteristics of the file formats identified by the media types. This section covers the basics of this registry and the key classes you can use to access the included type information.

4.2.1 The shared MIME-info database

Unix environments have traditionally had no standard way of sharing document type information among applications. This was a problem for popular open source desktop environments such as Gnome and KDE that are distributed with Linux. These environments strive to make the user experience more consistent with standard icons and program associations for all document types, akin to their commercial counterparts (Windows or the Mac desktop environment). To manage such document type information in a platform-independent manner, they came up with the Shared MIME-info Database specification (http://mng.bz/7Ylh), which among other things defines an XML format for media type information. This format, shown next, is used also by Tika.

Listing 4.1 Basic MIME-info database file

```
<mime-info xmlns="http://www.freedesktop.org/standards/shared-mime-info">

  <mime-type type="application/pdf">
    <alias type="application/x-pdf"/>              ◁──── Known aliases          ◁ Canonical
    <acronym>PDF</acronym>                         ◁──── Short acronym            name
    <expanded-acronym>                                                          ◁
      Portable Document Format
    </expanded-acronym>
    <comment xml:lang="en">                         │ Human-readable description
      PDF document                                 ◁─┘ in given language
```

```
    </comment>
    ...                                ◁—— Other details
    </mime-type>

    ...                                ◁—— Other media types

</mime-info>
```

A `mime-info` file contains a sequence of `mime-type` records that each describe a single media type. A type record specifies the official name of the type as well as any known aliases. For example, many officially registered media types are also known by experimental `x-*` names that predate the official type registration. A type record can also contain informal type names that are frequently used in human communications. Just like most people would call a domestic cat a *cat* rather than a "member of the *Felis catus* species," a term like *PDF document* is usually preferred to the more technically accurate `application/pdf` in informal language.

Capturing the media types in the `mime-info` file (called tika-mimetypes.xml in Tika's source) provides a single point of access for managing Tika's knowledge about media types. Tika ships with a rich, well-curated `mime-info` file, but nothing prevents you from adding to or removing from it to suit your needs. Just make sure that you try to fill in as much of the information shown in listing 4.1 as you can; it'll help Tika to detect the right file type, and your programs and operating systems to map that file to the right application.

Before going further into all the detailed type information that can be included in a `mime-info` database, let's first take a look at how you can access the recorded type information using Tika's APIs.

4.2.2   *The MediaType class*

Tika uses the `MediaType` class to represent media types. Instances of this class are immutable and contain only the media type's type/subtype pair and optional name=value parameters. The type and parameter names are all normalized to lowercase and the `MediaType` class supports the standard Java object equality and order comparison methods for easy use in all kinds of data structures. The class is depicted visually in the Unified Modeling Language (UML) notation in figure 4.4.

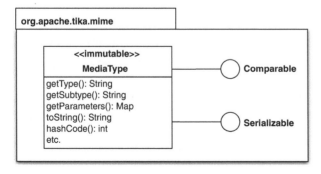

Figure 4.4   **Basic UML class diagram that summarizes the key features of the MediaType class. The class implements both the Comparable and Serializable standard Java interfaces. The type name, its subtype, and the associated type parameters are all available through getter methods, and the MediaType can be serialized to human-readable form by calling the toString method.**

The static `MediaType.parse(String)` method is used to turn media type strings such as `text/plain; charset=UTF-8` to `MediaType` instances. The type parser is flexible and tries to return a valid media type even for malformed inputs, but will return `null` if passed a string like "this is not a type" that simply can't be interpreted as a media type.

The following example shows how to use the key methods of the `MediaType` class. Full details of the class can be found in the API documentation on the Tika website:

```
MediaType type = MediaType.parse("text/plain; charset=UTF-8");

System.out.println("type:    " + type.getType());
System.out.println("subtype: " + type.getSubtype());

Map<String, String> parameters = type.getParameters();
System.out.println("parameters:");
for (String name : parameters.keySet()) {
    System.out.println("  " + name + "=" + parameters.get(name));
}
```

Individual `MediaType` instances don't do much, but they form the basis for higher-level concepts such as the `MediaTypeRegistry` class we'll encounter in the next section.

4.2.3 *The MediaTypeRegistry class*

The type information included in `mime-info` XML databases and other sources can be accessed through the `MediaTypeRegistry` class. As the name indicates, an instance of this class is a registry of media types and related information. The `MediaTypeRegistry` class and its important features are described in figure 4.5.

Tika contains a fairly extensive media type database that you can access using the static `MediaTypeRegistry.getDefaultRegistry()` method. The following example uses this method to print out all the media types and type aliases known to Tika. That's more than a thousand types!

```
MediaTypeRegistry registry = MediaTypeRegistry.getDefaultRegistry();

for (MediaType type : registry.getTypes()) {
    Set<MediaType> aliases = registry.getAliases(type);
    System.out.println(type + ", also known as " + aliases);
}
```

Now that we've studied the media type registry, we'll show you how the power and flexibility of Tika's media type detection mechanism is driven by the richness of the

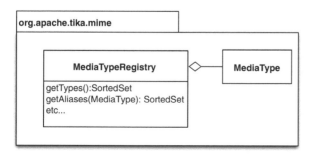

Figure 4.5 UML class diagram that summarizes the key features of the `MediaTypeRegistry` class. The class allows the set of loaded `MediaType` object instances to be returned as a `SortedSet`, and allows a user to obtain a `SortedSet` of aliases belonging to a particular `MediaType`.

information captured in its media type registry (aka MIME database, `mime-info` file, and the rest of the aliases we've given it so far). So, in other words, the more accurate, more fleshed-out, and more easily accessible and updateable Tika's media type registry is, the better your programs and software that leverage Tika will be able to discern the right application to handle files that you'll encounter.

A key part of the richness of the media type registry is the notion of media type hierarchies. Type hierarchies tell your applications things like the fact that the media type `application/xml` is a subtype of plain text (`text/plain`), and can be viewed in a text editor, not something like QuickTime for viewing movies.

4.2.4   *Type hierarchies*

Many media types are based on a more generic format. For example, all `text/*` types like `text/html` are supposed to be understandable even if treated as plain text, like when using the View Source feature included in most web browsers. It's thus accurate to say that `text/html` is a *specialization* of the more generic `text/plain` type.

These kinds of *type hierarchies* (parent-child relationships, or specializations) are different from the type/subtype categorization encoded in the standard internet media type system. Even though `text/plain` can be seen as a *supertype* of all `text/*` types, there's no similar generic format for all `image/*` types. In fact the Scalable Vector Graphics (SVG, `image/svg+xml`) format is based on XML (`application/xml`) and thus SVG images can also be processed as XML documents, the gist of which is demonstrated in figure 4.6. Such type relationships are often indicated with a name suffix like +xml. For example, the Electronic Publication (Epub, `application/epub+zip`) format used by many electronic books is actually a Zip archive (`application/zip`) with some predefined content.

Tika has built-in knowledge about handling text types and types with name suffixes such as +xml and +zip. Tika also knows that ultimately all documents can be treated as raw `application/octet-stream` byte streams. But more specific type hierarchy information needs to be explicitly encoded in the type database using `sub-class-of` elements as shown in the following example:

```
<mime-type type="application/vnd.apple.keynote">
  <sub-class-of type="application/zip"/>
</mime-type>
```
◁ **Keynote files as Zip**

```
<mime-type type="application/xml">
  <sub-class-of type="text/plain"/>
</mime-type>
```
◁ **XML documents as plain text**

image/svg+xml   application/xml   text/plain   octet-stream

Figure 4.6   Four levels of type hierarchy with the `image/svg+xml` type. The SVG image can be processed either as a vector image, as a structured XML document, as plain text, or ultimately as a raw sequence of bytes.

This kind of type hierarchy information is highly useful when trying to determine how a particular document can best be processed. For example, even if you don't have the required tools to process Keynote presentations, you may still be able to extract some useful information about the presentation by looking at the contents of the Keynote Zip archive.

Tika supports such use cases by making type hierarchy information easily available through the getSupertype() and isSpecializationOf() methods of the Media-TypeRegistry class. The former Java API method returns the closest supertype of a given media type (or null if the given type happens to be application/octet-stream), whereas the latter method checks whether a given type is a specialization of another more generic type. The use of the getSupertype() method is illustrated next:

```
MediaTypeRegistry registry = MediaTypeRegistry.getDefaultRegistry();

MediaType type = MediaType.parse("image/svg+xml");
while (type != null) {
    System.out.println(type);
    type = registry.getSupertype(type);
}
```

That's all there is to say about media types themselves. Let's move on to figuring out how you can tell the media type of any given file or document using this information about how to capture and represent. Even armed with this huge knowledge base of media type information, detecting the media type of a given file can be more complicated than you might expect. Tika simplifies this for you, and we'll show you how.

4.3   *File format diagnostics*

Biologists use details such as the shapes of leaves to detect different species of trees, and the color and patterns of feathers for bird species. Similarly, a researcher of document formats can use characteristic features of digital documents to detect the media types of those documents. This section is a guidebook for such a researcher, and provides you a full range of tools for detecting even the most unusual types of documents.

We'll begin with filename glob patterns, one of the most widely used and easy methods for media type detection. We'll cover content-type hints, magic bytes, and character encodings—a comprehensive set of digital fingerprinting techniques provided by Tika for identifying file types. The latter part of the chapter contains advanced techniques such as exploiting the structure of XML or combining both filename patterns and digital fingerprinting for detecting the underlying type of a file.

This entire section builds on the guidebook and information recorded and made available by Tika and its media type registry. Think of that registry as the biologist's sketchbook and additional literature that provide the necessary hints to make the species identification for the leaves that they're examining. See table 4.2 for a roadmap of the different detection types we'll cover in this chapter.

Table 4.2   Methods for detecting the type of a file using Tika. The methods build on top of the media type information curated in the Tika media type registry.

Method	Good for	Covered in
File globs	Well-known file types, with common extensions like *.txt, *.png.	Section 4.3.8
Content-type hints	When an application will touch a file before you do, and when it correctly identifies the right type (sometimes it won't!).	Section 4.3.9
MAGIC bytes	The general case. This approach works in most cases because nearly all file types have a unique digital fingerprint.	Section 4.3.10
Character encodings	When an odd charset was used and can be exploited in a fashion similar to MAGIC bytes as a digital fingerprint.	Section 4.3.11
Other mechanisms	If you're dealing with XML, whose digital fingerprint isn't always unique, but also whose schema can give away the underlying type.	Section 4.3.12
Combined approaches	In the most general case, as it combines the best capabilities of all of the underlying approaches.	Section 4.3.12

4.3.1   *Filename globs*

The simplest and most widely used mechanism for detecting file formats is to look at the filename. Most modern operating systems and applications use filename extensions such as .txt or .png to indicate the file type, even though this is mostly an informal practice with few guarantees that the extension actually matches the format of a file.

> **APRIL FOOLS'**   You can easily trick your computer using the concept of file extensions. For example, independent of whether you're using Windows or Mac, try taking an image file and changing its extension to .txt. Now, double click on the file. What happened? More than likely your computer tried to open the image file in a text editor program. It based this decision off of the file extension, which is as easy to change as the filename. Some modern operating systems try to use more information than the file extension to decide what application to open the file with.

Table 4.3 lists the name extensions of some of the more popular file formats.

Table 4.3   Popular file formats and their filename extensions

Extension	File format	Media type
.txt	Text document	text/plain
.html	HTML page	text/html
.xls	Microsoft Excel spreadsheet	application/vnd.ms-excel

Table 4.3 Popular file formats and their filename extensions *(continued)*

Extension	File format	Media type
.jpg	JPEG image	image/jpeg
.mp3	MP3 audio	audio/mpeg
.zip	Zip archive	application/zip

The practice of using filename extensions dates back to 40 years ago, when the operating systems of computers built by the Digital Equipment Corporation (DEC) started splitting filenames into a base name and a type extension. This practice was adopted by other vendors, including Microsoft who popularized the 8.3 filename format in their Disk Operating System (DOS) and early versions of Windows. Modern versions of Microsoft Windows no longer limit the filename length (in reality they limit length of the file path), but filename extensions are still used to determine which application should be used to process a file. Modern Mac OS and Unix systems handle filenames similarly.

In addition to filename extensions, there are also some more specific filenames and filename patterns that can be used to identify the type of a file. For example, many software projects contain text files such as README, LICENSE, and Makefile without any filename extensions. Unix systems also widely use textual configuration files whose names match the filename pattern .*rc (where * signifies any sequence of characters).

These and hundreds of other known filename patterns and extensions are included in Tika as <glob pattern="..."/> entries in the media type registry described in section 4.2. For example, here's how Tika represents the various file extensions typically used by C and C++ source files.

Listing 4.2 C and C++ filename patterns

```
<mime-type type="text/x-c">
  <glob pattern="*.c"/>
  <glob pattern="*.cc"/>
  <glob pattern="*.cxx"/>
  <glob pattern="*.cpp"/>
  <glob pattern="*.h"/>
  <glob pattern="*.hh"/>
  <glob pattern="*.dic"/>
  <sub-class-of type="text/plain"/>
</mime-type>
```

If you use file formats with specific extensions or filename patterns that Tika doesn't already know about, you can extend Tika with this information by modifying the tika-mimetypes.xml configuration file present in tika-core (recall section 2.3.7). Adding information to this file is as simple as pulling up the XML file in your favorite editor, quickly cutting and pasting some existing media type blocks, and then modifying the information for your new type and setting it to your liking.

Next, we'll study how to determine a file's media type leveraging information besides just the file extension, including leveraging hints *inside* the file.

4.3.2 *Content type hints*

Sometimes a document's filename isn't available, or the name lacks a type extension. This is common when the document is stored in a database, accessed over the network, or included as an attachment in another document. In such cases it's typical for the document to be associated with some external type information, most often an explicit media type.

For example, the HTTP protocol used by web browsers to request HTML pages and other documents from web servers specifies a `Content-Type` header that a server is expected to add to its response whenever it returns a document to the client.

Another example of this situation is when some application sets the `Content-type` metadata of a file, as when Microsoft Word saves a Word document for you. In these cases, regardless of the underlying extension that the application saves the Word document with (it could be named myfile.foo for all that it matters), Microsoft Word has still provided a *hint* to any other software that tries to detect the file's type.

We can exploit this information as part of our toolbelt, and we should when possible. But sometimes, this information isn't set, and even when it is, we're still not absolutely sure how much we can trust these content type hints, so Tika still goes the extra mile and employs more advanced techniques, such as magic byte detection.

4.3.3 *Magic bytes*

Filename extensions and other content type hints are usually fairly accurate, but there's no guarantee of that. In some cases such external information is either not available or is incorrect, so the only way to determine the type of a document is to look inside it and try to detect the document type based on its content.

A file format is just that: a format for expressing information in a file. Almost all file formats have some characteristic features or patterns that can be detected when looking at a file's raw byte contents. Many formats even include a *magic byte* prefix that's designed to accurately identify the file format. For example, the contents of GIF images always start with the ASCII characters GIF87a or GIF89a depending on the version of the GIF format used. More such magic byte patterns of common file formats are listed in table 4.4.

Using magic bytes as a means for media type detection is great, but it's only half of the problem. Another obstacle that presents itself is accurately identifying a file's character encoding, often referred to as its *charset*. In the next section, we'll explore this in detail.

Table 4.4 Magic byte patterns in popular file formats. Some of the patterns are represented as plain ASCII text, whereas others are shown in their hexadecimal equivalent.

Magic bytes	File format	Media type
`%PDF-` (ascii)	PDF document	`application/pdf`
`{\rtf` (ascii)	Rich Text Format	`text/rtf`
`PK` (ascii)	Zip archive	`application/zip`
`FF D8 FF` (hex)	JPEG image	`image/jpeg`
`CA FE BA BE` (hex)	Java class file	`application/java-vm`
`D0 CF 11 E0` (hex)	Microsoft Office document	`application/vnd.ms-excel,` `application/vnd.ms-word,etc.`

4.3.4 *Character encodings*

After the complexities of detecting magic bytes, file extensions, and content type hints, you might assume that at least the handling of plain text files should be simple. If only! The big problem with text is that there are so many ways of representing it as bytes. These representations are called *character encodings*, and there are hundreds of different encodings in active use.

As discussed earlier, the `test/plain` media type is often accompanied with a `charset` parameter that indicates the character encoding used in a text document. But even when this information is available, it's often incorrect. A better way of detecting the character encoding of a text document is clearly needed.

BOM MARKERS

The easiest way to detect a character encoding is to look for the optional *byte order mark* (BOM) used by Unicode encodings to indicate the order in which the encoded bytes are stored in the document. The Unicode character `U+FEFF` is reserved for this purpose and is included as the first character of an encoded Unicode stream. Table 4.5 shows how the BOM looks in the commonly used Unicode encodings.

If the first few bytes of a document match a known BOM pattern, you can be fairly confident that you're dealing with a text document in the character encoding indicated. Otherwise you're out of luck, since few of the other character encodings use byte order marks, and there are no other easy markers to be relied on.

Encoded BOM (hex)	Unicode encoding
`EF BB BF`	UTF-8
`FE FF`	UTF-16 (big endian)
`FF FE`	UTF-16 (little endian)
`00 00 FE FF`	UTF-32 (big endian)
`FF FE 00 00`	UTF-32 (little endian)

Table 4.5
BOM in common Unicode encodings

BYTE FREQUENCY

The best approach to detecting the type and encoding of such documents is to look at the frequency of different bytes within, say, the first few kilobytes of the document. Plain ASCII text hardly ever contains control characters except newline and tab, and most other character encodings avoid using those bytes for normal text. So if you see many control bytes (characters with code < 32), you can assume that you're not dealing with a plain text document.

If the document does look like plain text, you still need to determine the character encoding. There are a few tricks for detecting encodings such as UTF-8 that use easily recognizable bit patterns when encoding multibyte characters, and some character encodings never use certain byte values (for example, ASCII only uses the lowest seven bits).

STATISTICAL MATCHING

After you've checked for easy matches and ruled out impossible alternatives, the last resort is to use statistical matching to determine which character encoding is most likely to produce the bytes and byte sequences in the input document. Many character encodings are associated with a specific language or a group of languages for which the encoding is particularly designed, so the frequency of encoded characters or character pairs can be used for a reasonably accurate estimate of the language and encoding used in a document.

Tika's `MediaTypeRegistry` implements all of the aforementioned detection mechanisms and allows you to leverage them in your application. In the next section, we'll explore Tika's final type detection mechanisms, including XML root detection.

4.3.5 *Other mechanisms*

Some document formats are based on more generic formats like Zip archives (`application/zip`), XML (`application/xml`), or Microsoft's format for Object Linking and Embedding (OLE) or Compound File Binary File Format (MS-CFB: see http://mng.bz/gU1C) documents. Even if such a container format can be easily detected using magic bytes or other details, it may be difficult to determine if the format is used to host a more specific kind of document. The container format needs to be parsed to determine whether the content matches that of a more specific document type.

XML FORMAT

The most notable of such formats is XML, which has been used for countless more-specific document types such as XHTML (`application/xhtml+xml`) and SVG (`image/svg+xml`). To detect the specific type of a given XML document, the root element of the document is parsed and then matched against known root element names and namespaces.

OLE FORMAT

Microsoft's OLE format is another troublesome format to detect. Used by default by all Microsoft Office versions released between 1995 and 2003, many of which are still in production use, the OLE format is one of the most widely used document formats on the planet. The OLE format is essentially a miniature file system within a single file. Specifically named directories and file entries within such a file are used by specific programs, so the type of a document can be determined by looking at the directory tree of the OLE container. Unfortunately, the OLE format is somewhat complicated and requires random access to the document, which makes OLE type detection difficult for documents that are being streamed, for example, from a web server. Tika uses a best-effort approach for OLE detection that works pretty well in practice even within these constraints.

COMBINED HEURISTICS

These and other custom detectors are constantly being developed as Tika encounters new document formats that can't be detected using one or more of the simpler mechanisms we discussed earlier.

That's quite a load of different type detection mechanisms, and none of them promise to be absolutely accurate! Are we to announce defeat in the face of such complexity? Luckily the situation isn't that bad, as many of the preceding approaches can be used independently to verify the results of another detection method. Then, by combining the various detection heuristics at hand, we can come up with a highly accurate estimate of the media type of almost all kinds of documents. And the best part is that Tika does this automatically for you. The next section shows you how.

4.4   *Tika, the type inspector*

As you can probably remember from chapter 2, the `Tika` facade class has a `detect()` method that returns the detected media type of a given document. The `SimpleType-Detector` class shows how this works in practice.

Listing 4.3   Simple type detector example

```
import java.io.File;

import org.apache.tika.Tika;

public class SimpleTypeDetector {

  public static void main(String[] args) throws Exception {
      Tika tika = new Tika();

      for (String file : args) {
          String type = tika.detect(new File(file));
          System.out.println(file + ": " + type);
      }
  }

}
```

Pretty simple, right? Now let's look at what else you can do with type detection. The first thing is to switch to a customized type registry that contains some extra type information which you need in your application. The following shows how you can specify which media type configuration file is used by Tika. The default type configuration is included as an embedded classpath resource at /org/apache/tika/mime/tika-mimetypes.xml:

```
String config = "/org/apache/tika/mime/tika-mimetypes.xml";
Tika tika = new Tika(MimeTypesFactory.create(config));
```

In addition to passing java.io.File instances to the detect() method, you can also give it input streams, URLs, or even nothing but a filename string. In each of these cases Tika will do its best to combine all the available type information it has with the document details you've given. The result is usually the type you were looking for.

4.5   *Summary*

This completes our discussion of the taxonomy of document formats and the associated ways in which document types can be detected. We started by introducing the internet media type system and looking at how media types are handled in Tika using the mime-info database and the MediaType and MediaTypeRegistry classes. We then covered several heuristics for detecting document types, and finally brought it all together into the detect() method of the Tika facade.

By now you should know not only how to use Tika to detect document types, but also how Tika achieves this task internally and how you can extend Tika with custom type information. This knowledge will come in handy in the next chapters as we look at how to proceed from knowing the type of a document to being able to extract content and metadata from it.

Content extraction

5

This chapter covers

- Full-text extraction
- Working with the `Parser` interface
- Reading data from a stream
- Exporting in XHTML format

Armed with Tika, you can be confident of knowing each document's pedigree, so sorting and organizing documents will be a snap. But what do you plan on doing with those documents once they're organized?

Interactively, you'd likely pull the documents into your favorite editing application and start reading and updating their internal text. Programmatically, you're more than likely to do the same thing, and once you know what's what in terms of document types, and what applications are associated with them (like we showed you in chapter 4), you can make sure you're using the right parser toolkits and libraries to read and modify each document's text via your software program automatically.

But there are literally *scores* of those parsing toolkits and libraries, and each extracts the underlying text and information from documents differently. It'd help to have some software in your toolbelt that could assist you in choosing the right parsing library, and then normalizing the extracted text and information. Tika can

73

help you here. The original and most important use case for Tika is extracting textual content from digital documents for use in building a full-text search index—which requires dealing with all of the different parsing toolkits out there—and representing text in a uniform way.

This chapter describes Tika's content extraction capabilities in detail, and shows how this functionality can be used for full-text indexing and other related use cases.

We'll start with a simple full-text extraction and indexing example based on the Tika facade and the Apache Lucene search library. Then we'll proceed to cover the Parser interface that's the central abstraction for all the content extraction functionality in Tika. Finally, the latter half of this chapter discusses the inputs, outputs, and internals of Tika's parser classes. That's a lot of ground to cover, so let's get started!

5.1   Full-text extraction

The series of steps involved in generically extracting text from any type of document is somewhat involved. Though Tika exposes all of the steps as callable APIs and Java classes, allowing you to pick and choose how they're called, there's a common use case and ordering of the extraction steps.

We've codified that common use case as a method called parseToString within the Tika facade. Back when we first discussed the facade in chapter 2, we glossed over the internal steps that the method was abstracting. Not anymore. Let's take a deep dive into the method and see what it's doing. Once we know that, we'll show two ways to confidently integrate the facade method with Apache Lucene to perform full extraction and indexing.

5.1.1   Abstracting the parsing process

Let's look at the Tika facade and the parseToString method in action. Given a document as a file or an input stream, this method returns the text content of that document:

```
File document = new File("example.doc");
String content = new Tika().parseToString(document);
System.out.print(content);
```

What happens during this parseToString call when given the PDF version of this book as input? Figure 5.1 highlights the key steps of this process, and we'll discuss each of them in more detail next.

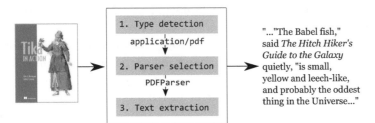

Figure 5.1   Overview of Tika's parsing process

1 First the `Tika` facade will use the heuristics described in chapter 4 to detect the given document's media type.

Our example document starts with the magic bytes `%PDF-`, which allow Tika to identify it as a PDF document, more precisely `application/pdf`.

2 Once the type of the document is known, a matching parser implementation is looked up. Tika comes with many different parser implementations, some based on external parser libraries and some included in Tika itself, and the one that can best parse the given document is automatically selected.

The `org.apache.tika.parser.pdf.PDFParser` class supports `application/pdf`, so Tika selects an instance of that class for parsing the example document.

3 The given document is then passed to the selected parser implementation, which interprets the bytes of the document according to the respective media type's rules. A `TikaException` is thrown if the document doesn't match these rules and thus can't be parsed. Alternatively, an `IOException` gets thrown if the input document can't be read.

The `PDFParser` class is a wrapper around the advanced PDF parsing capabilities of the *Apache PDFBox* library, so it passes the example document to PDFBox and converts the returned metadata and text content to a format defined by Tika.

The `parseToString()` method will also buffer the extracted text content in memory until the entire document has been parsed, and before the collected text gets returned to the client application as a single string. The buffer size is limited to 100,000 characters by default to avoid the risk of unexpectedly running out of memory.

This book is longer than the default limit, so somewhere around chapter 3 the buffer gets full and the rest of the book is ignored. The returned string starts with the foreword and continues with the text of the first few chapters of this book.

In sections 5.1.3 and 5.3.2 we'll cover how to deal with larger documents and other more complex topics, but let's first take a detour to see what we can do with the text we've just extracted.

5.1.2 *Full-text indexing*

Full-text search is the feature that makes it possible for a search engine to return all the documents that contain one or more words or phrases included in a user's query. Such search engines are increasingly important in our world of information overload, which makes full-text indexing one of Tika's key use cases.

Tika itself doesn't include indexing and querying capabilities, so you'll need to combine it with a search library such as Apache Lucene to implement full-text search. The `LuceneIndexer` class contains the essential piece of code needed for such integration.

Listing 5.1 Simple full-text indexer with Tika and Lucene

```
import java.io.File;
import org.apache.lucene.document.Document;
import org.apache.lucene.document.Field;
import org.apache.lucene.document.Field.Index;
```

```
import org.apache.lucene.document.Field.Store;
import org.apache.lucene.index.IndexWriter;          ⎤ Class for
import org.apache.tika.Tika;                          ⎥ full-text                        ⎤ Facade
public class LuceneIndexer {                         ⎦← indexing                        ⎥ instance for
                                                                                        ⎥ full-text
    private final Tika tika;                                                           ⎦← extraction
                                           ⎤ Lucene index writer for
    private final IndexWriter writer;     ⎦← indexing extracted text

    public LuceneIndexer(Tika tika, IndexWriter writer) {   ⎤← Create Lucene
        this.tika = tika;                                    ⎦  indexer instance
        this.writer = writer;
    }

    public void indexDocument(File file) throws Exception {      ⎤← Add file
        Document document = new Document();                       ⎦  to index
        document.add(new Field(
                "filename", file.getName(),
                Store.YES, Index.ANALYZED));
        document.add(new Field(
                "fulltext", tika.parseToString(file),
                Store.NO, Index.ANALYZED));
        writer.addDocument(document);
    }

}
```

A Lucene search index contains `Document` objects that themselves consist of named `Field` instances. Each `Field` can be stored as-is for later retrieval and/or indexed in various ways for searchability. For example, each `Field` may be tokenized on whitespace, to make it easier to search text by common keywords. Alternatively, `Fields` may be stemmed and their common roots be stored to make it easier to search on plural keywords. For example, this is useful when searching for the keyword *book* is expected to return hits containing the text *books*.

Once an index has been built and `Document` object instances have been recorded, users of Lucene can leverage the Lucene search API, which allows advanced searching against `DocumentFields` that have been indexed.

The code in listing 5.1 allows you to create a search index that can return the names of all files that contain selected words. The only missing piece is a `main()` method that opens an index for writing and adds selected documents to the index. Such a method is shown next:

```
public static void main(String[] args) throws Exception {
    IndexWriter writer = new IndexWriter(
            new SimpleFSDirectory(new File(args[0])),
            new StandardAnalyzer(Version.LUCENE_30),
            MaxFieldLength.UNLIMITED);
    try {
        LuceneIndexer indexer = new LuceneIndexer(new Tika(), writer);
        for (int i = 1; i < args.length; i++) {
            indexer.indexDocument(new File(args[i]));
        }
    } finally {
```

```
        writer.close();
    }
}
```

We're only scratching the surface of Lucene's indexing features here. Chapter 10 describes such Lucene integration and related search engine and web crawler projects in more detail. More comprehensive information on building search engines with Lucene can be found in the book *Lucene in Action*[1] or on the Lucene website at http://lucene.apache.org/.

With the preceding code you can already create a simple full-text search index, but a number of improvements could be made. The first and most obvious is the string size limitation of the parseToString method. In the next section we'll find out how to index documents of arbitrary length.

5.1.3 *Incremental parsing*

An average novel can easily contain more than 100,000 words, each about five characters long on average. Such an amount of text requires about a megabyte of memory when loaded into a string in Java. It's not uncommon for something like a Zip archive containing many e-books to expand to up to a gigabyte of text, which makes the parseToString method unsuitable for processing such documents.

The alternative is to use *incremental parsing*, which is supported by the parse method of the Tika facade. This method returns a java.io.Reader instance that the client application can use to incrementally read the text content of the parsed document. Lucene supports reader instances as field values, so it's easy to modify the indexDocument of our LuceneIndexer example to take advantage of this feature.

```
public void indexDocument(File file) throws Exception {
    Reader fulltext = tika.parse(file);
    try {
        Document document = new Document();
        document.add(new Field(
                "filename", file.getName(),
                Store.YES, Index.ANALYZED));
        document.add(new Field("fulltext", fulltext));
        writer.addDocument(document);
    } finally {
        fulltext.close();
    }
}
```

With this modification, our full-text indexer is capable of indexing the full contents of documents of all sizes. To query the search index created by our simple indexer example, you can use the IndexReader class from Lucene or a higher-level index browser tool like Luke.[2]

---

[1] *Lucene in Action*, written by Lucene developers Mike McCandless, Erik Hatcher, and Otis Gospodnetić and published by Manning, is the authoritative guide to Lucene. To find out more about the book, see the website at http://www.manning.com/hatcher3/.

[2] Luke is a development and diagnostic tool for Lucene search indexes. See the Luke website at http://sourceforge.net/projects/luke/ for downloads and documentation.

FIELD SIZE TRADE-OFF   In practice many search engines choose to sacrifice query accuracy for better performance and smaller index size. Lucene supports such trade-offs through the `IndexWriter` constructor's `MaxFieldSize` argument.

That's full-text extraction and indexing in a nutshell. Sounds simple, right? That's because the `Tika` facade was designed to make basic text extraction tasks as simple and easy to achieve as possible. Sometimes your needs are more complex, and that's where the `Parser` interface comes in. The rest of this chapter is dedicated to this interface and all the different ways it can be used to extract content from digital documents.

5.2   *The Parser interface*

The `Tika` facade simplifies and streamlines text extraction; it also, through its simplicity, insulates the user from being able to easily tweak each step in the process it automates.

Similar to its MIME identification system and metadata and language frameworks (which you'll read about in chapters 6 and 7, respectively), Tika's text extraction system is built on top of a set of extensible Java APIs. We'll elucidate those APIs to you in this section, walking you through Tika's `Parser` interface and its methods.

Once you have a working knowledge of the interface, we'll tell you about the existing `Parser` implementations in Tika, explaining how to customize them and using them as a model to write your own `Parsers` and integrate them back into the Tika text extraction process.

5.2.1   *Who knew parsing could be so easy?*

The `org.apache.tika.parser.Parser` interface is the cornerstone of the Tika API. It's used both as a public interface accessed by client applications and as an extension point implemented by parser plugins that each support different document formats. The interface has been carefully crafted over years based on experience and feedback from many different users and use cases. That's a lot of responsibility for a single interface, so let's see what it looks like.

Listing 5.2   Tika parser interface

```
package org.apache.tika.parser;

import java.io.IOException;
import java.io.InputStream;
import java.util.Set;

import org.apache.tika.exception.TikaException;
import org.apache.tika.metadata.Metadata;
import org.apache.tika.mime.MediaType;
import org.apache.tika.parser.ParseContext;
import org.xml.sax.ContentHandler;
import org.xml.sax.SAXException;

/** Tika parser interface. */
public interface Parser {
```

```
/** Returns the set of media types supported by this parser. */
Set<MediaType> getSupportedTypes(ParseContext context);

/** Parses a document stream into a XHTML SAX events and metadata. */
void parse(
        InputStream stream, ContentHandler handler,
        Metadata metadata, ParseContext context)
        throws IOException, SAXException, TikaException;

}
```

The Javadoc comments here have been trimmed to save space. The full Javadocs are available on the Tika website, and we'll discuss all the details of this interface shortly.

With just two declared methods, this interface is surprisingly compact when compared to the amount of functionality it hides. The first method, getSupported-Types(), is used internally by Tika when selecting the best parser implementation for parsing a given input document, a feature that we'll cover later in section 5.2.4. The second and more important method, parse(), is the real workhorse behind most of Tika's functionality. What's so special about this method? Read on to find out!

5.2.2   The parse() method

The parse() method takes four arguments that are used to pass information to and from the document parser. Instead of returning a formal return value, the parser implementation uses callbacks to pass parsed content back to the calling application. The information flows between the parse() method and its arguments are shown in figure 5.2.

The purpose of each of the four arguments is summarized in table 5.1.

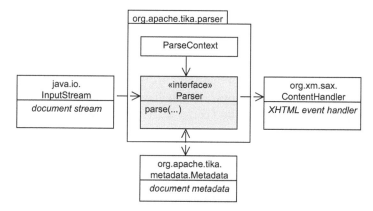

Figure 5.2   Information flows between the `parse()` method and its arguments. The input stream and metadata arguments are used as sources of document data, and the results of the parsing process are written out to the given content handler and metadata object. The context object is used as a source of generic context information from the client application to the parsing process.

Table 5.1 The arguments for the `org.apache.tika.parser.Parser`'s `parse()` method. Some of the arguments are only read, such as the `InputStream` and the `ParseContext`; some are callbacks (such as the `ContentHandler`); and some objects are actually written to, such as the `Metadata` argument.

Argument	Description
`InputStream stream`	The document input stream—The raw byte stream of the document to be parsed is read from this input stream. Note that this stream is read but *not closed* by the `parse()` method.
`ContentHandler handler`	XHTML SAX event handler—The structured text content of the input document is written to this handler as a semantic XHTML document. The use of XHTML as the output format allows Tika to represent structures like headings, paragraphs, and hyperlinks within the extracted text. Instead of serializing the XHTML output to a byte stream, it's delivered using the event-based SAX API which allows efficient and flexible post-processing of the extracted content.
`Metadata metadata`	Document metadata—The metadata object is used both as a source and a target of document metadata. Input metadata available to the client application, like the name of the document file, can be passed in the metadata object to help the parser better understand the document format. Parsed document metadata like the document title is written to the metadata object for use by the client application after the `parse()` method has returned. All aspects of metadata processing will be covered in chapter 6.
`ParseContext context`	Context of the parsing process—This argument is used in cases where the client application wants to customize the parsing process by passing custom context information. Things like custom XML parsers, alternative HTML mapping rules, and locale information can be injected through this context object.

If the parsing process fails for some reason, the `parse()` method throws an exception whose type indicates the kind of problem that was encountered, as shown in table 5.2.

Now that we know how `parse()` is supposed to behave, let's look at all the different ways in which it has been implemented by Tika.

5.2.3 *Parser implementations*

Tika supports dozens of different document formats through concrete parser classes that each support a single format or a family of closely related formats. There are also a few more generic implementations of the `Parser` interface, designed to simplify working with multiple different parsers. The class diagram in figure 5.3 summarizes these different kinds of parser classes and their relationships.

The format-specific parser classes support various document formats either by directly implementing the required parsing logic or preferably by relying on an external parser library. The goal of Tika is to provide a uniform API for content extraction, not to be the ultimate parser library that by itself understands all the document

Table 5.2 Potential problems that can be encountered during the `parse()` method. Outside of SAX parsing errors and I/O errors, Tika wraps the remaining parsing exceptions in its own custom `TikaException` class.

Error type	Description
IOException	Failure to read the input document—The parser reads the given `InputStream` in order to parse the document, but sometimes the stream fails with an exception, for example, if the underlying file, network resource, or other data source becomes unavailable. In such cases the parsing process is terminated and the exception gets thrown all the way up to the client application.
SAXException	Failure to process the XHTML SAX events—The extracted text is sent as XHTML SAX events to the given `ContentHandler` instance, which may sometimes have trouble processing the events. For example, a full-text indexer might need to throw an exception if the extracted text can't be written to the underlying search index. Like the `IOException`s discussed above, exceptions thrown by the content handler will terminate the parsing process and be delivered directly to the client application.
TikaException	Failure to parse the document format—The previous two kinds of exceptions indicate problems that come from outside the parsing process, either from reading the input document or from writing the extracted text content. What if the parser itself encounters an error, for example, when it fails to interpret the format of the given document? That's when a `TikaException` gets thrown.

formats in the world. Tika tries to leverage the existing content extraction capabilities of various open source parser libraries as much as possible, making the Tika parser classes behave as thin adapters between the uniform `Parser` interface and the custom APIs of the external parser libraries. For example, the `PDFParser` class uses the

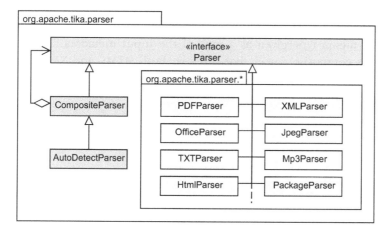

Figure 5.3 Class diagram that summarizes some of the most prominent implementations of the `Parser` interface. The generic classes in the `org.apache.tika.parser` package aren't tied to any specific document types, unlike the format-specific concrete parser classes organized in various subpackages.

`PDFTextStripper` class provided by the Apache **PDFBox** library to support the complex task of extracting text content from PDF documents.

The most notable of Tika's general-purpose parser classes are the `Composite-Parser` class and its subclass `AutoDetectParser`. The `CompositeParser` class implements the *composite pattern*[3] and allows a client to use a group of parser instances as a single parser that supports all the document types supported by any of the component parsers. Imagine being able to pick and choose which subsets of parsers out of Tika's bag you'd like to use for a given text extraction problem, and not needing to repeatedly configure and instantiate these parsers over and over again? Pretty useful, huh?

The `AutoDetectParser` subclass adds automatic type detection functionality, described in chapter 4, and uses it to automatically dispatch incoming documents to the appropriate component parsers using the composite methodology.

5.2.4   *Parser selection*

We've learned that there are multiple parser implementations in Tika, one for each document format and then some. How does Tika know which parser implementation to use for parsing a given document? That's what we'll find out in this section.

The simplest way to select a parser for a specific document format is to directly instantiate the corresponding parser class. For example, if you already know that you're processing an HTML document, then you can use the `HtmlParser` class directly like in the following example:

```
Parser parser = new HtmlParser();
parser.parse(stream, handler, metadata, context);
```

What if you need to support more than a single document format? Instead of using custom `if` or `case` statements to switch between different parser instances, you can use the `CompositeParser` class to automatically select a configured parser instance that matches the media type given as a part of the input metadata. The following example sets up a composite parser that supports both HTML and XML documents and that tries to parse any other input documents as plain text. The composite parser is then used to parse an HTML document:

```
Map<MediaType, Parser> parsersByType = new HashMap<MediaType, Parser>();
parsersByType.put(MediaType.parse("text/html"), new HtmlParser());
parsersByType.put(MediaType.parse("application/xml"), new XMLParser());

CompositeParser parser = new CompositeParser();
parser.setParsers(parsersByType);
parser.setFallback(new TXTParser());

Metadata metadata = new Metadata();
metadata.set(Metadata.CONTENT_TYPE, "text/html");
parser.parse(stream, handler, metadata, context);
```

---

[3] The composite design pattern is one of the most widely used patterns in object-oriented programming. It allows a client to treat a group of objects as a single instance, accessed using the same interface as any of the component objects.

An extra benefit of using the CompositeParser class is that you can use the setMedia-TypeRegistry() method to associate one of the media type registries discussed in chapter 4 with the composite parser. The parser will then automatically use the type inheritance rules encoded in the type registry to find the best match for a given input document type. For example, if the preceding code was given an XHTML document of type application/xhtml+xml, an associated type registry would automatically map that to text/html and cause the correct component parser to be selected.

Often the type of the input document isn't known in advance, so we need to use Tika's type detection capabilities described in the previous chapter. The easy way to do so is to use the AutoDetectParser class that extends the CompositeParser class with automatic type detection and other nice features. You can use AutoDetectParser as we just did by explicitly specifying the component parsers, but an easier way is to let it automatically look up and use all the available parser classes:

```
Parser parser = new AutoDetectParser();
parser.parse(stream, handler, metadata, context);
```

The preceding is just like our original example with the HtmlParser, but now we have a parser that automatically detects and supports all the document types known by Tika. How does this happen? The AutoDetectParser constructor first loads the default media type configuration included in Tika and then proceeds to look up all the available detector and parser implementations using Java's *service provider* mechanism. Type detectors are used to automatically identify the media type of the input document. Finally the appropriate parser for the detected media type is selected and used based on the type information returned by the component parsers' get-SupportedTypes() method.

> **SERVICE PROVIDERS IN JAVA**　A *service* in Java is a defined set of interfaces or classes, like the Parser interface and related classes in Tika. A *service provider* is a specific implementation of a service. For example, the XMLParser class is one provider of the Parser service.
>
> A particular service's available providers are configured in a *provider configuration* file located in the META-INF/services directory within a JAR archive. The provider configuration file for Parser services is called org.apache.tika.parser.Parser. This file lists the fully qualified class names of the service provider classes, and these classes get instantiated using the default constructor when the providers of the service are being looked up. In chapter 11 we'll look at how to use this mechanism to extend Tika with custom parser implementations.

Now we know what Tika's parsers look like and how they can be used separately or in combination. In the next sections we'll extend this knowledge by covering parser inputs, outputs, and internals in more detail.

5.3   *Document input stream*

At the core of Tika's `Parser` interface is the methodology by which Tika receives the input document: Java's `java.io.InputStream`. Standardizing on this class allows Tika to support streaming parsing for efficiency and for scalability.

This design decision also has some implications on how to feed Tika input documents from external sources, as well as how to best leverage the streaming interface for dealing with compression, and for dealing with parsing libraries that require the entire stream source for text extraction.

We'll discuss all of these challenges and how Tika's use of the Java `InputStream` class, as well as its own derivative input stream called `TikaInputStream`, help you overcome these difficulties with ease.

5.3.1   *Standardizing input to Tika*

The `java.io.InputStream` class is Java's lowest common denominator for reading any kind of raw byte streams. It defines a uniform API for reading digital documents regardless of their size or location, which is why the `Parser` interface uses an `Input-Stream` for reading the document to be parsed.

The following example shows how to pass a `java.io.FileInputStream` to a parser for parsing a document that's stored as a file in the local file system. Note how, as mentioned in the previous section, the responsibility to close the stream remains in the context where the stream was created:

```
InputStream stream = new FileInputStream(new File(filename));
try {
    parser.parse(stream, handler, metadata, context);
} finally {
    stream.close();
}
```

> **RESOURCE MANAGEMENT DONE RIGHT**   It's surprising how few APIs define proper resource management policies. Streams and other similar objects are often tied to costly system resources, and it's important that they be closed as soon as they're no longer needed. The best way to achieve such proper resource management is to make the creator of a resource also responsible for closing it, which is why the `parse()` method in Tika will explicitly *not* close the stream it's been given. Instead, the caller of the `parse()` method should use a `try-finally` block like in our example to guarantee that the stream is properly closed even if the parsing process fails with an exception.

The same mechanism can be used to parse documents that are stored in databases, accessed over the network, buffered in memory, or come from another source. Using an `InputStream` makes it also easy to apply decompression, decryption, or other filters before the parsing process. The following example shows how to parse a gzip-compressed network resource addressed with a URL:

```
InputStream stream =
    new GZIPInputStream(new URL(address).openStream());
```

```
try {
    parser.parse(stream, handler, metadata, context);
} finally {
    stream.close();
}
```

> **COMPRESSION NEVER STOPPED US BEFORE** Tika's built-in parsers for gzip and other common compression algorithms will automatically decompress the stream before recursively parsing the underlying document. Thus the text content extracted by Tika will be the same even if the client application doesn't apply a decompression filter like in our example. But the returned document metadata would refer users to the compressed stream, and, for example, the returned media type metadata would be application/x-gzip instead of the type of the underlying document. More about that later.

The InputStream class is a great least common denominator, but unfortunately it doesn't support random access reads, which are important for efficient processing of some file formats. For example, the OLE format used by older versions of Microsoft Office is designed for random access, and files such as Zip archives and PDF documents come with suffix sections at the end of the document stream that may affect the processing of earlier parts of the document.

One way to better support such formats would be to automatically spool the document input stream into a temporary file, but that would be highly inefficient if the document already exists on the local file system or is kept entirely in a memory buffer. Another approach would be to overload parse() with alternative ways to pass in the input document, but that would complicate the Parser interface and make it more difficult to use stream filters like in our decompression example. Is there a way to combine the benefits while avoiding the drawbacks of these different approaches? Yes, and it's called TikaInputStream.

5.3.2 *The TikaInputStream class*

The org.apache.tika.io.TikaInputStream class solves this problem by extending the InputStream class with methods for accessing the underlying file or other resource when it's available. The following example uses the TikaInputStream class to pass a local file to a parser:

```
InputStream stream = TikaInputStream.get(new File(filename));
try {
    parser.parse(stream, handler, metadata, context);
} finally {
    stream.close();
}
```

Here we're using the same parse() method as in the earlier examples, and a parser implementation that only needs normal InputStream functionality would behave as it did before. But a parser that needs access to the underlying file can do so using the extra methods provided by TikaInputStream:

```
TikaInputStream tikaInputStream = TikaInputStream.get(stream);
File file = tikaInputStream.getFile();
```

What if the `parse()` method is called with a normal `InputStream`? No problem, as the `TikaInputStream.get()` method will automatically wrap the given stream into a `TikaInputStream` instance that will spool the stream into a temporary file when the `getFile()` method is invoked. `getFile()` should be called before the stream has been processed; otherwise the method throws a `java.io.IOException`.

The extra functionality offered by `TikaInputStream` is summarized in the class diagram in figure 5.4. For example, the `hasFile()` method can be used to check whether the stream already has an underlying file that can be accessed directly. This is useful, for example, when parsing Zip archives, where direct access to the package index at the end of the file enables more accurate parsing results, but where the benefit isn't worth the extra cost of spooling the stream into a temporary file if the stream's not already backed by a file.

The static `get()` method, which is used to get or create `TikaInputStream` instances, is overloaded to allow multiple different document sources, ranging from byte arrays to network resources and database blobs. These factory methods also take an optional `Metadata` argument that's then filled with all available input metadata, including things such as the filename and length as well as any media type hint that's available when requesting resources from network servers.

As an extra benefit the `TikaInputStream` also includes efficient buffering and guarantees support for the `mark()` feature that's used by type detectors and many parser implementations. The `Tika` facade will automatically use the `TikaInputStream` wherever needed, and doing so is often a good idea, though not strictly necessary when you're dealing directly with the `Parser` interface.

THE MARK() FEATURE   This optional feature of the `InputStream` class allows a reader to `mark()` the current position of the stream and later `reset()` the stream to that earlier position. This is highly useful, for example, for parsers that need to look a few bytes ahead in the stream in order to decide how to proceed with the parsing process. Unfortunately many stream implementations that claim to support this feature fail to do so properly, especially around the end of the stream. Using `TikaInputStream` guarantees proper `mark()` support even in such corner cases.

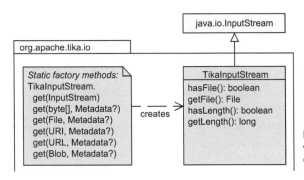

Figure 5.4   **Class diagram that shows the extra functionality provided by the `TikaInputStream` class**

That's pretty much all there is to say about passing documents to a parser. In the next section we'll look at what happens at the other end of the parsing process, where the extracted text content of the document is written back to the client application.

5.4 Structured XHTML output

The structured text content extracted by a parser is written out to the client application as a semantic XHTML document through a series of SAX events. That's a lot of advanced technology for something that could be covered by a simple character stream like the `Reader` returned by the `Tika` facade. To understand why Tika opts for the more complex solution, we need some background on how textual content is normally structured and why knowing that structure is useful to a computer program.

5.4.1 Semantic structure of text

Text is more than just a stream of characters. Starting with basic constructs like words and sentences, text is usually organized in increasingly large structures such as paragraphs, sections, chapters, and so on. Some pieces of text within such structures can serve special roles such as headings or captions. It's also possible for an author to specifically emphasize certain terms or phrases, for example, using italics or underlining. Finally, embedded links are an integral part of hypertext documents. The semantic structure of text is shown in figure 5.5.

These typographical constructs are used to organize and add meaning to written text, and are thus a part of the *semantic structure* of text. Document processing software and document formats typically include some of this structural information either directly (for example, by marking paragraph boundaries) or indirectly by including formatting information that a human reader or a sufficiently sophisticated program can use to deduce the structure. Having access to such information allows client applications to identify keywords, boost scoring of certain parts of the extracted text in a search index, follow hyperlinks to other related documents, and so on.

Deeper semantic details like the grammar of sentences, the meaning of words, or the overall style and composition of the document are still mostly beyond the capabilities of normal computer programs, so such information is only included implicitly in the text itself (see figure 5.6). The state of programmatic natural language processing tools like those provided by the Apache OpenNLP project[4] has been improving

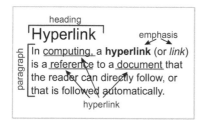

Figure 5.5 Structural breakdown of the beginning of the Wikipedia article on hyperlinks. In addition to the obvious heading, the authors of the text have used hyperlinks and different forms of emphasis to highlight key concepts in the opening paragraphs. These words—computing, hyperlink, link, reference, document—could well be treated as keywords of the document.

---

[4] http://incubator.apache.org/opennlp/

steadily over the last years and decades, which makes this level of information more readily available to computer programs. A good introduction to these topics is *Taming Text* (Ingersoll and Morton, Manning, publication projected for 2012).

Instead of trying to do such deep analysis of the document text, Tika strives to propagate the

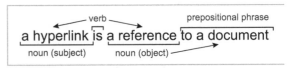

Figure 5.6 Grammatical breakdown of a simple sentence. Some computer programs and libraries can perform this kind of analysis of text, at times even more accurately than an average human, but the value of such analysis is limited without extensive knowledge about the meaning of words and their relationships. For now Tika doesn't attempt to parse such grammatical structures.

structural information encoded in the file format of the document. For example, the parser for Microsoft Excel spreadsheets produces normalized tables based on the worksheet structure of an Excel document. The design goal is to preserve all relevant structural information from the original document. If needed, more advanced semantic analysis tools (such as Apache UIMA) can then be used to post-process the output from Tika.

5.4.2 *Structured output via SAX events*

How should structural information be included in a Tika parser's output? The plain character stream returned by the Tika facade doesn't offer a place for such information, so a more complex output mechanism is needed. This is why the Parser interface uses a SAX content handler for the output.

SAX, or the *Simple API for XML*, is an event-based API for processing XML documents. SAX events that mark the opening or closing of XML elements, or the outputting of character data in between, are delivered as callbacks to the org.xml.sax .ContentHandler interface. This allows a parser implementation to easily annotate the extracted text with structural information. The callback mechanism avoids the need to build the entire XML document in memory or to serialize it into a byte stream that would then again be parsed to understand the contents. It also makes it easy for clients that are only interested in the extracted text stream to ignore the XML annotations by listening for only the character events.

> **PUSH AND PULL APIS**   SAX is a *push* API where the producer of content, in this case the parser instance, controls the flow of execution and uses callback methods to "push" out SAX events that carry information to the given event handler.
>
> This is different from the *pull* mechanism used, for example, by the Reader API as seen earlier with the Tika facade. Here the consumer of content, in our case the client application, controls the flow of execution and uses the read() method to "pull" characters from the reader instance.
>
> Most of the parser libraries used by Tika expect to be in control of the parsing process, so a push API like SAX is the best fit for the Parser interface. The

`org.apache.tika.parser.ParsingReader` class used by the `Tika` facade starts a background thread and an internal pipe to translate between these different API styles.

SAX is a perfect match for Tika's output needs, but as a generic XML API it doesn't specify any particular vocabulary that clients could use to understand the outputted XML elements. For example, a client that wants to extract all hyperlinks from a document needs to know which XML elements and attributes are used for the link annotations. Tika solves this problem by requiring all parsers to output strict XHTML markup. In addition, this information could also be codified as document metadata and extracted separately during the metadata processing step. We'll cover this in more detail in chapter 6.

5.4.3 *Marking up structure with XHTML*

The Extensible Hypertext Markup Language (XHTML, `application/xhtml+xml`) is a reformulation of the HTML standard using rigid XML instead of a more relaxed syntax. It supports familiar HTML markup elements and is easy to use with XML processing tools and APIs like SAX. To illustrate XHTML in action, the following shows how our earlier snippet from Wikipedia would appear in XHTML markup after processing by Tika's HTML parser:

```
<h1>Hyperlink</h1>
<p>In <a href="...">computing</a>, a <strong>hyperlink</strong>
(or <em>link</em>) is a <a href="...">reference</a> to a
<a href="...">document</a> that the reader can directly follow,
or that is followed automatically.</p>
```

MORE XHTML OUTPUT EXAMPLES   The Structured Text tab of the Tika GUI mentioned in chapter 2 is a good tool for reviewing Tika's XHTML output for different kinds of documents.

A `ContentHandler` instance passed as an argument to a `parse()` method call would see the preceding XHTML snippet as the following sequence of SAX events:

1 Start element `h1`
2 Output characters "Hyperlink"
3 End element `h1`
4 Start element `p`
5 Output characters "In"
6 Start element `a` with an `href` attribute
7 Output characters "computing"
8 End element `a`
9 Output characters ", a"
10 Start element `strong`
11 Output characters "hyperlink"
12 End element `strong`

13 Output characters "(or"

14 Start element em

15 Output characters "link"

16 End element em

17 Output characters ") is a "

18 Start element a with an href attribute

19 Output characters "reference"

20 End element a

21 Output characters "to a"

22 Start element a with an href attribute

23 Output characters "document"

24 End element a

25 Output characters "that the reader can ..."

26 End element p

That's a lot of tedious low-level processing, so Tika also provides utility classes in the org.apache.tika.sax package to make handling of SAX events easier. The most useful of these utilities are listed in table 5.3.

Table 5.3 Tika's SAX helper utility classes. These helper classes allow easy extensibility and customization of the output from Tika's text extraction functionality.

Class	Description
BodyContentHandler	The BodyContentHandler class picks the <body> part of the XHTML output and redirects it to another ContentHandler instance, writes the text content of the body to a java.io.Writer or java.io.OutputStream instance, or buffers the text in memory to be returned as a single string.
LinkContentHandler	The LinkContentHandler class detects all <a href="..."> elements in the XHTML output and collects these hyperlinks for use by tools such as web crawlers. Tika does its best to output fully resolved absolute URIs even if the document uses local URI references. This way you don't need to worry about tracking base URIs or correctly applying the sometimes complex URI resolution rules.
TeeContentHandler	The TeeContentHandler class delivers incoming SAX events to a collection of other event handlers, and can thus be used to easily process the parser output with multiple tools in parallel. Chapter 7 shows an excellent use case for this functionality.

The following example illustrates how these utility classes can be combined to write the text content of a document to a file while collecting any links for use in locating any referenced documents:

```
LinkContentHandler linkCollector = new LinkContentHandler();
OutputStream output = new FileOutputStream(new File(filename));
```

```
try {
    ContentHandler handler = new TeeContentHandler(
            new BodyContentHandler(output), linkCollector);
    parser.parse(stream, handler, metadata, context);
} finally {
    output.close();
}
```

You can mix and match such output processors as much as you like. Alternatively you could choose to use Java's TransformerHandler[5] class to serialize the XHTML output to be stored or transferred over the network as a byte stream. The serialized XHTML can later be parsed to run post-processing actions like the one shown here.

Now you know how Tika outputs the text content it has extracted and how you can process that output in your applications. Before wrapping up this chapter we'll look briefly at how you can use context to customize the parsing process and its output.

5.5 *Context-sensitive parsing*

The parser classes in Tika are mostly self-contained and need little external information apart from the actual document to be parsed and related input metadata. But there are a few cases where it's useful to be able to pass extra context information to a parser. This section summarizes the most important of such cases.

Context information is passed in the ParseContext argument to the parse() method, and parser implementations can use this information to customize the parsing process. A ParseContext instance is a simple container object that maps interface declarations to objects that implement those interfaces.

5.5.1 *Environment settings*

The simplest category of usable context information is various environmental settings such as the client application's locale or a specific XML library that should be used for parsing XML data.

Locale information specifies the way things such as numbers and dates should be represented in text. Some documents like Microsoft Excel spreadsheets contain such binary data that needs to be rendered to text when outputted by Tika. Since the spreadsheet documents usually don't specify the exact formatting or the output locale for such data, the parser needs to decide which locale to use. Using a hardcoded locale or the default locale of the Java runtime environment may not always be the correct solution, so a parser can allow the client application to explicitly specify which locale to use. The following shows how this is done:

```
ParseContext context = new ParseContext();
context.set(Locale.class, Locale.ENGLISH);
parser.parse(stream, handler, metadata, context);
```

---

[5] You can use the javax.xml.transform.sax.SAXTransformerFactory class to create SAX event handlers that transform SAX events to a DOM tree or serialize them to a byte stream.

Java supports multiple different XML parser libraries, but specifying which library and settings to use can be complicated. To address this problem, Tika allows a client application to explicitly specify which library should be used for parsing XML data both in entire XML documents and in XML snippets included as components of other document formats. To do this, a client application needs to pass a `javax.xml.parsers` `.SAXParserFactory` or a specific `javax.xml.parsers.SAXParser` instance through the parsing context.

5.5.2 *Custom document handling*

The environmental settings just described cause only minor modifications to a parser's functionality. Sometimes a client application needs more direct control over the parsing process to implement custom processing of specific kinds of documents. This can be achieved by passing custom handler objects through the parsing context.

The most notable of such handler interfaces is `HtmlMapper`, used by the `Html-Parser` class. The HTML parser first transforms the incoming HTML document to well-formed XHTML and then maps the included elements to a "safe" subset. The default mapping drops things such as `<style>` and `<script>` elements that don't affect the text content of the HTML page and applies other normalization rules. This default mapping produces good results in most use cases, but sometimes a client wants more direct access to the original HTML markup. The `IdentityHtmlMapper` class can be used to achieve this:

```
ParseContext context = new ParseContext();
context.set(HtmlMapper.class, new IdentityHtmlMapper());
parser.parse(stream, handler, metadata, context);
```

Another common case where custom processing is needed is handling of composite documents like Zip archives. When encountering such documents that contain other documents as components or embedded attachments, Tika will by default attempt to parse such component documents using a parser provided in the parsing context. The extracted text of the component document is then included in the output of the containing document.

Sometimes you'd rather process the component documents completely separately, for example, by adding all the entries in a Zip archive as separate entries of a full-text index. Such use cases can be implemented by passing a custom parser instance through the parsing context, as shown here:

```
ParseContext context = new ParseContext();
context.set(Parser.class, new ParserDecorator(parser) {
    @Override
    public void parse(
            InputStream stream, ContentHandler handler,
            Metadata metadata, ParseContext context)
            throws IOException, SAXException, TikaException {
        // custom processing of the component document
    }
});
parser.parse(stream, handler, metadata, context);
```

More information on the available customization options can be found in chapter 8 where we'll explore common document formats and the related parser classes in more detail.

5.6 *Summary*

This was a big chapter with lots of material, so let's take a moment to review what we've learned before moving on. We started with simple full-text extraction and indexing examples based on the `Tika` facade and the Lucene search library. Equipped with that background, we went on a tour through the `Parser` interface, its implementations, and the ways they can be used separately or in various combinations.

In the second half of this chapter we extended our coverage of the `Parser` interface to its inputs and outputs and the various utility classes Tika provides to support the parsing process. Finally, we looked at how context information can be used to customize the internal workings of Tika's parsers.

You should now have a good idea of the overall design and functionality of the content extraction features in Tika. To complete this picture we'll look at metadata extraction in the next chapter.

Understanding metadata

This chapter covers

- Metadata models and standards
- Metadata quality
- Capturing metadata with Tika

Conquering your fears of extracting text from files in a few lines of Java code has hopefully put Tika on your personal must-have list. The ease and simplicity with which Tika can turn an afternoon's parsing work into a smorgasbord of content handler plugins and event-based text processing is likely fresh on your mind. If not, head back to chapter 5 and relive the memories.

Looking ahead, sometimes before you've even obtained the textual content within the files you're interested in, you may be able to weed out which files you're not interested in, based on a few simple criteria, and save yourself a bunch of time (and processing power).

Take, for example, the use case presented in figure 6.1.

Figure 6.1 shows a user's perspective on a search engine. Much of the time is spent inspecting links—a critical step in the search engine process is deciding which links to follow (and which not to follow). Considering that some web pages may be larger than others, and unduly waste precious time and resources, a user's goal is to

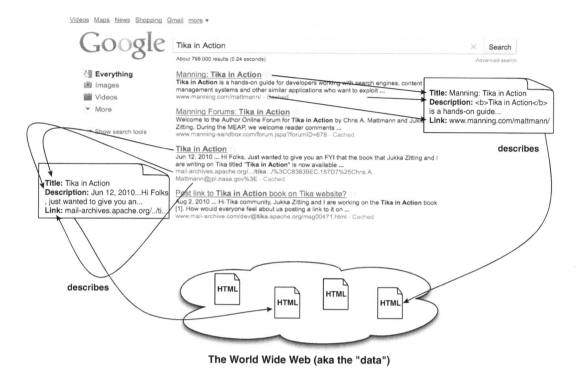

Figure 6.1 The search engine process and metadata. Metadata about a page, including its title, a short description, and its link are used to determine whether to "click" the link and obtain the content.

leverage the few pieces of *metadata*, or data about data, available in the web page's title, description, and so on, to determine whether the web page is worth visiting.

In this scenario, a user is searching for web pages about a new book on software technology written by a pair of good-looking gentlemen. The user is interested in purchasing the book and is ultimately searching for the first link returned from the Google search, but wants to consider at least a few other relevant web pages that may also yield the desired outcome. How should the user go about using the web pages returned from their query?

The user (often unconsciously) examines the few snippets of information available for each result in the list. These snippets of information include the web page's title, description, and URL. Whether they realize it or not, they're using metadata to make their decision. Clicking can be expensive, as sometimes web pages are large, and contain large numbers of scripts or media files that must be fetched by the browser upon requesting the web page.

This scenario illustrates the power of metadata as an effective summary of the information stored in web pages. But metadata isn't limited to a few simple fields—it can be much richer, and include date/time ranges, value ranges for particular data values, spatial locations, and a host of other properties.

Consider a set of PDF research paper files stored on a local hard disk. As a developer, you may be writing a program whose goal is to process papers written by a particular author (or set of authors), and to only consider those papers produced by a particular version of the PDF generation software. Since some of the files may be quite large, and contain fancy diagrams, tables, and figures, you may be interested in a quick means of deciding whether or not the PDF files are of interest to your program.

Metadata comes to the rescue again in this scenario, as often PDF files contain explicit document metadata that rapidly (without reaching into the file and extracting its textual content which may not even ultimately answer your question) exposes fields such as `Author` and `PDFVersion`, and that allows you to engage in the weeding out process quickly and with low memory footprint.

So, how does Tika help you deal with metadata? We'll spend the rest of this chapter answering that question in great detail. We'll first focus on exploring the existing metadata standards, and how Tika leverages these standards to provide a common vocabulary and representation of metadata across file formats. As the old saying goes, "The best thing about standards is that there are so many to choose from," but no need to worry—we'll point out which standards are more generic, and which are specific to concrete types of files.

Either way, you'll want to keep Tika close by, as it'll allow you to easily leverage all kinds of metadata standards, and to convert between them using metadata transformations. Capturing and exposing metadata from documents would be of little use without some quality control, so we'll explain how Tika helps you in that regard. Throughout the chapter, we'll build on top of the `LuceneIndexer` from chapter 5, focusing on making it metadata-aware.

To begin, let's discuss a few of the existing metadata standards to give you a feel for what types of metadata fields and relationships are available to you as a software developer, and more importantly, as a Tika user.

6.1   *The standards of metadata*

So metadata is useful summary information, usually generated along with the document itself, that allows you to make informed decisions without having to reach into the document and extract its text, which can be expensive. What are some of the types of things that you can do with metadata? And are there any existing metadata guidelines or specifications that you can leverage to help figure this out?

As it turns out, the answer to both questions is, *yes*! This section will teach you about the two canonical types of metadata standards as well as different uses of standards, including data quality assessment and validation, as well as metadata unification.

6.1.1   *Metadata models*

Though PDF file and HTML page properties are useful for making decisions such as *Do I want to read this research paper?* or *Is this the web page I was looking for?*, the property names themselves don't tell you everything you need to know in order to make use of them. For example, is `PDFVersion` an integer or an alphanumeric? This would be useful to know because it would allow you to compare different `PDFVersion` attributes. What about `Author`? Is it multivalued, meaning that a paper can have multiple authors, or is it only single-valued?

To answer these questions, we usually turn to *metadata standards* or *metadata models*. Standards describe all sorts of information about metadata such as cardinality (of fields), relationships between fields, valid values and ranges, and field definitions, to name a few. Some representative properties of metadata standards are given in table 6.1.

Table 6.1 Relevant components of a metadata standard (or metadata model). Metadata standards help to differentiate between metadata fields, allow for their comparison and validation, and ultimately clearly describe the use of metadata fields in software.

Property	Definition
Name	The name of the metadata field, such as `Author` or `Title`. The name is useful for humans to discern the meaning of the property, but doesn't help a software program to disambiguate metadata properties.
Definition	The definition of the metadata property, typically in human consumable form. If the metadata property were `Target Name` and the domain of discourse were planetary science, a definition might be, "The celestial body that the mission and its instruments are observing."
Valid values	The allowed or valid values for a particular metadata property. Valid values may identify a particular numerical range, for example, between 1 and 100. Valid values may also identify a controlled-value set of allowed values; for example, if the metadata property were CalendarMonth, a three-character representation of the 12 calendar months in a year, we may have a valid value set of {Jan, Feb, Mar, Apr, May, Jun, Jul, Aug, Sep, Oct, Nov, Dec}.
Relationships	Indicates that this property may have a relationship with another property, such as requiring its presence. For example, if the `Latitude` field is present, so should the `Longitude` field.
Cardinality	Prescribes whether the metadata property is multivalued, for example, metadata describing a file's set of `MimeType` names.

The *International Standards Organization* (ISO) has published a reference standard for the description of metadata elements as part of metadata models, numbered ISO-11179. Found at http://metadata-stds.org/11179/, ISO-11179 prescribes a generally accepted mechanism for defining metadata models.

Multitudes of metadata models are out there, and they can be loosely classified as either *general models* or *content-specific models*, as depicted in figure 6.2.

Tika supports both general and content-specific metadata standards.

GENERAL METADATA STANDARDS

General metadata standards are applicable to all known file types. The attributes, relationships, valid values, and definitions of these models focus on the properties that all

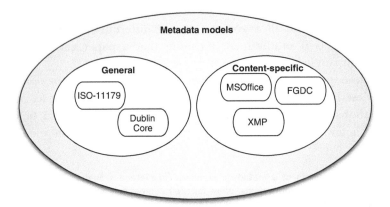

Figure 6.2   Classes of metadata models. Some are general, such as ISO-11179 and Dublin Core. Others are content-specific: they're unique to a particular file type, and only contain metadata elements and descriptions which are relevant to the content type.

electronic documents share (title, author, format, and so forth). Some examples of these models include ISO-11179 and Dublin Core, http://dublincore.org/. ISO-11179 defines the important facets of metadata attributes that are part of a metadata model. Dublin Core is a general metadata model consisting of less than 20 attributes (`Creator`, `Publisher`, `Format`) which are said to describe *any electronic resource*. Finally, the Extensible Metadata Platform (XMP: see http://www.adobe.com/products/xmp/) is a generic standard that provides a unified way for storing and transmitting metadata information based on various different *metadata schemas* such as Dublin Core or the more content-specific ones described next.

CONTENT-SPECIFIC METADATA STANDARDS

Content-specific metadata standards are defined according to the important relationships and attributes associated with *specific file types* and aren't exclusively generic. For example, attributes, values, and relationships associated with Word documents such as the number of words or number of tables aren't likely to be relevant to other file types, such as images. Other examples of content-specific metadata standards are Federal Geographic Data Committee (FGDC), a model for describing spatial data files, and the XMP dynamic media schema (xmpDM), a metadata model for digital media such as images, audio, and videos.

You can get a list of which standard metadata models your version of Tika supports via the `--list-met-models` option we saw in chapter 2:

```
java -jar tika-app-1.0.jar --list-met-models
```

The full output is a long list of supported metadata, so instead of going through it all, let's focus on a few good examples of both generic and content-specific metadata models. In appendix B you'll find a full description of all the metadata models and keys supported by Tika.

6.1.2 *General metadata standards*

Most electronic files available via the internet have a common set of metadata properties, the conglomerate of which are part of what we call *general metadata models* or *general standards* for metadata. General models describe electronic resources at a high level as in who authored the content, what format(s) the content represented is in, and the like.

To illustrate, let's look at some of the properties of the Dublin Core metadata model as supported by Tika. Recall the command we showed in the previous section. By using a simple `grep` command, we can augment the `--list-met-models` output to isolate only the Dublin Core part:

```
java -jar tika-app-1.0.jar --list-met-models | grep -A16 DublinCore
```

This produces the following output:

```
DublinCore
 CONTRIBUTOR
 COVERAGE
 CREATOR
 DATE
 DESCRIPTION
 FORMAT
 IDENTIFIER
 LANGUAGE
 MODIFIED
 PUBLISHER
 RELATION
 RIGHTS
 SOURCE
 SUBJECT
 TITLE
 TYPE
```

Looking at these attributes, it's clear that most or all of them are representative of *all* electronic documents. Think back to table 6.1. What would the valid values be for something like the `FORMAT` attribute? Most of the time the metadata field is filled with a valid MIME media type as we discussed in chapter 4. What would the cardinality be for something like the `AUTHOR` attribute? A document may be authored by multiple people, so the cardinality is one or more values.

We'll cover ways that Tika can help you codify the information from table 6.1 on a per-property basis later in section 6.1.4. For now, let's focus in on content-specific metadata models.

6.1.3 *Content-specific metadata standards*

Generic metadata standards and models are great because they address two fundamentally important facets of capturing and using metadata:

- *Filling in at least some value per field*—Content-specific metadata standards provide at least some value for each field (for example, for a PDF file the values for

FORMAT and TITLE might be application/pdf and mypdffile.pdf, respectively), reducing the generic nature of the metadata.

- *Being easily comparable*—Mainly due to having some default value, the actual attributes themselves are so general that they're more likely to mean the same thing (it's clear what TITLE is referring to in a document).

On the other hand, content-specific metadata standards and models are less likely to fulfill either of these properties. First, they aren't guaranteed to fill in any values of any of their particular fields. Take MS Office files and their field, COMPANY, derived from the same grep trickery we showed earlier:

```
java -jar target/tika-app-1.0.jar --list-met-models | grep -A28 MSOffice

MSOffice
 APPLICATION_NAME
 APPLICATION_VERSION
 AUTHOR
 CATEGORY
 CHARACTER_COUNT
 CHARACTER_COUNT_WITH_SPACES
 COMMENTS
 COMPANY
 CONTENT_STATUS
 CREATION_DATE
 EDIT_TIME
 KEYWORDS
 LAST_AUTHOR
 LAST_PRINTED
 LAST_SAVED
 LINE_COUNT
 MANAGER
 NOTES
 PAGE_COUNT
 PARAGRAPH_COUNT
 PRESENTATION_FORMAT
 REVISION_NUMBER
 SECURITY
 SLIDE_COUNT
 TEMPLATE
 TOTAL_TIME
 VERSION
 WORD_COUNT
```

COMPANY will only be filled out if the user entered a company name when installing MS Office on the computer that created the file. So, if you didn't fill out the Company field when registering MS Office, and you begin sharing MS Word files with your other software colleagues, they won't be able to use Tika to see what company you work for. (For privacy-minded people, this is a good thing!)

As for being easily comparable, this is another area where content-specific metadata models don't provide a silver bullet. The LAST_MODIFIED field in the Http-Headers metadata model doesn't correspond directly to the MODIFIED field in the

`DublinCore` model, nor does it correspond to the `LAST_SAVED` field from the `MSOffice` metadata model. So, content-specific metadata model attributes aren't easily comparable across metadata models.

Most document formats in existence today have a content- or file-specific metadata model associated with them (even in the presence of a general model, like Dublin Core). In addition to common models such as XMP, there are a slew of MS Office metadata formats, various models for science files such as Climate Forecast for climate sciences and FITS for astrophysics. A bunch of formats are out there, and their specifics are outside the scope of this book. The good news is this: Tika already supports a great number of existing content-specific metadata models, and if it doesn't support the one you need, it's extensible so you can add your own. We'll show you how throughout the rest of the chapter.

Let's not get too far ahead of ourselves though. First we'll tell you a bit about metadata quality, and how it influences all sorts of things like comparing metadata, understanding it, and validating it.

6.2 Metadata quality

Metadata is like the elephant in the room that no one wants to be the first to identify: how did it get there? What's it going to do? *What can we do with it?*

Metadata comes from a lot of different actors in the information ecosystem. In some cases, it's created when you save files in your favorite program. In other cases, other software that touches the files and delivers them to you over the internet annotates the file with metadata. Sometimes, your computer OS will create metadata for your file.

With so many hands touching a file's metadata, it's likely that the quality and abundance of the metadata captured about your files will be of varying *quality*. This can lead to problems when trying to leverage the metadata captured about a file, for example, for validation, or for making decisions about what to do with the file.

In this section, we'll walk you through the challenges of metadata quality and then see how Tika comes to the rescue, helping you more easily compare and contrast the collected metadata about your files. Onward!

6.2.1 Challenges/Problems

The biggest thing we've glossed over until now is how metadata gets populated. In many cases, the application that generates a particular file is responsible for annotating a file with metadata. An alternative is that the user may explicitly fill out metadata about the file on their own when authoring it. Many software project management tools (such as MS Project, or FastTrack on Mac OS X) prompt a user to fill out basic metadata fields (Title, Duration, Start Project Date, End Project Date, and so on) when authoring the file.

Sometimes, downstream software programs author metadata about files. A classic example is when a web server returns metadata about the file content it's delivering

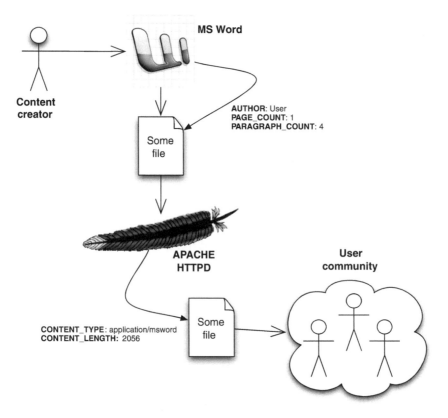

Figure 6.3   A content creator (shown in the upper left portion of the figure) may author some file in Microsoft Word. During that process, Word annotates the file with basic `MSOffice` **metadata. After the file is created, the content creator may publish the file on an Apache HTTPD web server, where it will be available for downstream users to acquire. When a downstream user requests the file from Apache HTTPD, the web server will annotate the file with other metadata.**

back to a user request. The web server isn't the originator of the file, but it has the ability to tell a requesting user things such as file size, content type (or MIME type), and other useful properties. This is depicted in figure 6.3.

With all of these actors in the system, it's no wonder that metadata *quality*, or the examination and assessment of captured metadata for file types, is a big concern. In any of the steps in figure 6.3, the metadata for the file could be changed or simply not populated, affecting some downstream user of the file or some software that must make sense of it later.[1] What's more, even if the metadata is populated, it's often difficult to compare metadata captured in different files, even if the metadata captured represents the same terminology. This is often due to each metadata model using its

---

[1] In a way, this is one of the main things that makes metadata extraction, and libraries that do so like Tika, so darned useful. So maybe we Tika community members should be happy this occurs!

own terms, potentially its own units for those terms, and ultimately its own definitions for those terms as well.

Metadata quality is of prime importance, especially in the case of correlating metadata for files of different types, and most often different metadata models. As a writer of software that must deal with thousands of different file types and metadata models every day, it's no easy challenge to tackle metadata correlation. You're probably getting used to this broken record by now, but here comes Tika to save the day again!

6.2.2 *Unifying heterogeneous standards*

Lucky for us, Tika's metadata layer is designed with metadata quality in mind. Tika provides a `Property` class based on the XMP standard for capturing metadata attributes. XMP defines a *property* (called `PropertyType` in Tika) as some form of metadata captured about an annotated document. XMP also defines *property values* that are captured for each metadata property. In Tika we call XMP property values `ValueTypes`. Let's take a quick look at a snippet of the Tika `Property` class.

Listing 6.1 `Property` class and support for XMP-like metadata

```
public final class Property {

    public static enum PropertyType {                    Maps to
        SIMPLE, STRUCTURE, BAG, SEQ, ALT                 XMP property
    }

    public static enum ValueType {
        BOOLEAN, OPEN_CHOICE, CLOSED_CHOICE, DATE, INTEGER, LOCALE,
        MIME_TYPE, PROPER_NAME, RATIONAL, REAL, TEXT, URI, URL, XPATH
    }                              Maps to XMP
    // ...                         property value
}
```

The `PropertyType` and `ValueType` enums allow Tika to define a metadata attribute's cardinality (is it a `SIMPLE` value, or a sequence of them—called `SEQ` for shorthand), its controlled vocabulary (a `CLOSED_CHOICE` or simple `OPEN_CHOICE`), and its units (a `REAL` or an `INTEGER`). Using Tika and its `Property` class, you can decide whether `LAST_MODIFIED` in the `HttpHeaders` metadata model is roughly equivalent in terms of units, controlled vocabulary, and cardinality to that of `LAST_SAVED` in the `MSOffice` metadata model.

These capabilities are useful in comparing metadata properties (recall from table 6.1 that these are important things to capture for each metadata element), in validating them, in understanding them, and in dealing with heterogeneous metadata models and formats. Tika's goal is to allow you to curate high-quality metadata in your software application.

So now that you're familiar with metadata models, Tika's support for the different properties of metadata models, and most of the important challenges behind dealing with metadata models, it's time to learn about Tika's metadata APIs in greater detail.

6.3   *Metadata in Tika*

In this section, we'll jump into Tika's code-level support for managing *instances* of metadata—the actual information captured in metadata, informed by the metadata models. Specifically we'll explore Tika's `org.apache.tika.metadata` package and its `Metadata` and `Property` classes, and their relationships. These classes will become your friend: transforming metadata and making it viewable by your end users is going to be something that you'll have to get used to. Never fear! Tika's here to help.

We've talked a lot so far about metadata *models*, but we've done little to show what *instances* of those models look like. Metadata instances are actual metadata attributes, prescribed by a model, along with their values that are captured for files. In other words, instances are the actual metadata captured for each file that you run through Tika. Let's get ourselves some metadata to work with in the following listing. When given a URL, the program will obtain the metadata corresponding to the content available from that URL.

Listing 6.2   Metadata instances in Tika

```
public class DisplayMetInstance {

  public static Metadata getMet(URL url) throws IOException, SAXException,
      TikaException {
    Metadata met = new Metadata();
    PDFParser parser = new PDFParser();
    parser.parse(url.openStream(), new BodyContentHandler(), met,
        new ParseContext());
    return met;                                          Get metadata
  }                                                   ❶ from URL

  public static void main(String[] args) throws Exception {
    Metadata met = DisplayMetInstance.getMet(new URL(args[0]));
    System.out.println(met);                      Print
  }                                                metadata

}
```

The output from this program is a Java `String` representation of the Tika `Metadata` instance. Run listing 6.2 on a PDF file (passed in via the URL parameter identified ❶) and the output may look like the following (reformatted for easier viewing):

```
created=Sun Jul 25 09:32:47 PDT 2010
producer=pdfeTeX-1.21a
creator=TeX
xmpTPg:NPages=20
PTEX.Fullbanner=This is pdfeTeX, Version 3.141592-1.21a-2.2 (Web2C 7.5.4) \
                kpathsea version 3.5.6
Creation-Date=2010-07-25T16:32:47Z
Content-Type=application/pdf
```

The preceding example contains seven metadata attributes—`created`, `producer`, `creator`, `xmpTPg:NPages`, `PTEX.Fullbanner`, `Creation-Date`, and `Content-Type`—and seven corresponding metadata values. The values and attributes used in this `Metadata` object instance in Tika were selected by the `PdfParser` class in Tika. Recall from chapter 5 that each Tika `Parser` class not only extracts text using XHTML as the representation, but also extracts and populates `Metadata`, provided to it in its `parse()` method:

```
void parse(
    InputStream stream, ContentHandler handler,
    Metadata metadata, ParseContext context)
    throws IOException, SAXException, TikaException;
```

Each Tika `Parser` is responsible for using the metadata models defined in the Tika metadata package to determine which metadata attributes to populate. Looking at the example, metadata attributes such as `Content-Type` come from the `HttpHeaders` model, others such as `creator` are defined by the `DublinCore` model, and for flexibility, Tika allows other attributes (and values) to be populated that may not yet have a defined metadata model in Tika's `org.apache.tika.metadata` package.

At its core, Tika provides a `Metadata` class and a map of keys and their multiple values to record metadata for files it examines. Let's wave the magnifying class over it and see what's inside.

6.3.1 *Keys and multiple values*

Tika's `Metadata` class, shown in figure 6.4, provides all of the necessary methods and functionality for recording metadata instances extracted from files. The class inherits and implements the set of metadata models (such as `DublinCore`) shown in the periphery of the diagram. The core class, `org.apache.tika.metadata.Metadata`, is a key/multivalued structure that allows users to record metadata attributes as keys using the `set(Property,...)` methods (which use the `Property` class previously discussed). The `Metadata` class allows a user to add multiple values for the same key (as in the case of `Metadata.AUTHOR` having multiple author values) using the `add(String, String)` method. The class also provides other methods that allow for introspection, including `names()`, which returns the set of recorded attribute names in the `Metadata` object instance, and the `isMultiValued(String)` method that allows users to test whether a particular metadata attribute has more than one value recorded. The `Metadata` class has a set of XMP-compatible `Property` attributes as we mentioned earlier, where each property is defined by its `PropertyType` (think *attribute name*) and its associated `PropertyValue` (think *attribute value*). `Property` classes provide facilities for validating and checking attributes, their units, and types, and for cross-comparing them.

To implement various metadata models, the `Metadata` class implements several model interfaces, such as `ClimateForecast`, `TIFF`, and `Geographic`, each of which provide unique metadata attributes to the `Metadata` object instance. The `Metadata` class has a one-to-many relationship with the `Property` class. Each `Property` provides necessary methods for validating metadata values, for example, making sure that they come from a controlled value set, or checking their units. This is accomplished using the XMP-like `PropertyType` and `PropertyValue` helper classes.

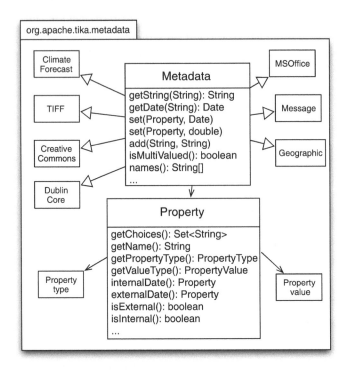

Figure 6.4 The code-level organization of the Tika metadata framework. A core base class, `Metadata`, provides methods for getting and setting metadata properties, checking whether they're multivalued, and representing metadata in the correct units.

Tika's `Parser` implementations can use the `Metadata` class, as can users of Tika who are interested in recording metadata and leveraging commonly defined metadata attributes and properties. Because of its general nature, the `Metadata` class serves as a great intermediate container of metadata, and can help you generate a number of different views of the information you've captured, including RSS and other formats.

6.3.2 *Transformations and views*

Since metadata extraction can be time-consuming, often involving the integration of parsing libraries, MIME detection strategies, text extraction, and other activities, once you have metadata for a corpus of files, you'll probably want to hold on to it for a while. But the metadata community is constantly defining new metadata standards that somehow better support a particular user community's needs.

Because of this, you'll inevitably be asked the question, "Can you export file X's metadata in my new Y metadata format?" It's worth considering what that request entails. Before you jump across the table and attack the person who caused you more work, consider how Tika can be of service to help defuse this situation.

REPRESENTING METADATA INSTANCES

Often, new metadata models are simply formatting variations and different representations of existing attributes defined in common metadata models, and already captured by Tika. Let's take the Really Simple Syndication (RSS) format as an example. RSS has been a commonly used XML-based format since the early 2000s, and is integrated into most web browsers and news websites as a means of publishing and subscribing to frequently changing content. RSS defines a *channel* as a set of recently published items. Each RSS document usually contains a single Channel tag (such as News Items or Hot Deals!), and several Item tags which correspond to the recent documents related to that channel.

TRANSFORMING RECORDED METADATA

As it turns out, turning basic key/multivalued metadata into RSS isn't as challenging as you may think. The same is true for changing basic key/multivalued metadata into a number of similar XML-based formats, or *views* of your captured metadata. The steps involved usually boil down to the following:

1 *Map the metadata attribute keys into the view's tag or item names*—This process amounts to deciding for each metadata attribute in your recorded metadata what the corresponding view tag's name is (for example, `Metadata.SOURCE` maps to RSS's `link` tag).

2 *Extract the metadata values for each mapped view tag and format accordingly*—For each mapped view tag, grab the values in the recorded metadata and shovel them into the view's output XML representation (for example, shove the value for `Metadata.SOURCE` into the value for the `link` tag, and enclose it within an outer `item` tag).

Now that you know how to represent metadata instances and values in Tika, and how to transform that recorded metadata, let's take a real use case and revisit the `Lucene-Indexer` example from chapter 5. We'll augment it to explicitly record `DublinCore` metadata, and then use that to feed an RSS service that shows the files recently indexed in the last 5 minutes. Sound difficult? Nah, you've got Tika!

6.4   *Practical uses of metadata*

Remember the `LuceneIndexer` from chapter 5? It was a powerful but simple example that showed how you could use the `Tika` facade class to automatically select a Tika `Parser` for any file type that you encountered in a directory, and then index the content of that file type inside of the Apache Lucene search engine.

One thing that we skipped in that prior example was using Tika to extract not just the textual content from the files we encountered, but the metadata as well. Now that you're a metadata master, you're ready for this next lesson in your Tika training. We'll show you two variations where we augment the `LuceneIndexer` with explicit recording of metadata fields. In the first example, we'll specifically index `DublinCore` metadata, leveraging Tika's support for metadata models. In the second example, you'll see how easily Tika can be used to extract content-specific metadata for *any* type of file encountered.

6.4.1 *Common metadata for the Lucene indexer*

Let's hop to it. The following listing rethinks the indexDocument(File) function from the existing LuceneIndexer and records some explicit file metadata using the Dublin-Core model.

Listing 6.3 Extending the Lucene indexer with generic metadata

```
public void indexWithDublinCore(File file) throws Exception {
  Metadata met = new Metadata();
  met.add(Metadata.CREATOR, "Manning");
  met.add(Metadata.CREATOR, "Tika in Action");
  met.set(Metadata.DATE, new Date());
  met.set(Metadata.FORMAT, tika.detect(file));
  met.set(DublinCore.SOURCE, file.toURL().toString());
  met.add(Metadata.SUBJECT, "File");
  met.add(Metadata.SUBJECT, "Indexing");
  met.add(Metadata.SUBJECT, "Metadata");
  met.set(Property.externalClosedChoise(Metadata.RIGHTS,
      "public", "private"), "public");
  InputStream is = new FileInputStream(file);
  tika.parse(is, met);
  try {
    Document document = new Document();
    for (String key : met.names()) {
      String[] values = met.getValues(key);
      for (String val : values) {
        document.add(new Field(key, val, Store.YES, Index.ANALYZED));
      }
      writer.addDocument(document);
    }
  } finally {
    is.close();
  }
}
```

It's worth pointing out that Tika's Metadata class explicitly supports recording metadata as Java core types—String, Date, and others. If you record metadata using a non-String type, Tika will perform validation for you on the field. At the time of this writing, Tika's support explicitly focuses on Date properties, but additional support is being added to handle the other types. Note the use of the add(String,String) method to record metadata that contains multiple values (like Metadata.CREATOR). The example in listing 6.3 also includes the use of an XMP-style explicit closed choice, recording whether the indexed file is public or private, in terms of its security rights (defined in DublinCore as DublinCore.RIGHTS).

Listing 6.3 is great because it uses a common, general metadata model like Dublin Core to record metadata (we saw in section 6.3.2 what this can buy us), but our example is limited to only using one set of metadata attributes. What if we wanted to use metadata attributes from all of the different metadata models that Tika supports?

Listing 6.4 Extending the Lucene indexer with content-specific metadata

```
public void indexContentSpecificMet(File file) throws Exception {
  Metadata met = new Metadata();
  InputStream is = new FileInputStream(file);          Leverage
  tika.parse(is, met);                                 Tika facade
  try {
    Document document = new Document();
    for (String key : met.names()) {
      String[] values = met.getValues(key);
      for (String val : values) {
        document.add(new Field(key, val, Store.YES, Index.ANALYZED));
      }
      writer.addDocument(document);                    Any metadata
    }                                                  model handled
  } finally {
    is.close();
  }
}
```

In this example, we leverage the `Tika` facade class and its `parse(InputStream, Metadata)` method, an entry point into all of Tika's underlying `Parser` implementations. By leveraging the `Tika` facade, we allow any of Tika's `Parsers` to be called, and to contribute metadata in their respective metadata models to the underlying file that we're indexing in Lucene. Pretty easy, huh?

Now that you have support for arbitrary metadata indexing and the ability to build up your corpus of metadata, let's see how you can easily transform that metadata and satisfy the inevitable questions you'll get from some of your downstream users. Just remember, Tika wants you to build bridges to your users, not choke them!

6.4.2 Give me my metadata in my schema!

Suppose one of your users asked you to produce an RSS-formatted report of all of the files your server received within the last 5 minutes. It turns out a hacker got into the system and the security team is doing a forensic audit trying to figure out whether the hacker has created any malicious files on the system.

Assume that you thought so highly of the metadata-aware `LuceneIndexer` that you created here that you put a variant of it into production on your system long before the hacker got in. So, you have an index that you incrementally add to, usually on the hour, which contains file metadata and free-text content for all files on your system.

In a few lines of Tika-powered code, we'll show you how to generate an RSS feed from your Tika-enabled metadata index. First, you'll need to get a listing of the files that have appeared within the last 5 minutes. The following takes care of this for you and provides the general framework for our RSS report.

Listing 6.5 Getting a list of recent files from the Lucene indexer

```
public String generateRSS(File indexFile) throws CorruptIndexException,
    IOException {
```

```
  StringBuffer output = new StringBuffer();
  output.append(getRSSHeaders());
  try {
    reader = IndexReader.open(new SimpleFSDirectory(indexFile));
    IndexSearcher searcher = new IndexSearcher(reader);
    GregorianCalendar gc = new java.util.GregorianCalendar();
    gc.setTime(new Date());
    String nowDateTime = ISO8601.format(gc);
    gc.add(java.util.GregorianCalendar.MINUTE, -5);
    String fiveMinsAgo = ISO8601.format(gc);
    TermRangeQuery query = new TermRangeQuery(Metadata.DATE.toString(),
        fiveMinsAgo, nowDateTime, true, true);
    TopScoreDocCollector collector =
        TopScoreDocCollector.create(20, true);
    searcher.search(query, collector);
    ScoreDoc[] hits = collector.topDocs().scoreDocs;
    for (int i = 0; i < hits.length; i++) {
      Document doc = searcher.doc(hits[i].doc);
      output.append(getRSSItem(doc));
    }
  } finally {
    reader.close();
  }
  output.append(getRSSFooters());
  return output.toString();
}
```

The key Tika-enabled part of listing 6.5 is the use of a standard metadata attribute, DublinCore.DATE, as the metadata key to perform the query. Since Lucene doesn't enforce a particular metadata schema, your use of the metadata-enabled Lucene-Indexer allows you to use a common vocabulary and presentation for dates that's compatible with Lucene's search system. For each Lucene Document found from the Lucene Query, listing 6.6 demonstrates how to use Tika to assist in unmarshalling the Lucene Document into an RSS-compatible item, surrounded by an enclosing RSS-compatible channel tag (provided by the getRSSHeaders() method and the getRSS-Footers() called in the following listing).

Listing 6.6 Using Tika metadata to convert to RSS

```
public String getRSSItem(Document doc) {
  StringBuffer output = new StringBuffer();
  output.append("<item>");
  output.append(emitTag("guid", doc.get(DublinCore.SOURCE), "isPermalink",
      "true"));
  output.append(emitTag("title", doc.get(Metadata.TITLE), null,
        null));
  output.append(emitTag("link", doc.get(DublinCore.SOURCE), null,
        null));
  output.append(emitTag("author", doc.get(Metadata.CREATOR), null,
        null));
  for (String topic : doc.getValues(Metadata.SUBJECT)) {
```

```
        output.append(emitTag("category", topic, null, null));
    }
    output.append(emitTag("pubDate", rssDateFormat.format(ISO8601.
            parse(doc
        .get(Metadata.DATE.toString())))), null, null));
    output.append(emitTag("description", doc.get(Metadata.TITLE), null,
            null));
    output.append("</item>");
    return output.toString();
}
```

The `getRSSItem(Document)` method shown in listing 6.6 is responsible for executing the processed we saw in listing 6.1, effectively using Tika's standard `DublinCore` metadata and its values and reformatting it to the RSS format and syntax. Scared of RSS reports, or metadata model–happy end users? Not anymore!

6.5 *Summary*

Phew! We just used Tika to leverage general and content-specific metadata models (Dublin Core and RSS, respectively), validated the outgoing RSS metadata by leveraging Tika's `Metadata` class and its underlying `Property` class, and built up a search engine index generated in large part by standardizing on Tika metadata and its models. After we constructed the index, we showed you how to transform your recorded metadata instances in Dublin Core into the language of RSS, using Tika APIs. Metadata is grand, isn't it?

In this chapter, we've covered a multitude of things related to the world of metadata. Let's review.

First, we defined what metadata is (data about data), and its ultimate utility in the world of text extraction, content analysis, and all things Tika. We also defined what a metadata model is, and its important facets: attributes, relationships between those attributes, and information about the attributes, such as their formats, cardinality, definitions, and of course their names! After these definitions, we looked at some of the challenges behind metadata management, and how Tika can help.

- *Metadata comparison and quality*—We discussed a bunch of different metadata models, and classified them into two areas: general models (like Dublin Core) and content-specific models (`HttpHeaders`, or MS Word) that are directly related to specific types of files and content. We also highlighted the importance of metadata quality and dealing with metadata transformation.

- *Implementation-level support for metadata*—With a background on metadata models and standards, we took a deep dive into Tika's support for representing metadata, looking at Tika's `Metadata` class. We discussed the simplicity and *power* of a basic key/multivalued text-based structure for metadata, and how Tika leverages this simplicity to provide powerful representation of metadata captured in both general and content-specific models for all the files that you feed through the system.

- *Metadata representation, validation and transformation in action*—The latter part of the chapter focused in on practical examples of Tika's `Metadata` class, and we brought the `LuceneIndexer` example from chapter 5 back to life, showing you how to augment the `LuceneIndexer` with common Dublin Core metadata, and how to extend the code to include property-specific metadata attributes (`Date`-related, `Integer`-related, and more). Finally, we showed you how to turn the metadata extracted by the `LuceneIndexer` into different metadata views, including some common XML formats you're probably familiar with (RSS), and even some that you probably aren't (remember: the metadata community is not out to cause you more work—well, maybe they are!).

It's been a great ride! Now that you're a bona fide Tika metadata expert, the time has come to understand how an important piece of per-file metadata gets populated by Tika: the file's *language*. It's a lot harder than it looks, and more involved than simply calling `set(Property, String)` on Tika's `Metadata` class—so much so that it warrants its own chapter, which is next up on your Tika training. Enjoy!

Language detection

Imagine you're in charge of developing a searchable document database for a multilingual organization like the European Union, an international corporation, or a local restaurant that wants to publish its menus in more than one language. Typically no single user of such a database knows all the languages used in the stored documents, so the system should be able to categorize and retrieve documents by language in order to present users with information that they can understand. And, to make things challenging, most of the documents added to the database don't come with reliable metadata about the language they're written in.

To implement such a multilingual document database, you need a language detection tool like the one shown in figure 7.1. This tool would act like a pipeline that takes incoming documents with no language metadata and automatically annotates them with the languages they're written in. The annotation should take the form of a `Metadata.LANGUAGE` entry in the document metadata. Our task in this chapter is to find out how this can be done.

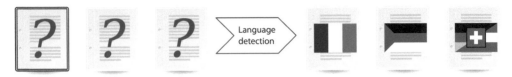

Figure 7.1   The language detection pipeline. Incoming documents with no language metadata are analyzed to determine the language they're written in. The resulting language information is associated with the documents as an extra piece of metadata.

Identifying written languages is in principle like the file format detection we covered in chapter 4, so the structure of this chapter follows a similar approach. After a quick look at our sample document and a simple code example in section 7.1, we re-encounter taxonomies in section 7.2, which describes the ISO 639 standard of language codes. Then, in section 7.2.1 we'll find out about different ways in which the language of a given text can be detected. Finally, section 7.3 shows how Tika implements language detection and how you can leverage this functionality in your applications. And as usual, we'll end the chapter with a brief summary that wraps up all the key points.

7.1   *The most translated document in the world*

The Universal Declaration of Human Rights (UDHR) is our sample document in this chapter. This famous declaration was adopted by the United Nations General Assembly in 1948 and has since become one of the best-known documents in the world. It has been translated into almost 400 languages.[1] In fact the UDHR holds the Guinness World Record for being the most-translated text in the world! It's the perfect example for studying language identification, especially since the United Nations makes all the translations easily available online at http://www.ohchr.org/. Figure 7.2 gives you an idea of the range of available translations by showing the UDHR opening sentence in the six official languages of the United Nations.

Let's see what Tika can tell us about these translations. The simplest way to do that is to use the Tika application's --language command-line option. This option tells Tika to detect the languages of given documents. The detection results are printed

يولد جميع الناس أحراراً متساوين في الكرامة والحقوق.

人人生而自由, 在尊严和权利上一律平等。

All human beings are born free and equal in dignity and rights.

Tous les êtres humains naissent libres et égaux en dignité et en droits.

Все люди рождаются свободными и равными в своем достоинстве и правах.

Todos los seres humanos nacen libres e iguales en dignidad y derechos.

Figure 7.2   The first sentence of the first article of the Universal Declaration of Human Rights, written in Arabic, Chinese, English, French, Russian, and Spanish— the six official languages of the United Nations.

---

[1]   As of late 2010 the UDHR was available in 375 different languages and new translation efforts were ongoing.

out as ISO 639 language codes. The following example shows Tika correctly detecting the English, French, Russian, and Spanish versions of the UDHR. Tika doesn't yet understand Arabic or Chinese, but it's learning fast!

```
$ java -jar tika-app-1.0.jar --language \
      http://www.ohchr.org/EN/UDHR/Documents/UDHR_Translations/eng.pdf \
      http://www.ohchr.org/EN/UDHR/Documents/UDHR_Translations/frn.pdf \
      http://www.ohchr.org/EN/UDHR/Documents/UDHR_Translations/rus.pdf \
      http://www.ohchr.org/EN/UDHR/Documents/UDHR_Translations/spn.pdf
en            ⟵ English
fr                      ⟵ French
ru                           ⟵ Russian
es                              ⟵ Spanish
```

What's the magic behind the `--language` option, and how can you use it in your applications? Let's find out!

7.2 Sounds Greek to me—theory of language detection

As discussed in chapter 4, the ability to consistently name and classify things is essential for fully understanding them. There are thousands of languages in the world, many with multiple dialects or regional variants. Some of the languages are extinct and some are artificial. Some don't even have names in English! Others, like Chinese, have names whose specific meaning is highly context-sensitive.[2] A standard taxonomy that can name and classify all languages is needed to allow information systems to reliably store and process information about languages.

There are a number of different increasingly detailed systems for categorizing and naming languages, their dialects, and other variants. For example, according to the RFC 5646: Tags for Identifying Languages standard, you could use `de-CH-1996` to identify the form of German used in Switzerland after the spelling reform of 1996. Luckily there aren't many practical applications where such detail is necessary or even desirable, so we'll focus on just the `de` part of this identifier.

The RFC 5646 standard leverages ISO 639 just like most of the other formal language taxonomies. ISO 639 is a set of standards defined by the *International Organization for Standardization* (ISO). The ISO 639 standards define a set of two- and three-letter language codes like the `de` code for German we encountered earlier. The two-letter codes that are most commonly used are defined in the ISO 639-1 standard. There are currently 184 registered two-letter language codes, and they represent most of the major languages in the world. The three-letter codes defined in the other ISO 639 standards are used mostly for more detailed representation of language variants and also for minor or even extinct languages.

---

[2] The Chinese language people normally refer to is Standard Mandarin, the official language of China and Taiwan. But Chinese is a complex family of related languages that span vast demographic, geographic, and historic spaces, though most of them share at least variations of the same written form. For example, the Chinese you hear in Hong Kong, Guangzhou, and Macau is Cantonese, a dialect that's about as far from Mandarin as German or French is from English.

The full list of ISO 639-1 codes is available from http://www.loc.gov/standards/iso639-2/ along with the larger lists of ISO 639-2 codes. Tika can detect 18 of the 184 currently registered ISO 639-1 languages. Here are the codes of these supported languages:

- `da`—Danish
- `de`—German
- `et`—Estonian
- `el`—Greek
- `en`—English
- `es`—Spanish
- `fi`—Finnish
- `fr`—French
- `hu`—Hungarian
- `is`—Icelandic
- `it`—Italian
- `nl`—Dutch
- `no`—Norwegian
- `pl`—Polish
- `pt`—Portuguese
- `ru`—Russian
- `sv`—Swedish
- `th`—Thai

After detecting the language of a document, Tika will use these ISO 639-1 codes to identify the detected language. But how do we get to that point? Let's find out!

7.2.1 Language profiles

Detecting the language of a document typically involves constructing a *language profile* of the document text and comparing that profile with those of known languages. The structure and contents of the language profile depend heavily on the detection algorithm being used, but usually consist of some statistic compilation of relevant features of the text. In this section you'll learn about the profiling process and different profiling algorithms.

Usually the profile of a known language is constructed in the same way as that of the text whose language is being detected. The only difference is that the language of this text set, called a *corpus*, is known in advance. For example, you could use the combined works of Shakespeare to create a profile for detecting his plays, those of his contemporaries, or modern works that mimic the Shakespearean style. Should you come across and old-looking book like the one shown in figure 7.3 you could use the Shakespearean profile to test whether the contents of the book match its looks. Of course, such a profile would be less efficient at accurately matching the English language as it's used today.

A key question for developers of language detection or other natural language processing tools is how to find a good corpus that accurately and fairly represents the different ways a language is used. It's usually true that the bigger

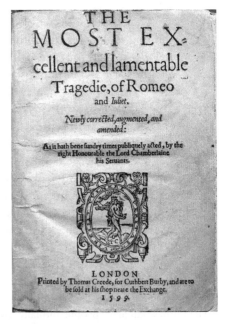

Figure 7.3 Title page of a 16th century printing of Romeo and Juliet by William Shakespeare

a corpus is, the better it is. Common sources of such sets of text are books, magazines, newspapers, official documents, and so forth. Some are also based on transcripts of spoken language from TV and radio programs. And the internet is quickly becoming an important source, even though much of the text there is poorly categorized or labeled.

Once you've profiled the corpus of a language, you can use that profile to detect other texts that exhibit similar features. The better your profiling algorithm is, the better those features match the features of the language in general instead of those of your corpus. The result of the profile comparison is typically a *distance* measure that indicates how close or how far the two profiles are from each other. The language whose profile is closest to that of the candidate text is also most likely the language in which that text is written. The distance can also be a percentage estimate of how likely it is that the text is written in a given language.

You're probably already wondering what these profiling algorithms look like. It's time to find out!

7.2.2 Profiling algorithms

The most obvious way to detect the language used in a piece of text is to look up the used words in dictionaries of different languages. If the majority of words in a given piece of text can be found in the dictionary of some language, it's likely that the text is written in that language. Even a relatively small dictionary of the most commonly used words of a language is often good enough for such language detection. You could even get reasonably accurate results with just the word *the* for detecting English; the words *le* and *la* for French; and *der*, *die*, and *das* for German!

Such a list of common words is probably the simplest reasonably effective language profile. It could be further improved by associating each word with its relative frequency and calculating the distance of two profiles as the sum of differences between the frequencies of matching words.[3] Another advantage of this improvement is that it allows the same profiling algorithm to be used to easily generate a language profile from a selected corpus instead of needing to use a dictionary or other explicit list of common words.

Alas, the main problem with such an algorithm is that it's not very efficient at matching short texts like single sentences or just a few words. It also depends on a way to detect word boundaries, which may be troublesome for languages like German with lots of compound words or Chinese and Japanese where no whitespace or other extra punctuation is used to separate words. Finally, it has big problems with *agglutinative* languages like Finnish or Korean where most words are formed by composing smaller units of meaning. For example, the Finnish words *kotona* and *kotoa* mean "at home" and "from home" respectively, which makes counting common words like *at*, *from*, or even *home* somewhat futile.

---

[3] The distance computation can more accurately be represented as calculating the difference of two n-dimensional vectors, where each dimension corresponds to a distinct word and the component along that dimension represents the relative frequency of that word in the profiled text.

Given these difficulties, how about looking at individual characters or character groups instead?

7.2.3   *The N-gram algorithm*

The profiling algorithm based on word frequencies can just as easily be applied to individual characters. In fact this makes the algorithm simpler, because instead of a potentially infinite number of distinct words, you only need to track a finite number of characters. And it turns out that character frequencies really do depend on the language, as shown in figure 7.4.

Obviously this algorithm works even better with many Asian languages that have characters which are used in only one or just a handful of languages. But this algorithm has the same problem as the word-based one in that it needs a lot of text for an accurate match. Interestingly enough, the problem here is opposite of that with words. Where a short sentence may not contain any of the most common words of a language, it's practically guaranteed to contain plenty of the common characters. Instead the problem is that there isn't enough material to differentiate between languages with similar character frequencies.

This detail hints at an interesting approach that turns out to be useful in language detection. Instead of looking at individual words or characters, we could look at character sequences of a given length. Such sequences are called 2-, 3-, and 4-grams or more generally *N-grams* based on the sequence length. For example, the 3-grams of a word like *hello* would be *hel, ell,* and *llo,* plus *_he* and *lo_* when counting word boundaries as separate characters.

It turns out that N-grams[4] are highly effective for isolating the essential features of at least most European languages. They nicely avoid problems with compound words or the oddities of languages like Finnish. And they still provide statistically significant matches even for relatively short texts. Tika opts to use 3-grams, as that seems to offer the best trade-off of features in most practical cases.

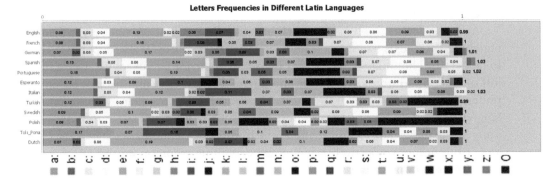

Figure 7.4   Frequency of letters in many languages based on the Latin alphabet

---

[4]   There are many research papers on N-grams for language detection. A simple search on scholar.google.com for "N-gram language identification" will reveal many of most relevant ones.

7.2.4 Advanced profiling algorithms

Other more advanced language profiling algorithms are out there, but few match the simplicity and efficiency of the N-gram method just described. Typically such algorithms target specific features like maximum coverage of different kinds of languages, the ability to accurately detect the language of very short texts, or the ability to detect multiple languages within a multilingual document.

Tika tracks developments in this area and may incorporate some new algorithms in its language detection features in future releases, but for now N-grams are the main profiling algorithm used by Tika.

Now that we've learned the basics of language codes and profiling algorithms, let's look at how to use them in practice. It's coding time!

7.3 Language detection in Tika

The language detection support in Tika is designed to be as easy to use as possible. You already saw the `--language` command-line option in action in section 7.1, and the Java API is almost as easy to use. The class diagram in figure 7.5 summarizes the key parts of this API.

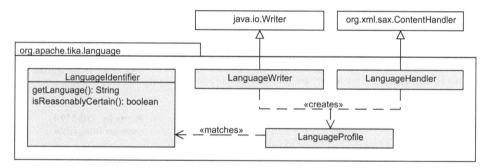

Figure 7.5 Class diagram of Tika's language detection API

The keys to language detection in Tika are the `LanguageProfile` and `Language-Identifier` classes in the `org.apache.tika.language` package. A `LanguageProfile` instance represents the language profile of a given piece of text. The default implementation in Tika 1.0 uses 3-grams for the language profile. Once you've constructed the language profile of a document, you can use the `LanguageIdentifier` class to map the profile into a matching ISO 639 language code. The following code shows how to do this:

```
LanguageProfile profile = new LanguageProfile(
        "Alla människor är födda fria och"
        + " lika i värde och rättigheter.");

LanguageIdentifier identifier =
    new LanguageIdentifier(profile);
System.out.println(identifier.getLanguage());
```

◁ **UDHR opening sentence in Swedish**

◁ **Prints sv, ISO 639-I code for Swedish**

Sometimes there's no clear match for a language profile, either because the language of the profiled text isn't yet known by Tika or because the profiling algorithm doesn't work optimally for that language or for that particular piece of text. You can use the isReasonablyCertain() predicate method of the LanguageIdentifier class to detect whether the language match is reliable. This method uses best-effort heuristics to estimate the accuracy of the language match, so even a positive result doesn't guarantee a 100% accurate match, but helps filter out most of the false matches encountered in practice.

7.3.1 *Incremental language detection*

You may have noticed that the LanguageProfile constructor used in the preceding example takes the entire input document as a single string. But as discussed in chapter 5, a better approach is usually to use a character stream or a SAX event handler to process document content. This way we don't need to keep the entire document in memory, and useful results can be obtained after accessing just part of the document. Tika supports such incremental language detection through the ProfilingWriter and ProfilingHandler classes.

The ProfilingWriter class is a java.io.Writer subclass that builds a language profile of the incoming character stream. The following example shows how this works:

```
ProfilingWriter writer = new ProfilingWriter();
writer.append("Minden emberi lény");                    UDHR opening
writer.append(" szabadon születik és");                 sentence in Hungarian
writer.append(" egyenl? méltósága és");
writer.append(" joga van.");

LanguageIdentifier identifier =                          Prints hu, ISO 639-I
    writer.getLanguage();                                code for Hungarian
System.out.println(identifier.getLanguage());
```

You can call the ProfilingWriter instance's getLanguage() method at any point, and it'll return the profile of the text that has already been seen. In practice even a few hundred characters is usually more than enough to get a fairly accurate language profile. For example, the language profile of the preceding example starts to match Hungarian after the second append() call.

What if you want to profile the XHTML output of a Tika parser? The answer to that question is the ProfilingHandler class. A ProfilingHandler instance listens to SAX character events and profiles the contained text just like the ProfilingWriter. The following shows how to detect the language of a document parsed from the standard input stream:

```
ProfilingHandler handler = new ProfilingHandler();
new AutoDetectParser().parse(
        System.in, handler,
        new Metadata(), new ParseContext());

LanguageIdentifier identifier = handler.getLanguage();
System.out.println(identifier.getLanguage());
```

With these tools we're now ready to address the task we set before ourselves at the beginning of this chapter!

7.3.2 *Putting it all together*

Remember the requirements of the multilingual document database described at the beginning of this chapter? It should be searchable and support categorization and filtering of documents based on the language they're written in. Chapter 5 showed how to do the search part based on extracted text, and the metadata features described in chapter 6 are ideal for categorizing and filtering documents. We've just learned how to build the automatic language detector. Now we only need to combine these tools to achieve our goal.

Assuming you've already implemented full-text and metadata processing based on the previous chapters, the easiest way to add language detection functionality is to decorate your existing parser instance. We can do that easily by extending the DelegatingParser class that by default delegates all parsing tasks to the Parser instance found in the parsing context. Our extension is to inject a ProfilingHandler instance to the parsing process and add the identified language to the document metadata once the parsing process is completed. Here's the complete source code for this solution.

Listing 7.1 Source code of a language-detecting parser decorator

```
import java.io.IOException;
import java.io.InputStream;

import org.apache.tika.exception.TikaException;
import org.apache.tika.language.LanguageIdentifier;
import org.apache.tika.language.ProfilingHandler;
import org.apache.tika.metadata.Metadata;
import org.apache.tika.parser.DelegatingParser;
import org.apache.tika.parser.ParseContext;
import org.apache.tika.sax.TeeContentHandler;
import org.xml.sax.ContentHandler;
import org.xml.sax.SAXException;

public class LanguageDetectingParser extends DelegatingParser {       ◁─┐ Custom
                                                                         │ parse()
    public void parse(                                                ◁─┘ method
            InputStream stream, ContentHandler handler,
            final Metadata metadata, ParseContext context)
            throws SAXException, IOException, TikaException {
        ProfilingHandler profiler =                               ◁─┐ Combine language profiler
            new ProfilingHandler();                                 │ with content handler
        ContentHandler tee =
            new TeeContentHandler(handler, profiler);
                                                                    ◁─┐ Call decorated
        super.parse(stream, tee, metadata, context);             ◁─┘ parser

        LanguageIdentifier identifier =              ◁── Get detected language
            profiler.getLanguage();
        if (identifier.isReasonablyCertain()) {                   ◁─┐ Avoid uncertain
            metadata.set(                                           │ matches
```

```
            Metadata.LANGUAGE,                    ◁┐ Set language
            identifier.getLanguage());              │ metadata
        }
    }
}
```

So how does this example work? We start by customizing the parse() method so we can inject language detection functionality. We use the TeeContentHandler class to direct the extracted text *both* to the original content handler given by the client application and to the ProfilingHandler instance we've created for detecting the document language. You may remember the TeeContentHandler class from chapter 5. It's perfect for our needs here, as it allows you to copy the parser output to multiple parallel handlers.

Once the setup is done, we invoke the original parse() method to parse the given document. Once the parsing is complete, we ask our profiler for the detected language identifier and use it to set the Metadata.LANGUAGE metadata entry if the language match was good enough to rely on.

You'd think that complex problems such as language detection would require lots of complicated code to achieve, but with the right tools it's pretty simple! The preceding code is all you need to make your application tell the difference between documents written in French, Russian, English, or a dozen other languages. And the best part is that your application will grow brighter every time a new Tika release adds new language profiles or improves its profiling algorithms.

7.4   Summary

Let's take a moment to look back at what we've learned in this chapter. Even though natural language processing is a fiendishly complex subject that has and probably will be a topic of scientific research for decades, certain areas are already useful in practical applications. Language detection is one of the simpler tasks of natural language processing, and can for the most part be implemented with relatively simple statistical tools. Tika's N-gram–based language detection feature is one such implementation.

We described this feature through the examples of the UDHR document and a multilingual document database. After the introduction we covered standard ISO 639 language codes and proceeded to discuss commonly used language detection algorithms. Armed with this theoretical background, we looked at how Tika implements language detection. Finally, we combined the lessons of this chapter to a Parser decorator that can be used to integrate language detection to the full-text and metadata processing features from previous chapters.

If you've read this book from the beginning, you'll by now have learned about type detection, text extraction, metadata processing, and, finally, language detection with Tika. These are the four main features of Tika, and the rest of this book will tell you more about how these features interact with the world around Tika. To begin, the next chapter takes you on a tour of the structure and quirks of many common file formats and the way Tika handles them.

What's in a file?

By now, your Tika-fu is strong, and you're feeling like there's not much that you can't do with your favorite tool for file detection, metadata extraction, and language identification. Believe it or not, there's plenty more to learn!

One thing we've purposefully stayed away from is telling you what's in those files that Tika makes sense of.[1] That's because files are a source of rich information, recording not only text or metadata, but also things like detailed descriptions of scenery, such as a bright image of a soccer ball on a grass field; waveforms representing music recorded in stereo sound; all the way to geolocated and time-referenced observations recorded by a Fourier Transform Spectrometer (FTS) instrument on a spacecraft. The short of the matter is that their intricacies and complexities deserve treatment in their own right.

---

[1] We covered some parts of the file contents, for example, we discussed BOM markers in chapter 4 while talking about file detection. In chapter 5, we discussed methods for dealing with file reading via `InputStreams`. In both cases, we stayed away from the *actual contents* of files in particular, since it would receive full treatment in this chapter.

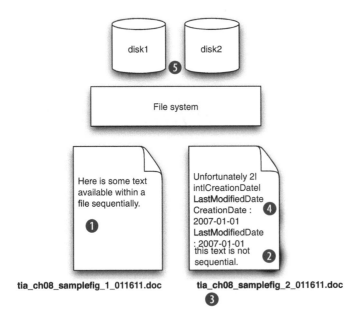

Figure 8.1 Several areas where content can be gleaned from a file

Files store their information using different methodologies as shown in figure 8.1. The information may be available only by sequentially scanning each byte of information recorded in the logical file, as shown at ❶ in the figure, or it may be accessible randomly by jumping around through the file, as ❷ in the figure demonstrates. Metadata information may be available by reading the file's header (its beginning bytes on disk) as shown at ❹, or it could be stored in a file's name or directory structure on disk as shown at ❸. Finally, files may be physically split across multiple parts on disk, or they may be logically organized according to some common collection somehow as shown at ❺. It sounds complex, and it is, but we'll hone in on Tika's ability to exploit these complexities.

In this chapter, we'll cover all internal and external aspects of files, as well as how Tika exploits this information to extract textual content and metadata. Files, their content, their metadata, and their storage representation are all fair game. The big takeaway from this chapter is that it'll show you how to develop your own Tika parsers and methodologies for extracting information from files using Tika, demonstrated by looking at how existing Tika parsers exploit file content for some common file formats like RSS and HDF. Let's dive in!

8.1   *Types of content*

The types of content within files vary vastly. We've picked two sample file format types to examine in this section: the Hierarchical Data Format (HDF), http://www.hdf-group.org/, a common file format used to capture scientific information, and Really Simple Syndication (RSS), the most commonly used format to spread news and rapidly changing information.

8.1.1 *HDF: a format for scientific data*

Consider a scenario in which a science instrument flown on a NASA satellite records data, which is then downlinked via one of a number of existing ground stations here on the earth, as shown in figure 8.2. The downlinked data is then transferred via dedicated networks to a science data processing center for data transformation, and ultimately for dissemination to the public.

In this scenario the raw data arriving at the science data processing center represents engineering and housekeeping information, including raw voltages from the instrument and rudimentary location information (such as an orbit number). This information is represented as a series of files, each corresponding to one channel of data from the instrument (three channels in total), and one set of three files per each orbit of the satellite around the earth.

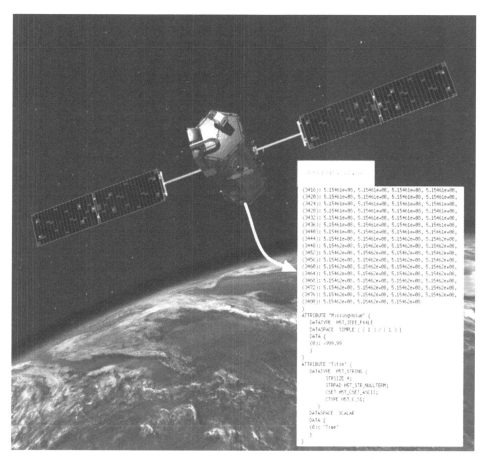

Figure 8.2 **A postulated satellite scenario, observing the earth and collecting those observations in data files represented in the Hierarchical Data Format (HDF). HDF stores data in a binary format, arranged as a set of named scalars, vectors, and matrices corresponding to observations over some space/time grid.**

Data within each channel file is stored initially in a binary data format; for the purposes of this example we'll assume the widely used Hierarchical Data Format (HDF), version 5 (HDF5). HDF provides an external user-facing API for writing to and reading from HDF5 files. The HDF5 API allows users to write data using a small canonical set of data constructs, specifically those shown in table 8.1.

Table 8.1 Simplified representation of content within Hierarchical Data Format (HDF) files. HDF represents observational data and metadata information using a small set of constructs: named scalars, vectors, and matrices.

Data type	Description
Scalar	Named scalar data, such as single-valued metadata information, numerical, or string-based. Examples might include Mission Name, with the associated scalar value Orbiting Carbon Observatory, as well as Instrument Type, with an associated scalar value of Spectrometer.
Vector (aka "1-dimensional Arrays" in HDF5)	Named vector data, including multivalued metadata or multivalued numerical arrays of integers and floats. Examples may include a set of latitudes corresponding to the satellite orbit path.
Matrix (aka "2-dimensional Arrays" in HDF5)	Named matrix data, including multidimensional numerical array data such as integers and floats. The information contained inside of these data types may correspond to a pixel matrix of some scene observed by the instrument, such as a 45 x 30 matrix of temperatures stored as float values (measured in some unit, such as kelvins), where each value in the 45 x 30 matrix has a corresponding latitude or longitude, stored in some associated additional matrices in the HDF5 file.

All of the data and metadata from our postulated scenario is represented in a set of three HDF5 files (corresponding to each channel of the instrument) for each orbit the satellite makes around the earth. That means that if the instrument is measuring a set of scientific variables, such as air temperature, wind speed, CO_2, or any number of other variables, that information is represented in the HDF5 files as sets of named scalars, vectors, and matrices.

8.1.2 *Really Simple Syndication: a format for rapidly changing content*

Let's consider another scenario, such as a Really Simple Syndication (RSS) feed file that lists the latest news stories provided by CNN.com, an example of which is provided in figure 8.3.

RSS files are based on a simple but powerful data model. Each RSS file is an XML file adhering to a prescribed XML schema that defines the RSS vocabulary. That vocabulary consists of two main data structures. First, each RSS file typically contains a *channel*, which aggregates a set of associated RSS *items*, each of which typically points to some news story of interest. Every RSS channel has a set of metadata associated with it, such as a URL and description (http://www.cnn.com/sports/ for the URL and "Latest news stories about sports within the last hour" as the description), as does each RSS item tag.

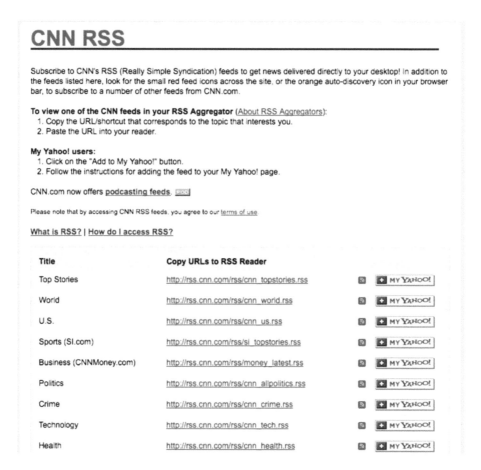

Figure 8.3 The CNN Really Simple Syndication (RSS) index page. CNN provides a set of RSS files that users can subscribe to in order to stay up to date on all of their favorite news stories, categorized by the type of news that users are interested in.

In the CNN example, CNN publishes sets of RSS files, each containing an RSS channel, one for each CNN news category (such as Top Stories, World, U.S., or any of the other categories in figure 8.3). Each RSS channel has a corresponding set of latest news stories and links that users can subscribe to via any number of different RSS readers, including most modern web browsers.

Understanding the types of content is the first step toward automatically extracting information from it. We'll go into the details of that in the next section, describing how Tika codifies the process of extracting content.

8.2 How Tika extracts content

By now, you've seen that engineers often must write applications that can understand many different file types, including HDF5 and RSS files as discussed earlier. The organization of content within different file types has a strong effect on the methodology

Tika uses to extract information from them, as well as the overall performance of the extraction process.

In particular, the organization of content within a file impacts Tika's two main approaches to content extraction. The first is Tika's ability to access a file in a streaming fashion, extracting content as it's read, in contrast to reading the whole file at once, extracting the content, and being able to access it randomly. The next section will demonstrate how Tika extracts content no matter how it's organized!

8.2.1   *Organization of content*

We'll spend this section examining how Tika makes sense of content, whether it supports streaming or random access in the context of RSS files and HDF5 files. We'll use Tika's `FeedParser` and `HDFParser` classes to demonstrate. Onward!

STREAMING

Content that's organized as a set of discrete, independent chunks within a file can be interpreted in a *streaming* fashion. Those independent chunks can be read in or out of order, and the entire file isn't required to make sense of those chunks—they make sense on their own. RSS is an XML-based file format that's amenable to streaming.

We'll start off by putting an RSS file under the microscope and by inspecting its organization:

```
<?xml version="1.0" encoding="ISO-8859-1"?>
<rss version="2.0">
  <channel>
    <title>CNN.com</title>
    <link>http://www.cnn.com/?eref=rss_topstories</link>
    <description>
      CNN.com delivers up-to-the-minute news and information ...
    </description>
    <language>en-us</language>
    <copyright>© 2010 Cable News Network LP, LLLP.</copyright>
    <pubDate>Tue, 07 Dec 2010 22:25:36 EST</pubDate>
    <ttl>5</ttl>
    <image>...</image>
    <item>
      <title>Elizabeth Edwards dies ...</title>
      <guid isPermaLink="false">...</guid>
      <link>http://rss.cnn.com/...</link>
      <description>Elizabeth Edwards, the ...</description>
      <pubDate>Tue, 07 Dec 2010 22:15:33 EST</pubDate>
    </item>
    <item>
      <title>Obama slams GOP, ...</title>
      ...
    </item>
    <item>
      <title>WikiLeaks founder sent to jail</title>
      ...
    </item>
    ...
  </channel>
</rss>
```

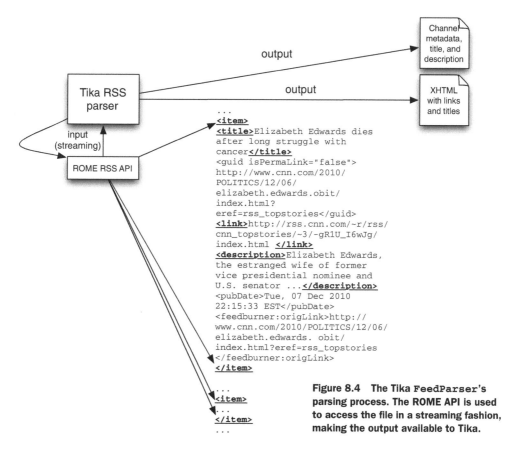

Figure 8.4 The Tika `FeedParser`'s parsing process. The ROME API is used to access the file in a streaming fashion, making the output available to Tika.

One advantage of RSS is that it's implemented using a specific XML dialect as mentioned earlier. An RSS document consists of a single `channel` tag, wrought with `item` tags with descriptive information such as links to the actual content (in this case, the news story), along with information about when the story was published, who published it, an optional media file, and so on.

Tika's `org.apache.tika.parser.feed.FeedParser` class exploits the underlying content structure of the RSS file to extract its text and metadata information, as depicted in figure 8.4. The open source RSS parser library ROME is used for handling the nitty-gritty details of the RSS format.

The following listing starts off with the gory details. We'll discuss the listing shortly after.

Listing 8.1 Tika's RSS feed parser exploiting RSS's XML-based content structure

```
public void parse(
      InputStream stream, ContentHandler handler,
      Metadata metadata, ParseContext context)
      throws IOException, SAXException, TikaException {
   try { //
```

❶ Leverage ROME
   API for parsing

```
    SyndFeed feed = new SyndFeedInput().build(        ❷ Parse using
        new InputSource(stream)); //                     SAX parser

    String title = stripTags(feed.getTitleEx()); //
    String description = stripTags(feed.getDescriptionEx());
                                                          Extract
    metadata.set(Metadata.TITLE, title);                 core channel
    metadata.set(Metadata.DESCRIPTION, description);      metadata  ❸

    ... //                         ⟵── See next listing

    xhtml.endDocument();
  } catch (FeedException e) {
    throw new TikaException("RSS parse error", e);
  }
}
```

As should be second nature by now (if not, head back over to chapter 5), Tika parsers implement the parse(...) method defined in the org.apache.tika.parser.Parser interface. The FeedParser begins by leveraging the ROME API for RSS feed processing, as shown in ❶. ROME allows for stream-based XML parsing via its SAX-based parse interface, as shown in ❷. In doing so, Tika is able to exploit the SAX parsing model for XML and take advantage of a number of its emergent properties, including low memory footprint and faster result processing. Once Tika hands off the RSS input stream to ROME, ROME provides methods, as shown in the bottom portion of the listing, that allow extraction of information from the RSS channel, which Tika's Feed-Parser flows into its extracted metadata, as shown in ❸.

> **WHEN IN ROME**   The Java ROME API (humorously subtitled *All feeds lead to ROME*) is the most widely developed and most actively used Java API for RSS feed parsing. ROME handles a number of the modern RSS formats in development including RSS 2.0 and ATOM. Tika uses ROME's RSS parsing functionality because, well, it rocks, and there's no reason to write it again.

Here's the second half of the parse method.

Listing 8.2   The latter half of the FeedParser's parse method: extracting links

```
XHTMLContentHandler xhtml =
    new XHTMLContentHandler(handler, metadata);
xhtml.startDocument();

xhtml.element("h1", title);
xhtml.element("p", description);

xhtml.startElement("ul");                            ❶ Use ROME to
for (Object e : feed.getEntries()) {                    extract feed items
    SyndEntry entry = (SyndEntry) e;
    String link = entry.getLink();                   ❷ Obtain item links
    if (link != null) {
        xhtml.startElement("li");
        xhtml.startElement("a", "href", link);         Output Tika
                                                        XHTML links
        xhtml.characters(stripTags(entry.getTitleEx()));  ❸ and title text
```

```
        xhtml.endElement("a");
        SyndContent content = entry.getDescription();
        if (content != null) {
            xhtml.newline();
            xhtml.characters(content.getValue());
        }
        xhtml.endElement("li");
    }
}
xhtml.endElement("ul");
```

After the channel `Metadata` has been extracted, the `FeedParser` proceeds to iterate over each `Item` in the feed as shown in ❶. The first step is to use ROME's `SyndEntry` class, which represents a single `Item` from the `Channel`. For each `Item`, its links and metadata are extracted as shown in ❷. Once the information has been extracted, it's output as XHTML in the final step ❸ of listing 8.2.

Tika was able to exploit the underlying content organization of an RSS file and the associated ROME library's easy API. ROME provided access to RSS file information to extract both RSS metadata and link text in a streaming fashion, sending the information to Tika's `FeedParser` class.

Now that we've seen streaming, let's take another example, this time looking at an HDF5 file and how Tika's `HDFParser` is affected by the underlying file content organization. The HDF5 file format prohibits random access of information, requiring the user to have an API which loads the entire file into memory before accessing it.

RANDOM ACCESS

Tika's `HDFParser` builds on top of the NetCDF Java API. NetCDF is a popular binary scientific format, similar to HDF5 except for how data and metadata are stored, as shown in figure 8.5. In HDF5 (and prior versions), data and metadata can be grouped into different associations, connected by a common group name. In NetCDF, all of the data and metadata within the file is assumed to be "flat," and all within the global group.

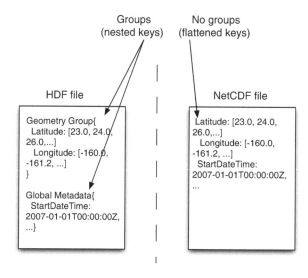

Figure 8.5 A side-by-side comparison of HDF and NetCDF. HDF supports grouping of keys like putting Latitude and Longitude inside of the Geometry group. NetCDF doesn't support grouping, and the keys are all flattened and ungrouped.

As it turns out, the underlying content model of scalars, vectors, and matrices (remember table 8.1?) is so similar for HDF5 and NetCDF4 that we can leverage the same Java API (originally intended for NetCDF4) to read HDF5. Let's take a look at Tika's `HDFParser` and see.

Listing 8.3 The Tika `HDFParser`'s parse method

```
public void parse(InputStream stream, ContentHandler handler,
        Metadata metadata, ParseContext context) throws IOException,
        SAXException, TikaException {
    ByteArrayOutputStream os = new ByteArrayOutputStream();
    this.writeStreamToMemory(stream, os);                      ◁┐  Must read entire
                                                                   file in memory
    NetcdfFile ncFile = NetcdfFile.openInMemory("", os.toByteArray());  ◁┐
                                                                Use NetCDF API
                                         Helper function to      to parse file
                                         extract string met
    this.unravelStringMet(ncFile, null, metadata);     ◁┘
}
```

Much of the magic of the `HDFParser` lies in the `unravelStringMet` function which we'll look at shortly. But there's one important aspect of the parser to point out, and it has to do directly with the way that the HDF5 content is organized. HDF5 does *not* support random access (in contrast to RSS, which as we saw in the prior section, *does* support random access). Because of this limitation, the API used to read the HDF5 file must be given the *entire* file contents as a `ByteArray` as shown in upper portion of the following listing.

Listing 8.4 The Tika `HDFParser`'s `unravelStringMet` method

```
protected void unravelStringMet(NetcdfFile ncFile, Group group,
  Metadata met)
{
    if (group == null) {
        group = ncFile.getRootGroup();
    }

    // unravel its string attrs                               Only consider
    for (Attribute attribute : group.getAttributes()) {   ◁  HDF scalars
        if (attribute.isString()) {
            met.add(attribute.getName(), attribute.getStringValue());
        } else {
            // try and cast its value to a string
            met.add(attribute.getName(), String.valueOf(attribute
                .getNumericValue()));                  ◁┐  Typecast values
        }                                                  to Strings
    }

    for (Group g : group.getGroups()) {              ┐ Flatten and
        unravelStringMet(ncFile, g, met);            ◁ unpack recursively
    }
}
```

Luckily Tika supports both types of files: those that support random access, and those that don't. We should note that file formats that support random access typically also support file streaming, as was the case with the `FeedParser` example from listing 8.1.

Now that we've seen how the organization of a file's content can influence the way that Tika extracts information from it, we'll focus on how a file's header structure and naming conventions can also play a big role in how Tika extracts metadata information. File creators codify information in all sorts of different ways; we'll have to do some detective work for the upcoming sections, but luckily Tika is like your Watson to help unravel the mystery!

8.2.2   File header and naming conventions

A file's metadata information can take many forms and be locked away in a number of places. In some cases, you can examine the first few bytes of information (sometimes called a *file header*) and obtain rich semantic information. In other cases, you're forced to look elsewhere to find metadata to extract from a particular file, including the file's name and (in some cases) its directory structure.

In this section, we'll examine both areas of metadata that a file presents, and we'll show you how Tika is the right tool for the job no matter which one the file uses to codify its metadata.

FILE HEADERS

Depending on the file type, it's possible to focus on just the file header information in order to extract useful information. Let's take a real HTML page as an example:

```
<!DOCTYPE html PUBLIC "-//W3C//DTD XHTML 1.0 Transitional//EN"
"http://www.w3.org/TR/xhtml1/DTD/xhtml1-transitional.dtd">
<!-- -->
<html><!-- InstanceBegin template="/Templates/book.dwt"
codeOutsideHTMLIsLocked="false" -->
<head>
<!-- InstanceBeginEditable name="doctitle" -->
<title>Manning: Tika in Action</title>
<!-- InstanceEndEditable -->
<link href="../styles/main.css" rel="stylesheet" type="text/css" />
<!-- InstanceBeginEditable name="head" --><!--
InstanceEndEditable -->
<meta name = "keywords" content = "Apache, Tika, content analysis,
language
identification, mime detection, file format, Lucene, Solr, Nutch,
search engine,
indexing, full text, parser, MIME-INFO, freedesktop.org, Office Open
XML, PDF,
Zitting, Mattmann, metadata, Dublin Core, XMP, ISO 11179, MIME type,
media type,
magic bytes, IETF" />
</head>

<body>
<!-- ... -->
</body>
</html>
```

In the sample HTML file, note the <meta> tag and its attribute name, which lists a set of keywords about the HTML page. In this particular example, we've omitted much of the actual page in between the <body> tags, focusing only on the *header* of the file.

HEAD HUNTING   The HTML file format uses the tag <head> to denote the HTML file header, a pointer to the location of header information. This is an area where meta information about the page is placed, including stylesheets, JavaScript, base links, and other global page information.

Most HTML parsers provide a mechanism to extract header information fron the HTML file, and Tika's HtmlParser leverages this functionality to pull out the file meta-data as shown next.

Listing 8.5   Snippet of Tika's HtmlHandler class that deals with meta tags

```
if ("META".equals(name) && atts.getValue("content") != null) {

    if (atts.getValue("http-equiv") != null) {
        metadata.set(
                atts.getValue("http-equiv"),
                atts.getValue("content"));
    } else if (atts.getValue("name") != null) {          Parse and add
        metadata.set(                                    meta keywords
                atts.getValue("name"),
                atts.getValue("content"));
    }
}
```

Other file formats have similar notions of file header information. JPEG and other image formats are good examples of this behavior. For example, most image formats encode the size, color depth, and other similar facts about a image within the first few hundred bytes of the file.

But it's not always possible to get all the metadata information present in a file by examining its header. In other cases, the entire file needs to be parsed. (Remember the HDFParser from the previous section?) In some other cases, we don't even need to crack open the file to get the metadata information. We'll specifically look at those cases in the next section, where we examine file naming conventions as a means of metadata extraction.

FILE NAMING CONVENTIONS

File naming conventions sometimes convey metadata. Many people name their files intuitively based on some hierarchy of how the files should be organized in their mind, or attributing to some other criteria.

For example, let's look at the following output from a UNIX /bin/ls command run on a local machine of ours. Note that this command was run on Mac OS X 10.6, with the -FG option also provided as an alias to ls (in other words the command is actually ls -lFG). We've redacted the host names and other identifying information to protect the innocents.

```
[host:~/src/tikaInAction] unixuser% ls -1
total 25944
-rw-r--r--@  1 unixuser   unixgrp      5590 Sep 30 14:07 Tika-in-Action.xml
-rw-r--r--@  1 unixuser   unixgrp       585 Jun 18 08:53 assembly.xml
-rw-r--r--@  1 unixuser   unixgrp    268853 Sep 30 14:07 cover.jpg
drwxr-xr-x  13 unixuser   unixgrp       442 Nov 22 20:42 figs/
drwxr-xr-x   4 unixuser   unixgrp       136 Apr 19  2010 misc/
-rw-r--r--@  1 unixuser   unixgrp      3373 Sep 30 14:07 pom.xml
drwxr-xr-x   8 unixuser   unixgrp       272 Sep 30 22:07 src/
drwxr-xr-x  11 unixuser   unixgrp       374 Nov 22 16:33 target/
-rw-r--r--@  1 unixuser   unixgrp     73088 Nov 22 12:53 tia-ch01.xml
-rw-r--r--@  1 unixuser   unixgrp     50181 Nov 22 12:56 tia-ch02.xml
-rw-r--r--@  1 unixuser   unixgrp     49612 Sep 30 14:07 tia-ch03.xml
-rw-r--r--@  1 unixuser   unixgrp     71947 Nov 22 13:02 tia-ch04.xml
-rw-r--r--@  1 unixuser   unixgrp     77175 Nov 22 13:50 tia-ch05.xml
-rw-r--r--@  1 unixuser   unixgrp     63988 Nov 22 13:45 tia-ch06.xml
-rw-r--r--@  1 unixuser   unixgrp     30700 Nov 22 13:27 tia-ch07.xml
-rw-r--r--@  1 unixuser   unixgrp      7076 Nov 22 21:18 tia-ch08.xml
-rw-r--r--@  1 unixuser   unixgrp      1917 Nov 21 20:21 tia-ch09.xml
-rw-r--r--@  1 unixuser   unixgrp       223 Sep 30 14:07 tia-ch10.xml
-rw-r--r--@  1 unixuser   unixgrp       167 Sep 30 14:07 tia-ch11.xml
-rwx------@  1 unixuser   unixgrp  12085010 Nov 22 21:20 tika.pdf*
```

This listing output holds a lot of information. First, we can gather information such as who created the file, when it was created, how big it is, and the permissions for reading, writing, and executing the file. We'll see later that the actual file path, including both its directory path and filename, provide metadata that we can extract.

For the first part of information available from the /bin/ls output, we can leverage Tika's `Parser` interface to write a `Parser` implementation which will allow us to extract `Metadata` from the /bin/ls output. Let's cook up the example next.

Listing 8.6 Leveraging directory information to extract file metadata

```
public void parse(InputStream is, ContentHandler handler, Metadata metadata,
      ParseContext context) throws IOException, SAXException, TikaException {

  List<String> lines = FileUtils.readLines(TikaInputStream.get(is).
        getFile());
  for (String line : lines) {
    String[] fileToks = line.split("\s+");
    if (fileToks.length < 8)                    ❶ Ignore
      continue;                                      nonlisting entries
    String filePermissions = fileToks[0];
    String numHardLinks = fileToks[1];          ❷ Parse line cols
    String fileOwner = fileToks[2];                  from /bin/ls
    String fileOwnerGroup = fileToks[3];
    String fileSize = fileToks[4];
    StringBuffer lastModDate = new StringBuffer();
    lastModDate.append(fileToks[5]);
    lastModDate.append(" ");
    lastModDate.append(fileToks[6]);
    lastModDate.append(" ");
    lastModDate.append(fileToks[7]);
    StringBuffer fileName = new StringBuffer();
    for (int i = 8; i < fileToks.length; i++) {
```

```
        fileName.append(fileToks[i]);
        fileName.append(" ");
    }
    fileName.deleteCharAt(fileName.length() - 1);
    this
        .addMetadata(metadata, filePermissions, numHardLinks,
                fileOwner,
            fileOwnerGroup, fileSize, lastModDate.toString(),
            fileName
                .toString());                        ⟵──❸ Add extracted file meta
    }
}


private void addMetadata(Metadata metadata, String filePerms,
    String numHardLinks, String fileOwner, String fileOwnerGroup,
    String fileSize, String lastModDate, String fileName) {
  metadata.add("FilePermissions", filePerms);
  metadata.add("NumHardLinks", numHardLinks);            ⟵──❹ Add scalar meta
  metadata.add("FileOwner", fileOwner);
  metadata.add("FileOwnerGroup", fileOwnerGroup);
  metadata.add("FileSize", fileSize);
  metadata.add("LastModifiedDate", lastModDate);
  metadata.add("Filename", fileName);

  if (filePerms.indexOf("x") != -1 &&
          filePerms.indexOf("d") == -1) {
    if (metadata.get("NumExecutables") != null) {
      int numExecs = Integer.valueOf(
              metadata.get("NumExecutables"));
      numExecs++;
      metadata.set("NumExecutables", String.valueOf(numExecs));
    } else {
      metadata.set("NumExecutables", "1");          ⟵──❺ Add derived meta
    }
  }
}
```

In effect, our `Parser` implementation is a glorified streaming line tokenizer, pulling out the relevant pieces of the /bin/ls output as shown in ❷ and ❸. The `Parser` implementation tokenizes each line on whitespace, and ignores lines such as the first line where the information provided is summary information—specifically the total size of the directory as shown in ❶.

One nice feature of the provided `Parser` implementation is that it not only extracts scalar metadata (shown in ❹) from the /bin/ls output, but it extracts derived metadata (shown in ❺). In this case, it extracts the number of executables it could find by counting the number of files that contain the x permission in their File-Permissions extracted metadata field.

We can see the output of listing 8.6 by running a command similar to the following:

```
ls -l | java -classpath \
tika-app-1.0.jar:tika-in-action-SNAPSHOT.jar:commons-io-1.4.jar \
tikainaction.chapter8.DirListParser
```

Or, you can also use Maven to execute the command:

```
ls -l | mvn exec:java -Dexec.mainClass="tikainaction.chapter8.DirListParser"
```

Now that we've seen how to examine basic file and directory information available as output from a listing command,[2] let's look at what metadata information we can extract if we examine the full file path including both its directory and filename components. Figure 8.6 magnifies a particular file from the directory listing output and demonstrates the file's conceptual parts.

Taking an example from the /bin/ls command output, note the different components of the full file path. Information including who created the file, which book the file is associated with, and the chapter number are all available by examining the file and directory naming conventions.

The file includes information such as its creator (denoted by the particular user ID part of the /Users/ folder on the file system), the book that the file is associated with (the first set of information *after*/src/ and before tikaInAction), as well as the chapter number (the information available after the hyphen in tia-ch and before .xml in the filename). These rules that we've codified in parentheses provide a recipe for exploiting filename and directory information to extract useful and relevant metadata that we may use in processing the associated file.

There's one other major place where metadata information may lie. Files often point to *other files* which may themselves have metadata associated with *both files* or all files in a particular collection. Let's see how we can extract and leverage this link information using Tika.

LINKS TO OTHER FILES

Often files, in order to cut down on the amount of direct metadata and text they capture, will reference other files. In the MS Office suite, you can create explicit hyperlinks between Word documents and Excel files, or Excel files and PowerPoint files, and so on. In HTML files, you can create <a> tags with an href attribute, a hyperlink pointing at related content from the origin HTML file. In content management

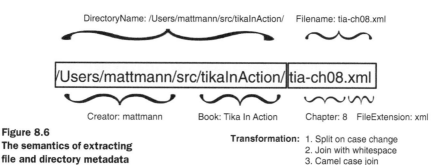

Figure 8.6
The semantics of extracting
file and directory metadata

---

[2] We used /bin/ls, a basic UNIX utility. Similar information would have been available if we used the Windows dir command.

systems, you can also explicitly create links between web pages, documents, and other forms of media as part of the content metadata information. There are numerous examples of file-based linking; these are only a representative few.

File links themselves are valuable metadata information because they may point us to other forms of rich associated content, ripe for extraction. So, how does Tika help you with deciphering things such as links to other files?

Tika uses a SAX ContentHandler interface mechanism to allow output from its XHTML extraction step to be customized in some specific way. One of the useful ContentHandler implementations included in Tika is the LinkContentHandler class. This class is responsible for taking document link information extracted by the underlying parser, and making it easily available to downstream Tika API users. The main snippet of the LinkContentHandler class is highlighted next.

Listing 8.7   Tika's `LinkContentHandler` class makes extracting file links a snap

```
public void startElement(
        String uri, String local, String name, Attributes attributes) {
    if (XHTML.equals(uri)) {
        if ("a".equals(local)) {                           ←─❶ Detected <a> tag
            LinkBuilder builder = new LinkBuilder("a");
            builder.setURI(attributes.getValue("", "href"));
            builder.setTitle(attributes.getValue("", "title"));
            builderStack.addFirst(builder);                ←─❷ Cache extracted link
        } else if ("img".equals(local)) {
            LinkBuilder builder = new LinkBuilder("img");
            builder.setURI(attributes.getValue("", "src"));
            builder.setTitle(attributes.getValue("", "title"));
            builderStack.addFirst(builder);                ←┐ Cache extracted
                                                           ❸ image link
            String alt = attributes.getValue("", "alt");
            if (alt != null) {
                char[] ch = alt.toCharArray();
                characters(ch, 0, ch.length);
            }
        }
    }
}

public void endElement(String uri, String local, String name) {
    if (XHTML.equals(uri)) {
        if ("a".equals(local) || "img".equals(local)) {
            links.add(builderStack.removeFirst().getLink());
        }                                     ←┐ Commit extracted
    }                                         ❹ links to link set
}
```

The LinkContentHandler first determines whether it's encountered an <a> tag within the XHTML as shown in ❶. If it has found an <a> tag, the LinkContentHandler extracts its href and title attributes as shown in ❷. The LinkContentHandler also inspects <img> tags and extracts their relevant links as demonstrated in ❸. All of the extracted links are then passed onto the downstream handler, shown in ❹.

The last section of the chapter is up next. In it, we'll explain how the physical and logical representation of how a file is stored affects methods for information extraction, and throws off ordinary toolkits that purport to do text and metadata extraction. Good thing you have Tika, and good thing it's no ordinary toolkit!

8.2.3 Storage affects extraction

The mechanism by which a file is stored on media may transmit useful information worthy of Tika's extraction. These mechanisms include the logical representation of files via storage, such as through links (such as symbolic links), as well as the notion that files can be sets of independent physical files linked together somehow.

Files can be physically stored on a single disk or via the network. Sometimes files may be physically distributed—as in the case of networked file systems like Google File System (GFS) or Hadoop Distributed File System (HDFS)—but centrally represented via a collection of network data blocks or some other higher-order structure. We'll discuss how Tika's use of the InputStream abstraction hides some of this complexity and uniqueness.

Individual files may be stored on disk as part of a larger whole of logically or physically linked files via some mechanism such as a common collection label, or a unique directory to collect the files. Tika doesn't care because it can exploit information from either case. Madness, you say? Read on!

LOGICAL REPRESENTATION

Let's postulate a simple example of software deployment to illustrate how logical representation of files and directories may convey otherwise-hidden meaning that we'll want to bring out in the open using Tika. Take, for example, the software deployment scenario in figure 8.7.

In our postulated scenario, software is extracted from a configuration management system—let's say Apache Subversion—and then run through a deployment process which installs the latest and greatest version of the software into the /deploy directory, giving the installed software a unique version number. A symbolic link, titled *current*, is also updated to point to the most recent installed version of the software as a result of this process.

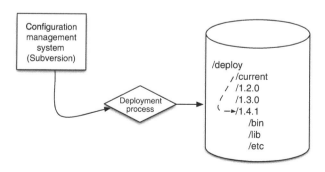

Figure 8.7 A software deployment scenario in which the system is pulled out of configuration management, run through a deployment process that copies and installs the software to a directory path, and codified with the unique software version number. A symlink titled *current* points to the latest and greatest installed version of the software.

What if we wanted to write a quick software program that would roll back the software to the last prior working version when there's some critically identified bug as a result of the latest software deployment process? Let's whip something up with Tika that could address this problem for us!

Listing 8.8   A sample program to roll back a software version using Tika

```
public void rollback(File deployArea) throws IOException, SAXException,
    TikaException {
  LinkContentHandler handler = new LinkContentHandler();
  Metadata met = new Metadata();
  DeploymentAreaParser parser = new DeploymentAreaParser();
  parser.parse(IOUtils.toInputStream(deployArea.getAbsolutePath()),
        handler,
     met);                                              ◁┐ Extract versions
  List<Link> links = handler.getLinks();                 │  from deploy area
  if (links.size() < 2)
    throw new IOException("Must have installed at least 2 versions!");
  Collections.sort(links, new Comparator<Link>() {      ◁┐ Sort by
    public int compare(Link o1, Link o2) {                │  version desc
      return o1.getText().compareTo(o2.getText());
    }
  });

  this.updateVersion(links.get(links.size() - 2).getText());  ◁┐ Roll back to
}                                                              │  prior version
```

The example program from listing 8.8 first passes along the path of the deployment area to the `DeploymentAreaParser` class, whose `parse` is shown in listing 8.9. The `DeploymentAreaParser` reads the underlying logical file structure, determining which files are actual deployed software versions in contrast to symlink files pointing to the current version. The returned software version directories are made available by calling `LinkContentHandler`'s `getLinks` method, and then the directories are sorted in descending order. To roll back, we pass along the second-to-last version directory to a function called `updateVersion`, where we update the version to the prior stable software. Not too shabby, huh?

Listing 8.9   A custom Tika `Parser` implementation for our deployment area

```
public void parse(InputStream is, ContentHandler handler,
    Metadata metadata, ParseContext context) throws IOException,
    SAXException, TikaException {

  File deployArea = new File(IOUtils.toString(is));      ◁┐ Obtain deploy
  File[] versions = deployArea.listFiles(new              │  area path
        FileFilter() {

    public boolean accept(File pathname) {
        return !pathname.getName().startsWith("current");
    }
  });
```

```
XHTMLContentHandler xhtml = new
  XHTMLContentHandler(handler, metadata);          Iterate over
xhtml.startDocument();                              deployed
                                              ◁⌐   versions
for (File v : versions) {
  if(isSymlink(v)) continue;
  xhtml.startElement("a", "href", v.toURL().toExternalForm());
  xhtml.characters(v.getName());        ◁⌐  Extract file info,
  xhtml.endElement("a");                     ignore symlink
}

}
```

PHYSICAL REPRESENTATION

If we expand our focus beyond the logical links between files and consider how those files are actually represented on disk, we arrive at a number of interesting information sources ripe for extraction. For example, considering that more and more file systems are moving beyond simple local disks to farms of storage devices, we're faced with an interesting challenge. How do we deal with the extraction of information from a file if we only have available to us a small unit of that file? Even worse, what do we do if that small unit available to us is *not* a "power" unit like the file header?

The reality is that we need a technology that can abstract away the mechanism by which the file is actually stored. If the storage mechanism and physical file representation were abstracted away, then the extraction of text and agglomeration of metadata derived from a file could easily be fed into Tika's traditional extraction processes that we've covered so far.

This is *precisely* why Tika leverages the `InputStream` as the core data passing interface to its `Parser` implementations via the `parse(...)` method. `InputStreams` obfuscate the underlying storage and protocol used to physically represent file contents (or sets of files). Whether it's a GFS URL pointer to a file that's distributed as blocks over the network, or a URL pointer to a file that's locally on disk, Tika still deals with the information as an `InputStream` via a call to `URL.openStream`. And URLs aren't the only means of getting `InputStreams`—`InputStreams` can be generated from `Files`, `byte[]` arrays, and all sorts of objects, making it the right choice for Tika's abstraction for the file physical storage interface.

8.3   Summary

Bet you never thought files had such an influence over how their information is consumed! This chapter served as a wake-up call to the reality that a file's content organization, naming conventions, and storage on disk can greatly influence the way that meaning is derived from them.

- *File content and organization*—We started out by showing you how file content organization can affect performance and memory properties, and influence how Tika parses out information and metadata. In the case of RSS, its content organization (based on XML) allows for easy streaming and random access, whereas in the case of HDF5, the entire file had to be read into memory, precluding streaming, but supporting random access.

- *Extracting file header information and exploiting naming conventions*—The middle portion of the chapter focused on file header metadata and file naming conventions, showing how in many cases metadata can be extracted from a file without even having to open the file. This feature can greatly affect the ability to easily and quickly catalog metadata about files, using Tika as the extractor.
- *File storage and how it affects extraction*—The last important aspect of files is the physical location of a file (or set of associated files) on disk. In many cases, individual files are part of some larger conglomerate, as in the case of directories and split files generated by archive/compression utilities. We examined how this information can be exploited by Tika to extract text and metadata that would normally be impossible to extract when considering each file in isolation.

The next fork in the road will take us to the advanced use and integration of Tika into the larger search ecosystem. You should be well prepared for this journey by now and hopefully eager to see where Tika fits with other information technologies!

Part 3

Integration and advanced use

Many traditional crafts are taught using an apprentice system where students work under the guidance of a master craftsman. They learn each aspect of the craft, starting from the basics and moving up to more advanced tasks as their understanding and skills grow. Once the apprentice has learned everything their master has to teach, they move on to independent practice. Through knowledge and experience from practice they eventually become masters themselves.

The previous part of this book was our attempt to carry you through a Tika apprenticeship. By following the chapters and trying out the included examples, you've had a chance to work your way through all of Tika's key features and should now be ready to start using these skills in practice. Perhaps you'll go on to become a master Tika craftsman!

But in a complex world it's often not enough to master just your own craft. You need to be aware of and understand the world around you and the ways in which it affects your work. This is why the apprentices of even traditional crafts like woodworking are encouraged to study topics like marketing, finance, and other business skills before they go on to start their own practice. Similarly, in this part of our book we want to give you a picture of the world around Tika and perhaps give you ideas of how to most successfully apply your newfound Tika skills within this world.

We'll start with a look at various kinds of information-processing systems and architectures in chapter 9. Many of these systems are related to search in various ways, so chapter 10 looks at how Tika fits together with a comprehensive stack of open source search tools. Finally, in chapter 11 we'll discover Tika's plugin model and how you can use it to easily extend Tika functionality.

Welcome to the next stage in your Tika studies!

The big picture

It's time to start thinking big. After looking at the details of how Tika works, you're probably already thinking of how to integrate it with your applications. The purpose of this chapter is to give you ideas about where and how Tika best fits with different kinds of applications, architectures, and requirements.

We'll do this in two parts. First we'll focus on functionality and look at common information-processing systems. We'll start with search engines and then look at document management and text mining as examples of other information-processing systems where Tika comes in handy. The question is about *what* such systems can achieve with Tika and *where* Tika fits in the system architecture. Then in the latter part of this chapter we'll turn to nonfunctional features such as modularity and scalability. The question there is *how* to use Tika to best meet such requirements.

145

9.1   *Tika in search engines*

Throughout this book we've mentioned search engines as common places where Tika is used, so let's take a closer look at what a search engine does and where Tika fits in. If you already know search engines, you can probably skip this section. If not, we'll start with a quick reminder of what a search engine does before a more detailed discussion of the components in a search engine.

9.1.1   *The search use case*

As outlined in figure 9.1, a search engine is broadly speaking an information-processing system that makes it possible to efficiently search for documents by maintaining an index of a document collection. Users look for information within a possibly unbounded collection of documents. They express what they're looking for as a search query that can consist of keywords, phrases, or more complex constraints.

A classic example is a web search engine such as Google Search or Microsoft's Bing, where the document collection is the entire web, the documents are web pages and other web resources, and the index is maintained by constantly "crawling" the web for new or updated documents.

The search engine works by indexing documents in the specified collection. A user then issues queries to the search engine and receives results through some addressing mechanism such as URLs for web resources or ISBN codes for printed books. The user can then find and access the matching document from the source collection.

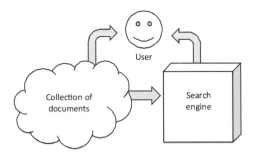

Figure 9.1   Overview of a search engine. The arrows indicate flows of information.

9.1.2   *The anatomy of a search index*

What does a search engine look like internally, and where does Tika fit in there? The architectural diagram in figure 9.2 answers these questions by showing the key components of a typical search engine.

If we follow the flow of data within such a search engine, we first encounter the crawler component, whose task is to fetch documents to be indexed. There are many strategies for finding and fetching documents, but typically a crawler will either traverse a structured collection like a file system or follow document links in an unstructured collection like the public web. Often a crawler also has an update strategy by which it refetches already-indexed documents to check whether they've been modified. In the next chapter we'll look at the Apache Nutch project, which contains a highly versatile and scalable crawler. The Apache ManifoldCF project (that we will cover later in chapter 10) provides another crawler example, optimized for ingestion into Apache Solr (also covered in chapter 10).

After a document has been fetched by the crawler, it's handed to the extraction component whose task is to extract text and other data from the document. As discussed in chapters 5 and 6, the extracted text content and metadata of a document are much more useful to a search engine than raw bytes. In some search engines, the extraction component is also used to feed interdocument links back to the crawler component for use in traversing the document collection. These tasks are exactly what Tika does, so the extraction component of a search engine can easily consist of nothing but Tika and a bit of related glue code.

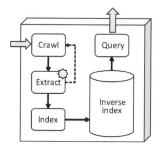

Figure 9.2   Architecture of a search engine. Blocks identify key components and the arrows show how data flows between them. Tika is typically used in the starred extraction component.

The next component in line is the indexer that converts the extracted document information into records stored in the search index. A typical search engine uses an *inverse index* that consists of a mapping from individual words or other search terms to the documents that contain them. The index is called "inverse" because instead of mapping a document identifier to the contents of the document, the mapping is from the content of a document to its identifier. Often the indexer uses a special analyzer tool to preprocess the previously extracted text; for example, to normalize words and other tokens into their base forms and to exclude common words such as *the* or *and* from being indexed. The Apache Lucene project discussed in the next chapter contains everything you'd need to build an indexer like this.

Finally, after the document has been indexed, there needs to be some way for the user to query the search index. The query component takes queries expressed by the user and translates them into the index access operations needed to find all the matching documents. The query component is normally tightly related to the indexer component, because they both contain information about the structure and organization of the inverse index and typically need to use the same analyzer configuration to map both documents and queries to the same underlying index terms. Because of this interdependence, you'll normally use the same library or framework for both of these components.

Search is useful as a standalone service, but elements of search engines are often found also in other types of information-processing systems. This is natural, both because search is such an important feature and because the crawling and extraction components of a search engine are useful also in other applications. In the next section we'll look at two broad categories of such applications.

9.2   *Managing and mining information*

A classic search engine as described in the previous section deals with documents that are stored and managed elsewhere and produces results that typically point to those external resources. What if your application is in charge of managing all those documents or needs to produce high-level reports that summarize or combine the contained information in some intelligent manner? These are the two categories of information-processing systems that we'll cover next.

The first category is document management systems, of which there are quite a few different types, ranging from personal information management systems to huge record archives. The second is the emerging field of text mining, which has experienced some nice advances in recent years. Let's start with document management.

9.2.1 *Document management systems*

Understood broadly, a *document management system* combines a document collection and search engine into a single service. Such a system takes care of storing, classifying, archiving, and tracking documents or other sorts of digital assets, and provides support for accessing the documents in various different ways, including searching and reporting. Often a document management system also includes things such as workflow support and integration with various other systems, for example, Documentum, SharePoint, and so on.

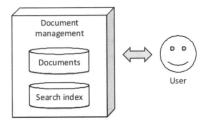

Figure 9.3   Overview of a document management system

Common examples of document management are content, asset, and records management systems used by many companies. Even tools such as customer relationship management systems have similar features or contain an embedded document database, because they need to efficiently track and access documents such as sales quotes, customer requests, and other related correspondence.

Figure 9.3 shows a high-level overview of the typical architecture of a document management system. The system consists of a document database and a search index for locating documents within the database.

A document management system can use Tika not only as a part of the embedded search index, but also as a tool for helping automatically classify documents and report document characteristics. The metadata extraction (see chapter 6) and language detection (see chapter 7) capabilities of Tika are often highly useful, as they allow the system to better understand and categorize a document that might otherwise look like a bunch of bits that a user would need to explicitly classify. Even the basic type detection feature discussed in chapter 4 can be important for such a system.

DOWNLOADS DONE RIGHT   A web-based document management system normally needs to provide a way for users to download documents for local review and editing. An important part of such a feature is annotating the download with a `Content-Type` header that contains the correct media type of the document, because without that information it's difficult for the browser to determine how to best handle the document. With Tika's automatic type detection there's no excuse not to provide that information.

Search engines and different kinds of document management systems are probably the most important environments where Tika is being used, but there's also an exciting new category of tools that's quickly becoming mature. Read on to learn more about text mining and how to use Tika in that context!

9.2.2 *Text mining*

Traditional search engines or document management systems mostly just organize or manage information and are typically judged in quantitative terms such as how many documents they cover. Text mining applications are different in that they take existing documents but produce qualitatively different information, for example, in the form of relationships or key concepts.

Consider a task where you're given an archive of all the email messages and other documents from your company over the last three years, and asked to provide a summary of all information related to a particular product or event. How would you go about achieving such a task? The sheer magnitude of raw data even in a small company rules out any manual approaches. You'll need a computer (or a whole set of them) to mine through the data and report back with the information you're looking for.

This is one example of the large class of information-processing tasks that are nowadays being performed using text mining tools. The key elements of such tasks are their large scale and the unstructured nature of the information being processed. A more traditional data mining task would typically consist of correlating and summarizing individual data points stored as structured rows in a relational database. With text mining, we don't have the luxury of predefined structure. The relevant data is usually stored within the ambiguity of natural language and scattered around among multiple kinds of documents, messages, and databases.

Figure 9.4 shows a high-level overview of a typical data mining system. The system consumes documents from a large collection, processes the information contained in the documents, and outputs the mining results in the form of reports, databases, or other high-level summaries that users can often use directly without having to reach back to any individual source document.

Text mining systems like these are normally designed to work on plain text, from which they then extract structure and meaning through natural language processing or other text processing methods. But the source data to be mined is usually stored in formats such as email messages, web pages, or office documents. A text extraction step is needed to make such data useful to a text mining system, and this is where Tika comes in handy.

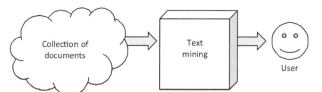

Figure 9.4   Overview of a text mining system

Many text mining systems use an internal processing pipeline to convert the incoming data from raw bytes or characters to increasingly meaningful units of information such as grammar trees or word occurrence vectors. Tika can usually be plugged into an early part of such a pipeline in order to convert incoming documents from bytes to text that can then be used as input to later stages of the pipeline.

That's where Tika fits within text mining. Together with earlier points about search engines and document management systems, you should now have a good picture of the most common kinds of applications where Tika is being used. Next we'll turn our attention to some key nonfunctional features that are relevant to all these and other kinds of applications.

9.3   Buzzword compliance

When talking about software components and applications, modularity or scalability come up often. Such features are so desirable that they've become buzzwords. If you trust marketing materials, virtually all software is highly scalable and modular. But what do these features mean in practice, and how does Tika scale on this buzzword-meter? Read on to find out!

9.3.1   Modularity, Spring, and OSGi

Most information-processing systems are complex applications composed of many smaller libraries and components. Being able to incrementally upgrade, customize, or fix individual components without breaking the rest of the system is therefore very useful. Complex deployment requirements (cloud, mobile, and so on) and the increasingly distributed organization of software development teams also benefit from good component architectures. Modularity has been a goal of software architects for decades, but it's never been as important as today!

How does Tika fit within a modular component architecture? As discussed in previous chapters, Tika's internal architecture is designed to be as pluggable and modular as possible. Most notably, one of the key design criteria for the `Parser` API covered in chapter 5 was to support easy integration with external parser libraries and components. Thus a Tika deployment with parser components from multiple different sources could easily look like the one featured in figure 9.5. In chapter 11 we'll go into more detail on how and why to implement such custom or third-party parser plugins.

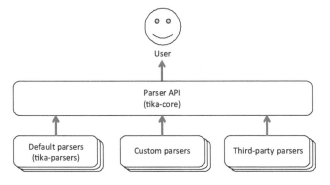

Figure 9.5   Tika deployment with parser implementations from multiple different sources

In addition to being easy to implement, Tika parsers are also easy to use in a component environment. For example, all parser classes are expected to have a zero-argument constructor and be configurable dynamically through the parsing context mechanism discussed in chapter 5. The following Spring bean configuration snippet illustrates this by wiring up a simple composite parser that understands both plain text and PDF documents:

```
-->
  <bean id="tika" class="org.apache.tika.parser.AutoDetectParser">
    <constructor-arg>
        <list>
            <ref bean="txt"/>
            <ref bean="pdf"/>
        </list>
    </constructor-arg>
  </bean>

  <bean id="txt" class="org.apache.tika.parser.txt.TXTParser"/>
  <bean id="pdf" class="org.apache.tika.parser.pdf.PDFParser"/>
<!
```

A component configuration like the one shown here creates a static composition of parsers. Modifying the configuration requires restarting your application or at least reloading the configuration and all components that depend on it. But sometimes a more dynamic mechanism is needed. Imagine being able to replace the PDF parser with a commercially licensed alternative, upgrade the plain text parser for a version with the latest bug fixes, and add a new parser for a custom file format without having to restart or even reload any other components of the system! This is what the OSGi framework makes possible.

The *OSGi framework* is a modular service platform for the Java environment. Originally designed for embedded systems with complex deployment and management requirements, OSGi is also quickly becoming popular on the server side. Tika supports OSGi through the `tika-bundle` component, which combines Tika core classes and all the default parsers into a single package that can easily be deployed into an OSGi container. Once deployed, the Tika bundle will provide all the standard Tika classes and interfaces that we've already covered. And as an extra twist, the bundle will automatically look up and use possible parser services from other bundles.

9.3.2 *Large-scale computing*

What if your modules are entire computers instead of individual software components? Especially in large search and text mining applications, it's becoming increasingly common to spread the processing load to hundreds or thousands of commodity servers. Cloud services like Amazon's Elastic Computing Cloud (EC2) make such environments readily available at low cost and minimal overhead. But how do you run Tika on such systems?

Such large-scale deployments typically use sharding or map-reduce algorithms for controlling their workload. The basic idea is that the data to be processed is distributed over the computing cluster, and each individual computer is only responsible for handling a small subset of the data. This approach works well with Tika, which only really cares about a single document at a time.

For example, consider a case where you need to create a full-text index of millions of documents. In chapter 5 we outlined how to build a simple full-text indexer with Tika, but it may take months for such an application to index all the documents on a single computer.

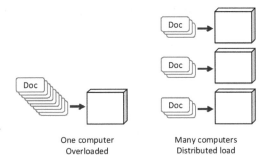

One computer
Overloaded

Many computers
Distributed load

Figure 9.6   Distributing a large workload over multiple computers can dramatically improve system throughput.

Now what if you're given 1,000 computers to achieve this task? Figure 9.6 illustrates what a difference distributing such computations over multiple computers can make.

The only requirements for such distribution of computing work is that the processing can be split into independent pieces that can be processed in parallel and that the results of these partial processes can be combined easily. Luckily, an inverse search index meets both these requirements in that documents can be indexed in parallel and it's easy to merge two or more independent indexes into a single larger index. This suggests a straightforward map-reduce solution illustrated in figure 9.7.

What happens here is that we split our collection of input documents into parts that each contain a few hundred documents. These parts are then sent to individual computers for producing an index that covers just those documents. This is the "map" part of our map-reduce solution. The resulting small indexes are then "reduced" into a big index by merging them together.

An important concern in such a solution is being able to properly handle computer failures. The more computers you're using, the more likely it becomes that at least one of them will fail while it's doing important work. The solution to such cases is to restart the failed computation on another computer.

There's a fast-growing ecosystem of tools and communities focused on such large-scale information systems. A good place to start is the Apache Hadoop project which,

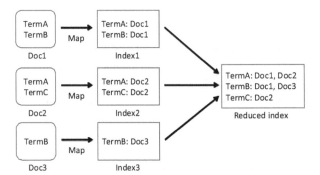

Figure 9.7   Building an inverse index as a map-reduce operation

together with related Apache projects, implements a comprehensive suite of cloud computing tools.

9.4 *Summary*

This completes our high-level overview of where and how you might find yourself using Tika. We started with a search engine walkthrough and a brief overview of document management and text mining as examples of related information-processing systems. Then we turned to modularity and scalability as key nonfunctional features. As we found out, Tika supports component systems such as Spring and OSGi, and it also fits in nicely with large-scale architectures such as map-reduce operations.

A single chapter is only enough to scratch the surface, but you'll find a lot more information in books and other resources dedicated to these topics. Good starting points are other books in Manning's *In Action* series, which covers pretty much all the projects and technologies mentioned in this chapter. Since Tika is such a new tool, it's not yet widely referenced in existing literature, and the information from this chapter should help you fill in those blanks where appropriate.

The next chapter is dedicated to a sprawling collection of open source tools and projects that are often found in applications and systems described in this chapter. Read on to discover the Lucene search stack!

Tika and the Lucene
search stack

This chapter covers

- ManifoldCF and Open Relevance
- Lucene and Solr
- Nutch, Droids, and Mahout

We're going to take a break from our in-depth tour of the Tika framework. By now, those topics should be second nature to you. But you may not be so comfortable with phrases like *Mahout*, or *Droids*, or (eep!) *Open Relevance*.

Though these terms might sound foreign, they're common terminology to those familiar with the Apache Lucene[1] family of search-related applications. Lucene is an Apache *Top Level Project*, or *TLP*, originally home to a number of search-related software products that themselves have grown to TLP-level status, including Tika.

---

[1] The name Lucene was Doug Cutting's wife's middle name, and her maternal grandmother's first name as detailed at http://mng.bz/XyTG.

It's our job in this chapter to educate you about these projects, and frame your understanding of Tika's usefulness and relationship to this family of software applications. We'll keep it high-level, focusing more on the architecture and less on the actual implementations. Those are dutifully covered in other fine Manning books.[2]

> **VIEW FROM THE TOP** An Apache Top Level Project (TLP) signifies a level of maturity for a particular software product. TLP indicates that the project has attracted a diverse base of committers, across multiple organizations; made frequent software releases under the Apache license, adhering to Apache standards in terms of dependent libraries, attribution, and legal protection; and demonstrated the ability to self-govern, elect new committers, and effectively manage itself. Tika reached this tremendous milestone on April 21, 2010.

10.1 Load-bearing walls

We'll begin by explaining the high-level diagram shown in figure 10.1, indicative of the rich and blossoming Lucene ecosystem.

Each of the boxes shown in the diagram represents a current Apache Lucene subproject, or Apache Top Level Project, with its own diverse community, release cycle, and set of software products released under its umbrella.

The diagram is layered to demonstrate the architectural properties of the system. In traditional software architecture, the layered architectural style has the following characteristics. Each *layer* represents some component (or set of related components) providing computation and functionality. Communication may occur intralayer (between components in the same layer) or interlayer, indicating that two adjacent layers are communicating. Interlayer communication may only occur between adjacent layers, originating from a top layer (the service consumer), and being responded to by a bottom adjacent layer (the service provider). Layers at the bottom of the architecture have little abstraction—they provide core functionality upon which all top layers rely.

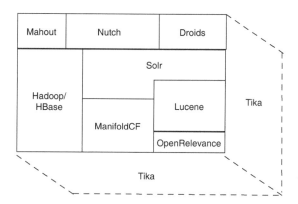

Figure 10.1 The Apache Lucene ecosystem and its family of software products. Some of the software products (such as Mahout, Nutch, Tika, and Hadoop) have graduated to form their own software ecosystems, but they all originated from Lucene. Tika is the third dimension in the stack, servicing each layer in some form or fashion.

---

[2] Specifically, we encourage you to check out *Mahout in Action*, *Lucene in Action* (1st and 2nd editions), and *Solr in Action*, because they cover Tika in some form and will help as a supplement to this book.

Layers at upper levels of the architecture have increasing layers of abstraction, depending on those services provided by the directly adjacent service provider layer. Some layers are cross-cutting (Hadoop/HBase and Solr) and are shown as layers spanning multiple levels in the architecture. In addition, Tika is shown as the three-dimensional layer, since its applicability spans each one of the service consuming and providing layers in the Lucene ecosystem.

The technologies at the lower portion of the stack in figure 10.1 form the load-bearing walls on which the rest of the ecosystem stands tall. In this section, we'll restrict our focus to ManifoldCF and Open Relevance and their relationship to Tika. As can be seen from the diagram, even though ManifoldCF and Open Relevance form the load-bearing walls, there's still room for some Tika "mortar" to hold those walls together!

10.1.1 ManifoldCF

The Apache Manifold Connectors (or ManifoldCF) project[3] is an Apache Incubator podling focused on building connections between external enterprise document repositories (for example, SharePoint, Documentum, and so on) and higher-level content technologies such as Apache Solr (which we'll talk about in section 10.2.2). ManifoldCF was originally conceived and implemented as a closed source set of software made available by the MetaCarta company, but was donated to the Apache Software Foundation in January 2010. The home page for the project is shown in figure 10.2.

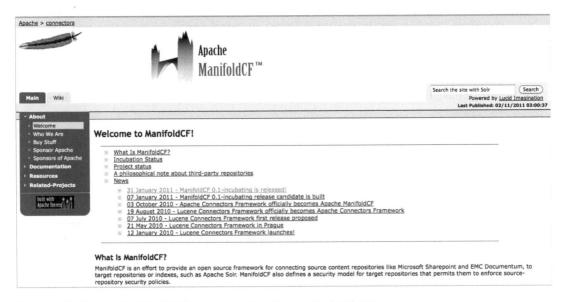

Figure 10.2   The Apache ManifoldCF home page from the Apache Incubator

---

[3] For more information see http://incubator.apache.org/connectors/ or check out *ManifoldCF in Action* at http://manning.com/wright/.

PEAS IN A POD An Apache Incubator *podling* is a project not yet fully endorsed by the Apache Software Foundation. All projects enter Apache through the Apache Incubator, a super-project whose sole responsibility is to guide new podlings through the ins and outs of Apache. Specifically, the goal is to attract a diverse set of committers, encourage frequent releases under the Apache license, and to move toward the ability to self-manage and self-govern. It should be no surprise that the next step for projects after graduating from the Incubator is Apache TLP status.

The project originally entered the Apache Incubator under the title *Lucene Connectors Framework*, or *LCF*, but was later renamed ManifoldCF to avoid confusion with other Apache connector-related products, including the Apache Tomcat connector framework.

The main goal of ManifoldCF is to make it easy to connect to existing enterprise-level document sources, including Microsoft SharePoint, EMC Documentum, and Windows File Shares, to name a few. Once connected, ManifoldCF extracts content from those sources. Once extracted, ManifoldCF provides a set of tools to easily make the extracted content available to send to output sinks, with a specific focus on Lucene and Solr. In addition, ManifoldCF also extracts security-related information and passes it along to the Lucene and Solr index for use in downstream policies.

There has been some light discussion[4] in the ManifoldCF community about using Tika's MIME detection capabilities (recall chapter 4) to identify content as it travels from input source to output sink, but nothing beyond discussion has materialized to date. Beyond identifying content, Tika may also prove useful in ManifoldCF as an output content transformer, extracting information from content traveling across the wire and making that extracted information easily available to the ManifoldCF framework.

We'll see in section 10.2.2 how ManifoldCF currently integrates Tika via Apache Solr's `ExtractingRequestHandler`, more commonly known as `SolrCell`. ManifoldCF sends output content as `Document` constructs directly to `SolrCell`, which then uses Tika to parse out metadata and text to send to Apache Solr.

Let's take a look at the Open Relevance project (ORP) next. Open Relevance is a community of volunteers whose goal involves making large document collections easily available for analysis and relevancy identification.

10.1.2 Open Relevance

Open Relevance (http://lucene.apache.org/openrelevance/) started out as an Apache Lucene subproject in June 2009, with the stated goals of making large corpuses of web content available under the Apache license. Search ranking techniques require these corpuses in order to train their algorithms to identify content relevant to return in search results. Since search ranking must be fairly content agnostic, corpuses of web content such as those provided by OpenNLP must be comparatively large, and representative of the entire web.[5] The home page for the Open Relevance project is shown in figure 10.3.

---

[4] See, in particular, http://mng.bz/4018.
[5] Though smaller corpuses are also useful for specific relevancy training and algorithms.

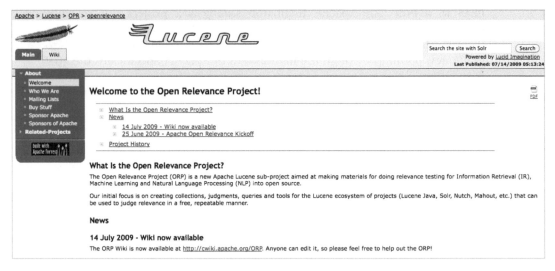

Figure 10.3 The Apache Open Relevance home page

To date, three data sets are part of the Open Relevance collection in Apache SVN (http://mng.bz/04Tk):

1 *Hamshahri corpus*—This is a moderately sized data set (~350MB) of newspaper articles from 1996 to 2002 covering 82 categories of interest including politics, arts, and so on.

2 *OHSUMED corpus*—This is a larger data set (~850MB) of analyzed medical documents from 1987 to 1991.

3 *Tempo corpus*—This is a small data set (~45MB) of newspaper articles from 2000 to 2002.

In making these datasets available, and providing a community for discussion of them, Open Relevance serves to inform other search-related projects in the Lucene ecosystem. For example, Lucene `Analyzer` classes[6] can be trained to recognize the same patterns and concepts identified as part of each corpus. In addition, Solr `Analyzers` can take advantage of these. Nutch also uses a custom set of Lucene `Analyzers`, which can be furthered informed by the data sets in Open Relevance. In addition, ranking algorithms in Solr, Lucene, and Nutch can be tuned according to the suggested importance and relevancy of the documents as identified in each training corpus from Open Relevance.

So, where does Tika play into this equation? Open Relevance expects as input a number of document collections, containing document IDs, relevant textual summaries, and other queries that help ascertain the relevancy of documents to common categories and queries of interest. This is *precisely* the type of information that Tika can extract and provide from a corpus of documents. For example, consider the following listing:

---

[6] Don't worry—we'll explain what these are shortly.

Listing 10.1 Integrating Tika into Open Relevance

```
public TrecDocument summarize(File file) throws FileNotFoundException,
    IOException, TikaException {
  Tika tika = new Tika();              ◁——— Use Tika facade        Extract text
  Metadata met = new Metadata();                                  and metadata

  String contents = tika.parseToString(new FileInputStream(file), met);  ◁┘

  return new TrecDocument(met.get(Metadata.RESOURCE_NAME_KEY),
        contents, met
      .getDate(Metadata.DATE));        ◁——— Build ORP TREC document

}
```

The only code developed so far for Open Relevance is a set of utility code to represent documents according to *TREC (Text Retrieval Conference)* standards. These document contain three attributes: a document identifier, a date associated with the document, and its text summary.

By this point in the book, you should know that Tika excels in extracting *all three* of the TREC document attributes that are modeled by ORP. The program in listing 10.1 shows how simple the integration is in Tika. A single call to the `Tika` facade takes care of all the work!

So far, we've shown you the load-bearing walls on which the rest of the Lucene ecosystem stands, and how Tika helps those walls (and can be thought of as their mortar). In the next section, we'll discuss the core search technologies in the next layer of the Lucene ecosystem: Lucene Core and Solr.

10.2 *The steel frame*

The "bread and butter" technologies that stand on top of the load-bearing walls in the Lucene ecosystem are the flagship Apache Lucene library itself (sometimes called *Lucene Core*), as well as Apache Solr, which builds on top of Lucene, but still belongs in this level.

10.2.1 *Lucene Core*

Apache Lucene[7] is a Java-based library that provides a few basic constructs which, when brought together, form a powerful, flexible mechanism to implement search. Its home page is shown in figure 10.4.

At its core is the `Document` model, allowing for the arbitrary storage of named `Fields` per `Document`, with multiple values per `Field`. This allows metadata to be stored per `Document` in the index, as shown in table 10.1.

Table 10.1 A table-oriented view of a Lucene `Document`

Field	Value(s)
Title	Tika in Action
Author	Chris A. Mattmann, Jukka Zitting
Number of Pages	250

---

[7] See http://lucene.apache.org/ or check out *Lucene in Action* at http://manning.com/hatcher3/.

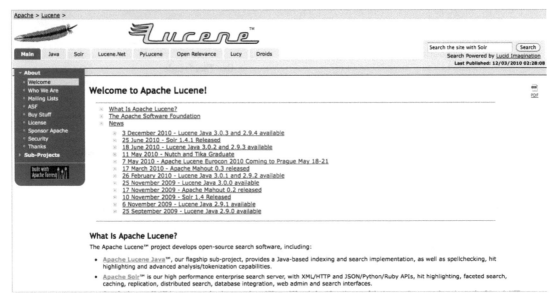

Figure 10.4   The Apache Lucene Top Level Project home page

Table 10.1 represents a Lucene `Document` that itself represents metadata about an upcoming important book. The `Document` contains three `Fields`: *Title, Author,* and *Number of Pages,* where *Author* is a multivalued field containing two values, separated by a comma, and the other two fields are single-valued entries.

In addition to the `Document` model for representing content in a search index, Lucene provides a query model and a set of tools for analysis and tokenization of both text and numeric data. Lucene also contains a number of additional modules, for highlighting (partial) word matches, for indexing content from dictionaries like WordNet,[8] and even for geographic information system (or spatial) search!

Tika has grown to provide a number of useful features to the core Lucene library. We saw some of these in action when we saw the `LuceneIndexer` from chapter 5, and the `MetadataAwareLuceneIndexer` from chapter 6. In short, Tika can feed *both* text and metadata to a Lucene index for *any* type of file that Tika knows about.[9] Not only can Tika extract text and metadata to feed into a Lucene index, it can also dynamically pick and choose the type of files (using its MIME detector, which you read about in chapter 4) to send to the Lucene index.

Once files have been indexed in Lucene, Tika can also help out, as we saw in the `RecentFiles` example from chapter 6, where Tika's standard metadata field names were used to automatically determine the names of the document metadata field names to query on.

Tika's utility doesn't stop at Lucene Core. One of Tika's most frequent usages within the Lucene family in is connection with Apache Solr, as we'll read about in the next section.

---

[8]   A large lexical database of English words. Read more about it at http://wordnet.princeton.edu/.

[9]   And by now, we know that includes many types of files, more than 1200!

10.2.2 *Solr*

Apache Solr (http://lucene.apache.org/solr/) builds on top of Lucene but offers many of the same functions (highlighting, query parsing, tokenization, analysis, and so forth), exposing these capabilities over a RESTful interface. Solr also extends Lucene to support concurrent index writing and reading, leveraging an HTTP Servlet Application server such as Apache Tomcat or Jetty to assist in concurrency and transaction management. The home page for the Apache Solr project is shown in figure 10.5.

Solr originally began as an internal project at CBS Interactive (or CNET), but was donated to the Apache Software Foundation in January 2006 via the Apache Incubator. After graduating from the Incubator, Solr became a Lucene subproject. Over the years, the Lucene and Solr communities have grown closer together, resulting in a merge of their development activities in March 2010.

One of Solr's flagship capabilities is its plugin mechanism, and one of the most useful plugins developed for Solr to date *directly* integrates Tika into Solr's toolkit. The `ExtractingRequestHandler`, or `SolrCell` as it's more commonly known, is a Solr `UpdateHandler` implementation that allows any arbitrary document to be sent to Solr via its HTTP update interface. Once the document arrives in Solr, Tika is leveraged to extract text and metadata from the document, and to map that text and metadata into fields stored per `Document` in the Lucene/Solr index. Recall in section 10.1.1 we discussed that one of ManifoldCF's key features is its easy integration with `SolrCell` and Tika, by sucking documents out of proprietary enterprise document and content repositories and ingesting them into Solr via Tika and `SolrCell`.

Other areas of integration between Tika and Solr include a recent project to integrate Tika's language identifier (recall chapter 7) as an `UpdateProcessor` interface in Solr known as the `LanguageIdentifierUpdateProcessor`. More information on `LanguageIdentifierUpdateProcessor` can be found on the Solr JIRA system.[10]

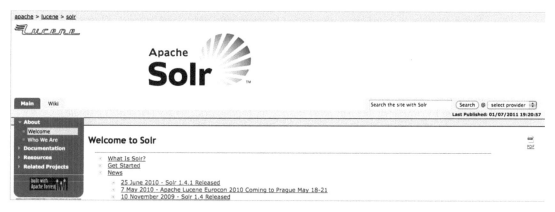

Figure 10.5 The Apache Solr Project home page

---

[10] http://issues.apache.org/jira/browse/SOLR-1979

Now that we've covered the steel frame of the Lucene search ecosystem, it's time to talk about some of the advanced applications that sit on top of the frame. You probably won't be surprised at this, but Tika is used a lot in each of the applications and software systems we're about to discuss.

10.3 *The finishing touches*

With a strong foundation and core, it's no wonder that higher-level applications and frameworks have blossomed in the Lucene ecosystem. The oldest of these frameworks was the original home to Apache Hadoop—the Apache Nutch project. Nutch's goal is to leverage Lucene, Solr, and various content-loading and extraction technologies to provide web-scale (tens of *billions* of web pages) search, in an efficient and effective matter. *Apache Droids* is an Incubator podling whose focus is developing a lightweight extensible crawler that can integrate into projects such as Nutch, Lucene, and Solr, without all the complex features and functions that those technologies provide. Finally, though we discussed Mahout earlier (in section 3.3), we'll revisit it in the context of the Lucene ecosystem discussion, and discuss the applications that sit on top of the core and load-bearing walls of Lucene.

The best thing about our upcoming foray into these technologies? They all leverage Tika!

10.3.1 *Nutch*

Apache Nutch entered the Apache Incubator in January 2005, and quickly graduated that June to Lucene subproject status. At its core, Nutch's primary goal was (and remains) opening up the "black box" that is web search and allowing for infinite tinkering and exploration in order to improve user experience and advance the state of the practice. According to Doug Cutting (Nutch's creator), Nutch came about for this reason:

> *Nutch provides a transparent alternative to commercial web search engines. Only open source search results can be fully trusted to be without bias. (Or at least their bias is public.) All existing major search engines have proprietary ranking formulas, and will not explain why a given page ranks as it does. Additionally, some search engines determine which sites to index based on payments, rather than on the merits of the sites themselves. Nutch, on the other hand, has nothing to hide and no motive to bias its results or its crawler in any way other than to try to give each user the best results possible.*
>
> —Doug Cutting
> Founder of Nutch, 2004

After a period of years and eventual 1.0 release under the Lucene umbrella, Nutch graduated to Top Level Project status in April 2010. Its home page (http://nutch.apache.org/) is shown in figure 10.6.

Nutch is the integration architecture that leverages most or all of the components from the Lucene ecosystem as shown in figure 10.7.

At its core, Nutch provides a crawling framework (similar to what we'll discuss when we talk about Droids) that leverages different `Protocol` plugins responsible for

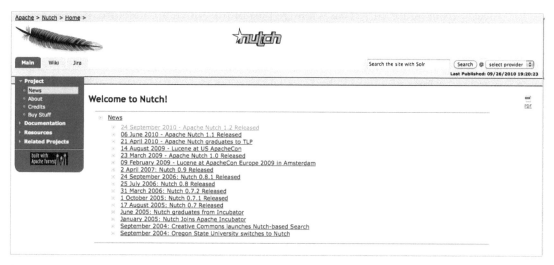

Figure 10.6   The Apache Nutch Top Level Project home page

downloading file content (over HTTP, FTP, SCP, and so on). Once content is obtained, it's fed through Tika for parsing and metadata extraction. Once the metadata and text has been extracted, that information is passed along to Solr for indexing, and made available for search via Solr's REST APIs. The original content is cached in *Apache Gora* (http://incubator.apache.org/gora/), a new Apache Incubator podling responsible for data storage and object-relational mapping. Nutch's crawling process is run on top of Apache Hadoop as a set of distributed crawling jobs, efficiently distributing the load of crawling *billions* of web pages across a set of clustered computing resources.

What we've just described is the current Nutch2 architecture, and it represents a huge advancement over the 1.x series. Nutch2's goal is to leverage the rest of the projects in the Lucene ecosystem to do its heavy lifting, and to make construction and experimentation with a web-scale search engine possible by forging the necessary connections between these powerful (but complex) software technologies.

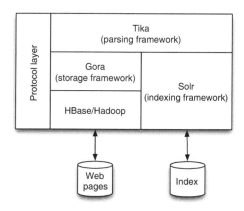

Figure 10.7   The Apache Nutch2 Architecture. A major refactoring of the overall system, Nutch is now a delegation framework, leaving the heavy lifting to the other systems in the Lucene ecosystem.

Clearly, from figure 10.7, Tika is a huge part of the Nutch architecture. Besides assisting in content extraction and metadata extraction for parsing, Tika's MIME detection system is also heavily used to help determine which content should be pulled down and crawled, how it should be parsed (which parser to leverage), and how to flow the extracted information into Solr. As we've seen with the search engine examples (from chapters 1 and 9 and as you'll see in chapter 15), it's hard to build a search engine *without* leveraging a framework like Tika since parsing, metadata extraction, MIME detection, and language identification are all critical functions of search.

Next we'll cover Apache Droids, an Incubator podling whose focus is restricted to extensible file crawling and delivery to systems such as Solr and Nutch. Don't worry; Tika will pop up there again, too!

10.3.2 Droids

One of the more serious complaints about Nutch over the years came from users who felt it was *too* configurable.[11] Nutch's plentiful configuration parameters threw off users who wanted to start crawling and indexing information about files and documents out of the box. Additionally, many potential users didn't have access to a 100-node cluster to see the benefits of deployment over Hadoop and thus wanted a more minimal, out-of-the-box crawler to begin experimenting with a corpus of documents.

Enter Apache Droids, an effort to refactor and reconfigure the crawler portion of Nutch into an independent, easy-to-use framework for text extraction and crawling. Droids entered the Apache Incubator in October 2008, and has been an Incubator project ever since. The home page for Droids is shown in figure 10.8.

Droids has no qualms about leveraging Tika as a core component in its framework. The Droids home page (http://incubator.apache.org/droids/) says it all.

Figure 10.8   The Apache Droids Project home page

---

[11] Yes, it's possible for users to get annoyed with too much extensibility in a system. Good software frameworks make the appropriate trade-off between sensible defaults and existing functionality at the expense of total configuration, but usually that lesson is learned over a *looong* time.

Apache Tika, the parser component, is just a wrapper for Tika since it offers everything we need. No need to duplicate the effort.

A `Handler` *is a component that uses the original stream and/or the parser (*`ContentHandler` *coming from Tika) and the url to invoke arbitrary business logic on the objects.*

That pretty much covers web-crawling and file-crawling frameworks built on top of the Lucene stack. At this point, we hope you appreciate how Tika fills in as the mortar connecting most of these technologies, providing the common functionality that Lucene components require to implement world-class search software.

We'll wrap up the section with a short revisit to the Apache Mahout project, and its role in the overall Lucene ecosystem.

10.3.3 *Mahout*

Apache Mahout[12] started out as a Lucene subproject in January 2008, when a number of Lucene project members realized that they shared a common interest in implementing scalable machine learning algorithms on top of the Apache Hadoop framework. The home page for Mahout is shown in figure 10.9. In April 2010, Mahout become an Apache Top Level project.

Figure 10.9   The Apache Mahout Top Level Project home page

---

[12] See http://mahout.apache.org/ or check out *Mahout in Action* at http://manning.com/owen/.

Since its inception, Mahout has grown to focus on the field of machine learning, opting to add capabilities for collaborative filtering (finding common products and recommending them), clustering, and (automatic) categorization. Mahout gels nicely with Lucene in that it can load data from Lucene indexes and feed the information into its machine learning algorithms to run analyses and assist in decision making in software applications, such as suggest a book you should buy on Amazon (based on your purchase history), or categorize a new product you've added to your website based on its features and extracted information.

We covered Mahout pretty extensively in section 3.3, but let's summarize in case you've forgotten by this point.[13] Tika can be leveraged in Mahout's algorithms as a means of turning files and documents into extracted text, which is in turn fed into Mahout's software framework for collaborative filtering, clustering, and so forth. Since Mahout algorithms are Hadoop-enabled, Mahout represents another real-world example (akin to Nutch) of bringing Tika to Hadoop, which remains a large load-bearing wall in the Lucene ecosystem.

For an in-depth look at Mahout and Tika, we recommend heading back to section 3.3 and checking out figure 3.8. Now that we've covered all of the core portions of the Lucene architecture and ecosystem, it's time for a quick recap and wrap-up of the chapter.

10.4 *Summary*

The goal of this chapter was to introduce you to the vibrant Lucene ecosystem, and all of the supporting cast involved in it, including Mahout, Lucene, ManifoldCF, and others. We tried to keep it high-level and focus on the architecture and broader details of each of these projects, as an in-depth treatment of them is beyond the scope of this book.

We framed Tika's relationship to each of these technologies, and tried to indicate the overall layered architecture and commonalities between each of these software products, taking special care to show you where Tika fit in along the way. The key takeaways should include these points:

1 *The architecture of the Lucene ecosystem*—Identifying which technologies fit where, and why.

2 *The broad infection of Tika into each layer of the architecture*—There's no getting around it—Tika forms the mortar that holds the "bricks" or layers of the architecture together.

Now that you can tell your Tikas from your Solrs, it's time to wrap up this part of the book and discuss some advanced usage of Tika, focusing on the cases where Tika as shipped requires some extensions and additional functionality to meet your needs. It's called "Extending Tika" and it's up next!

---

[13] We wouldn't blame you, seven chapters later!

Extending Tika

This chapter covers

- Teaching Tika about new media types
- Custom type detection
- Building custom parsers

There are thousands of document formats in the world and new ones are constantly being introduced, so it's impossible for a library like Tika to support all of them out of the box. Thus even though each Tika version adds support for new formats, there will be times when Tika won't be able to extract content from or even detect the type of a document you're trying to use. This chapter is about what you can do in such a situation.

Imagine that you're working with a new XML-based file format for medical prescriptions. Each file describes a single prescription and consists of a set of both fixed and free-form fields of information. Optionally the prescription documents can be digitally signed and encrypted for better security and privacy. Figure 11.1 shows how such digital prescriptions can be used in practice.

It'd be useful to make such documents searchable based on both free-form text and selected metadata fields like the patient name or identifier. The easiest way to implement such a search engine is to use an existing search stack like the one we

Figure 11.1   Illustration of how a digital prescription document can be used to securely transfer accurate prescription information from a doctor to a pharmacy. A digital signature ensures that the document came from someone authorized to make prescriptions, and encryption is used to ensure the privacy of the patient.

described in the previous chapter, and to do that you simply need to teach Tika how these documents should be parsed.

We'll use such digital prescription documents as our example for extending Tika. First we'll teach Tika how to detect and identify such documents, and then we'll see how to make Tika correctly parse these documents.

11.1   *Adding type information*

The first step in dealing with a new document type is identifying it with a media type. Let's tentatively name our prescription format `application/x-prescription+xml`. The x- prefix marks this as an experimental type that hasn't been officially registered, and the +xml suffix signals that the type is XML-based.

We also need some information to help automatic detection of prescription documents. As discussed in chapter 4, the file extension and the XML root element are good hints for type detection. So let's assume that the prescription files are named with a .xpd extension for *extensible prescription document*. Furthermore let's assume that the XML documents start with an `<xpd:prescription>` element whose prefix `xpd` is mapped to the namespace `http://example.com/2011/xpd`. The following listing shows what such a document might look like:

```
<xpd:prescription xmlns:xpd="http://example.com/2011/xpd">
  <xpd:doctor>...</xpd:doctor>
  <xpd:patient>...</xpd:patient>
  <xpd:medicine>...</xpd:medicine>
  <xpd:instructions>...</xpd:instructions>
</xpd:prescription>
```

All this type information can be described in the media type record shown next. Please refer back to chapter 4 where we covered the MIME-info database for more details about the media type record structure:

```
<mime-info>
<mime-type type="application/x-prescription+xml">
  <sub-class-of type="application/xml"/>
  <acronym>XPD</acronym>
  <expanded-acronym>Extensible Description Document</expanded-acronym>
  <comment xml:lang="en">Digital prescription</comment>
  <glob pattern="*.xpd"/>
  <root-XML localName="prescription"
            namespaceURI="http://example.com/2011/xpd"/>
</mime-type>
</mime-info>
```

The most obvious way to teach Tika about new document types is to extend the existing media type database, so that's what we'll focus on first.

11.1.1 Custom media type configuration

Let's look at the shared MIME-info database file we covered earlier in chapter 4. The database contains details of all the media types known to Tika, so to support a new type you'll need to add it to the database. This section shows how to do that.

By default Tika will load this database from the org/apache/tika/mime/tika-mimetypes.xml file inside the tika-core JAR. But you can also instruct Tika to load an alternative file using the `MimeTypesFactory` class. For example, the following listing shows how to load an alternative MIME-info database and use it to set up a `Tika` facade instance for use in type detection:

```
String path = "file:///path/to/prescription-type.xml";
MimeTypes typeDatabase = MimeTypesFactory.create(new URL(path));
Tika tika = new Tika(typeDatabase);
String type = tika.detect("/path/to/prescription.xpd");
```

When executed with the described custom settings, this code snippet will return the expected `application/x-prescription+xml` media type. You can also use the `Mime-Types` object returned by the `MimeTypesFactory` for constructing `AutoDetectParser` instances or anywhere you need a `Detector` object.

Tika currently doesn't support merging multiple MIME-info databases, so the best way to create a customized database is to start with the default version included in the tika-core JAR. This unfortunately means that you should update your customized version whenever a new Tika release is made. A future Tika release will no doubt add support for incremental database updates to make it easier to maintain these kinds of custom extensions.

Now that Tika knows our custom types, our next step is to look at adding more generic type detection strategies through custom `Detector` classes.

11.2 Custom type detection

Customizing the MIME-info database is all it takes to teach Tika about new types and new type detection rules based on common features such as file extensions, magic bytes, or XML elements. But what if you're dealing with a more complex format for which none of these simple detection mechanisms work? The answer lies in Tika's `Detector` interface, which allows you to plug in custom type detection algorithms.

To better understand the `Detector` interface and how to use it as an extension point, we'll first go through a quick overview of how the interface works. Then we'll dive in and implement a complete custom type detector for encrypted prescription documents. Finally we'll see how custom detectors can be plugged into Tika.

11.2.1 *The Detector interface*

The Detector interface specifies a generic API for type detection algorithms. The detect method defined in this interface detects the type of a document based on the document's raw byte stream and any available document metadata. The diagram in figure 11.2 outlines how this works.

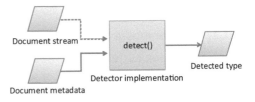

Figure 11.2   Overview of a generic type detector

One detector implementation can look at the byte stream for known byte patterns while another can inspect the available document metadata for known filename suffixes or other media type hints. Detector implementations should also be prepared for the absence of either of these inputs, for example, when dealing with just a filename or a raw byte stream. If the detector can't determine the document type based on the available information, it should return the generic application/octet-stream media type.

Tika will automatically load all available detector implementations using Java's service provider mechanism. When detecting the type of a document, all these available detectors are invoked in sequence and the most specific media type is returned to the client application as the detection result. You can add custom detection algorithms by implementing the Detector interface and adding the required service provider settings. The next section shows how this is done in practice.

11.2.2 *Building a custom type detector*

For example, let's assume that the pharmacy automation system we described earlier is supposed to automatically detect and process digital prescriptions sent as encrypted email attachments. We have the decryption key but can't rely on things such as file extensions or other external type hints for detecting these documents.

So how would we go about detecting such documents? As described earlier, the solution is to create a custom Detector class and plug it into Tika's type detection mechanism. The example class shown next does exactly this. Take a moment to study the code, and read on for a more detailed description.

Listing 11.1   Custom type detector for encrypted prescription documents

```
public class EncryptedPrescriptionDetector implements Detector {

    public MediaType detect(InputStream stream, Metadata metadata)
            throws IOException {
        Key key = Pharmacy.getKey();                        ◁┐ ❶ Pharmacy's
        MediaType type = MediaType.OCTET_STREAM;               private key

        InputStream lookahead =                             ◁┐ Look at beginning
            new LookaheadInputStream(stream, 1024);         ❷ of stream
        try {
            Cipher cipher = Cipher.getInstance("RSA");      ◁─❸ Decrypt stream
```

```
            cipher.init(Cipher.DECRYPT_MODE, key);
            InputStream decrypted =
                new CipherInputStream(lookahead, cipher);

            QName name = new XmlRootExtractor()
                .extractRootElement(decrypted);
            if (name != null
                    && "http://example.com/
    xpd".equals(name.getNamespaceURI())
                    && "prescription".equals(name.getLocalPart())) {
                type =
                    MediaType.application("x-prescription");
            }
        } catch (GeneralSecurityException e) {
            // unable to decrypt, fall through
        } finally {
            lookahead.close();
        }
        return type;
    }

}
```

④ **Does it look like XML?**

⑤ **Found digital prescription!**

What's happening here? Let's go through the code in steps.

1 First, detector classes are instantiated using the public default constructor and can't access extra settings through the `ParseContext` object that the `Parser` classes can. Thus in this case we need a static reference to the pharmacy's decryption key ❶.

2 Then in the `detect()` method we start trying to detect the document type. This method can assume that the given stream supports the mark feature, and is only expected to reset the stream to its original position before returning. The `org.apache.tika.io.LookaheadInputStream` (introduced in Tika 1.0) utility class ❷ is a perfect tool for this, as it takes care of all the details of properly managing the stream state. See the Javadocs of that class for more details.

3 We then try to decrypt ❸ the `lookahead` stream using the standard cryptography API in Java. If the decryption fails for whatever reason, we can assume that the document is either not encrypted or that we don't have the correct key for that document. In either case this detector can return `application/octet-stream` as the fallback type.

4 If we do manage to decrypt the stream, our next task is to check whether it looks like XML and starts with the `xpd:prescription` element. The `org.apache.tika.detect.XmlRootExtractor` utility class ❹ is designed for this purpose, and is also used by the default type detection code in Tika.

5 Finally, if all signs point to this being an encrypted digital prescription, we can inform Tika of that fact by returning the `application/x-prescription` media type ❺. Note that we've dropped the +xml suffix from the type name, as the encryption makes the document unusable for standard XML-processing tools. This new media type should also be added to the MIME-info database as a sibling of the already declared XML type.

11.2.3 *Plugging in new detectors*

The one last thing you need after compiling this custom detector class is to plug it into Tika. The easiest way to do that is to place the compiled class into a JAR archive together with a META-INF/services/org.apache.tika.detect.Detector file that contains the fully qualified name of this class on a line by itself. Then include that JAR in your classpath, and Tika will automatically pick up and use the new detector.

If you want more control over the set of detectors used by your application, you can also use the `CompositeDetector` class to explicitly compose a combination of them. The following code snippet shows how to extend our previous detection example with support for encrypted prescription documents:

```
String path = "file:///path/to/prescription-type.xml";
MimeTypes typeDatabase = MimeTypesFactory.create(new URL(path));
Tika tika = new Tika(new CompositeDetector(
        typeDatabase,
        new EncryptedPrescriptionDetector()));
String type = tika.detect("/path/to/tmp/prescription.xpd");
```

By now you've learned how to extend Tika's media type database and type detection capabilities to cover pretty much any new document type you encounter. The next step is to let Tika parse such documents, and that's what we'll focus on in the next section.

11.3 *Customized parsing*

Knowing the type of a document is useful, but even better is being able to extract information from the document. To do this you need to be able to parse the document format, and for that you use the `Parser` interface described in chapter 5. To enable Tika to extract information from a new document type, the first step is to implement a new parser class or to extend an existing one. In this section we'll do both.

Consider the digital prescription documents we've been discussing. In their unencrypted form they're XML documents with a specific structure, and the encrypted form wraps a digital signature and encryption around the underlying XML document. To best handle such documents, we need two new parser classes, one for the basic XML format and another for the encrypted form. The relationship between these custom parser classes and the greater Tika parser design is outlined in figure 11.3.

As shown in this diagram, we'll first implement support for the unencrypted prescription documents by extending the standard `XMLParser` class in Tika. Once we have that class, it'll be

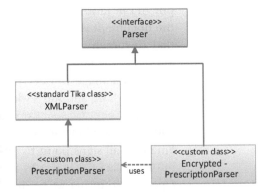

Figure 11.3 Custom parser classes for handling digital prescription documents

easy to combine it with our earlier work on detecting encrypted documents to implement a custom parser for encrypted digital prescriptions.

11.3.1 *Customizing existing parsers*

Let's start with the existing parsers that you can already find in Tika. Most of the time they work pretty well, but what if you need to make some minor adjustments to help them better understand the kinds of documents you're working with? The Parse-Context object that we covered in chapter 5 allows some level of customization, but sometimes you need to make more extensive changes to parser behavior.

Many parser classes in Tika have been designed with such customization in mind, so you can often extend them with a subclass that overrides selected methods. See the Javadocs of the parser classes for more information on the ways in which they can be extended. A good example of such extensibility is the XMLParser class that we'll be using next.

Remember the simple XML outline of a basic prescription document in section 11.1? The document contains separate elements for the doctor, the patient, the medicine, and any instructions associated with the prescription. The default XML parser will take the text content of all these elements and make it available as the output of the parsing process. Wouldn't it be useful if at least some of these fields were also made available as structured metadata fields?

An example class that does this is shown in the following listing. It retains the default behavior of the XMLParser class while also mapping the contents of the xpd:doctor and xpd:patient elements into similarly named metadata fields.

Listing 11.2 An `XMLParser` subclass for parsing prescription documents

```
public class PrescriptionParser extends XMLParser {

    @Override                                              ❶ Override with
    protected ContentHandler getContentHandler(              custom behavior
            ContentHandler handler, Metadata metadata,
            ParseContext context) {
        String xpd = "http://example.com/2011/xpd";       ❷ Capture
                                                             element
        ContentHandler doctor = new ElementMetadataHandler(  metadata
                xpd, "doctor", metadata, "xpd:doctor");
        ContentHandler patient = new ElementMetadataHandler(
                xpd, "patient", metadata, "xpd:patient");  ❸ Combine with
                                                             default behavior
        return new TeeContentHandler(
                super.getContentHandler(handler, metadata, context),
                doctor, patient);
    }
                                                           ❹ Report
    @Override                                                supported type
    public Set<MediaType> getSupportedTypes(
            ParseContext context) {
        return Collections.singleton(
                MediaType.application("x-prescription+xml"));
    }
}
```

Let's step through the code to better understand how it works.

1   To start with, the class extends the existing XMLParser class and overrides the protected getContentHandler() method ❶. This method controls how the SAX events from the parsed XML document are mapped to Tika's XHTML output. The default implementation strips out all elements and passes only the text content to the client. In this case we customize this project to map selected parts of the XML document into corresponding metadata fields.

2   To achieve this we use the ElementMetadataHandler utility class from the org.apache.tika.parser.xml package ❷. This class interprets an incoming SAX event stream and maps the text content of selected elements to a given metadata field. In our case we're interested in the names of the doctor and the patient mentioned in the prescription, so we construct two such handlers.

3   We use the TeeContentHandler class ❸ to tie these metadata handlers together with the default XMLParser behavior as returned by the superclass method. See chapter 5 for more details on how the TeeContentHandler class works.

4   Finally we override the getSupportedTypes() method ❹ to only return the application/x-prescription+xml media type. This allows our custom class to coexist with the default XMLParser class that supports just the standard application/xml media type.

That wasn't too hard, was it? Let's move on to creating an entirely new parser class.

11.3.2 *Writing a new parser*

You probably guessed it already: we also need a way to parse the encrypted prescription documents. Since there's currently no generic parser in Tika for encryption formats, we need to write a new one to be able to extract information from encrypted prescriptions.

We already have all the basic building blocks we need from previous examples, so the only thing left to do is to put those block together into a fresh new parser class. The result is shown in the following listing.

Listing 11.3 Parser class for encrypted prescription documents

```
public class EncryptedPrescriptionParser          ❶ New parser class
        extends AbstractParser {
                                                   ❷ Implement
    public void parse(                                parse() method
            InputStream stream, ContentHandler handler,
            Metadata metadata, ParseContext context)
            throws IOException, SAXException, TikaException {
        try {                                      ❸ Decrypt incoming
            Key key = Pharmacy.getKey();              document stream
            Cipher cipher = Cipher.getInstance("RSA");
            cipher.init(Cipher.DECRYPT_MODE, key);
            InputStream decrypted =
                new CipherInputStream(stream, cipher);
```

```
        new PrescriptionParser().parse(
                decrypted, handler, metadata, context);
    } catch (GeneralSecurityException e) {
        throw new TikaException(
                "Unable to decrypt a digital prescription", e);
    }
}

public Set<MediaType> getSupportedTypes(
        ParseContext context) {
    return Collections.singleton(
            MediaType.application("x-prescription"));
}

}
```

Delegate
to parser
❹ we created

❺ Report
supported type

You can probably tell what each part in this code does, but let's still go through it so we don't miss any details.

1 Instead of implementing the `Parser` interface directly, we start by extending the `AbstractParser` base class ❶. This simple class comes with default implementations for deprecated old methods so we don't need to worry about them in our code.

2 The main functionality goes into the `parse()` method ❷ whose behavior we covered in detail in chapter 5. Here we want to first decrypt the encrypted document stream ❸ and then pass the XML content to the extended XML parser we already created ❹.

3 Since we're delegating detailed processing to another parser class, we don't need to worry about producing XHTML output in this class. Otherwise we could use the `XHTMLContentHandler` utility class that we also covered in chapter 5.

4 And like before, we implement the `getSupportedTypes()` method ❺ in this class to tell Tika about the kinds of documents it should be using this parser class for. The returned media type should match the type returned by the corresponding detector.

Now we have two new parser classes: one for encrypted and one for unencrypted digital prescriptions. We still need to tell Tika to use these parsers, which is what we'll do next.

11.3.3 *Plugging in new parsers*

Parser plugins are just like new detectors, in that Tika by default uses the service provider mechanism to load all available implementations from the classpath. To tell Tika about your two new parsers, you need to place the compiled classes into a JAR file together with a META-INF/services/org.apache.tika.parser.Parser file that lists the fully qualified names of these two classes on separate lines. When you include that JAR in your classpath, Tika will automatically start using these new parsers.

JAR archives like this are an easy way to extend Tika. For example, you can put all the code from this chapter into a new tika-xpd-1.0.0.jar file together with the two service provider files in META-INF/services. Then you'll have a complete Tika plugin that you can easily use to enable support for digital prescriptions in any system that uses Tika for metadata and content extraction.

So what happens if you want to override an existing parser in case you have two parsers that both claim to support the same MIME type (such as application/x-prescription+xml)?

11.3.4 *Overriding existing parsers*

When you have two `Parsers` that both claim to support the same type, a simple bit of code can help you ensure the `Parser` you want to be selected is called by Tika, as shown next.

Listing 11.4   Overriding `Parsers` in Tika

```
Parser custom = new MyCustomPrescriptionParser();        ⟵──❶ Declare custom parser
Parser parser = new AutoDetectParser(
  parser.getDetector(),
  ParserDecorator.withTypes(custom,                       ⟵──❷ Call custom parser first

  Collections.singleton("application/x-prescription+xml")));
        parser.parse(...);
```

In listing 11.4, first you declare an instance of the `MyCustomPrescriptionParser` in ❶. This is the `Parser` that you'd like to be called instead of the default parser for the type `application/x-prescription+xml`. Then, to link that `Parser` to the media type, you can decorate your `MyCustomPrescriptionParser` by creating an `AutoDetectParser` instance with your `MyCustomPrescriptionParser` as the first `Parser` in the list provided to the constructor, as shown in ❷. The combination of the `ParserDecorator` and the ordered set of `Parser` passed to the `AutoDetectParser` constructor helps ensure that no matter what `MyCustomPrescriptionParser` purports to deal with in terms of MIME types, it'll be called and selected as the `Parser` for the application-x-prescription+xml type.

That's a lot of functionality packed into a few small classes and some lines of configuration, and a good place to end our coverage of how to extend Tika. It's time to summarize what we've learned here.

11.4 *Summary*

In this chapter we learned about a digital prescription document format, which despite being fictional is a good example of the kinds of new document formats that are being developed and used every day. Being able to easily detect, index, and search such documents is often an important requirement. Tika and the tools it integrates with can be a major help in implementing such requirements. You only need to extend Tika to understand such new document formats, which is what we've done in this chapter.

After briefly explaining our example document format, we looked at how to add information about that type into Tika's media type database along with basic type detection details. Then, we covered more complex detection strategies by writing a custom `Detector` class. Finally, we implemented two custom `Parser` classes, one extended and one standalone, to allow Tika to extract text and metadata from our example documents. All this functionality was wrapped into a simple JAR archive that can be used as a drop-in plugin to extend the capabilities of any Tika-enabled system.

This concludes the third part of this book. By now you should know pretty much everything there is to know about Tika and should be able to start using it even in complex ways in your own applications. In the next part of this book we'll discuss of how others are using Tika.

Part 4

Case studies

Welcome to the last major section of the book. It's hard to imagine we've come this far, but here we are!

You should have a fundamental understanding of Tika, its features and functionality, its methods for extension, and its placement among other leading technologies in the search space and overall information landscape.

This portion of the book focuses on one of the basic methods of human learning: *by example*. What better way to get more ideas of how to use Tika in your particular software application than seeing how others have done so successfully?

In chapter 12 we'll show you how the National Aeronautics and Space Administration (NASA) has been using Tika as a major component of its ground data processing system pipelines. We'll follow that in chapter 13 by sharing our experience using Tika to help manage content with the Apache Jackrabbit content repository. Chapter 14 gives you a feel for how Tika has been used in the context of a bioinformatics data collection system at the National Cancer Institute. And we'll wrap up the book the same way we started it: with a classic real-world case study of Tika's use in the search engine community in chapter 15.

Powering NASA
science data systems

This chapter covers

- The Planetary Data System
- The Earth Science Enterprise systems
- How Tika fits in

Welcome to the first of four deep dives showing Tika's use in a real-world system. We'll assume that, by now, you have a firm grasp of what Tika can do, how you can use its functionality in your application, and how you can extend Tika and add new functionality to it.

In this chapter, we'll spend less time covering Tika's nuts and bolts, and we'll spend more time showing you how a real-world, huge-scale organization like the National Aeronautics and Space Administration (NASA) uses Tika in some of its newer, large-scale data system efforts.

One of Tika's flagship deployments has been within NASA. We've used Tika to help power search for NASA's Planetary Data System, the archive for all planetary science information collected over the past 40 years. Tika's helped us extract information from PDS datasets and index them for a revamp of PDS's search architecture, helping to turn its online data distribution system into a Google-like, free-text and facet-based search. We'll explain Tika's role in this revamp early in the chapter.

Besides planetary science, Tika has also helped NASA in the Earth science domain. Tika now helps power many of NASA's Earth Science Ground Data Systems, augmenting the power of another Apache technology called *Object Oriented Data Technology* (OODT) to identify files for cataloging and archiving, delivery to geospatial information systems, and processing and distribution to the general public. We'll briefly discuss examples of Tika's use within the Orbiting Carbon Observatory (OCO), the National Polar-orbiting Operational Environmental Satellite System (NPOESS) Preparatory Project (NPP), Sounder Product Evaluation and Analysis Tool Element (PEATE), and the Soil Moisture Active Passive (SMAP) missions. Yes, that was a ton of acronyms—welcome to the world of NASA and let's dive in!

12.1   *NASA's Planetary Data System*

We'll cover the important aspects of the NASA's Planetary Data System (PDS) search engine redesign project in this section, starting with some basic information about PDS, including discussion on its core data model and its improved search engine architecture. Along the way, we'll explain where Tika fits in, and how it helped.

The PDS is NASA's archive for all of its planetary science information. All of the planetary missions as far back as Viking[1] are cataloged in the PDS.

The system accepts data and metadata processed from instrument science data teams after those teams receive raw data records downlinked from the spacecraft. The data can be arbitrarily represented and formatted (Word documents, engineering datasets, images—sound familiar?) as long as there's a plain-text, ASCII metadata file (called a *label*) describing the data delivered along with it. This architecture is depicted in figure 12.1.

In the next section, we'll provide some brief background on the PDS data model.

12.1.1   *PDS data model*

All metadata in the Planetary Data System is guided by a domain data model, built around familiar NASA mission concepts. A *Mission* is flown with one or more science *Instrument*s, concerned with observing a *Target* which could be a planet, star, or some small celestial body (a comet or asteroid). The full PDS data model is beyond the scope of what we could cover in this chapter (let alone this whole book), but we have enough to go on with the previous.

THE GREAT THING ABOUT STANDARDS   The full PDS standards reference is a 14 MB, 531-page document describing the PDS data and metadata model in glorious detail. If you're interested in learning more about PDS data, check out http://mng.bz/6r1B.

---

[1] For a full list of NASA planetary missions, see http://science.nasa.gov/planetary-science/missions/.

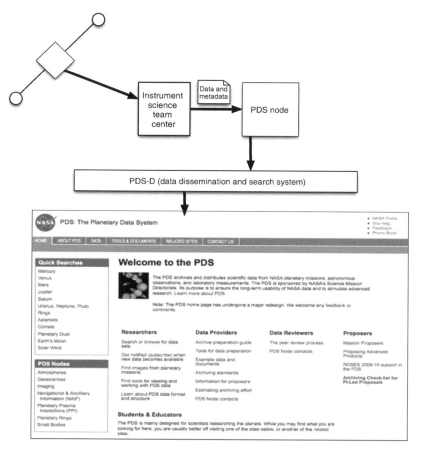

Figure 12.1   The flow of data through NASA's Planetary Data System

Every (set of) data file(s), or as PDS and NASA in general call them *product(s)*, delivered to PDS must have a label associated with it that in some form captures this data model. So, for example, if the Cassini mission sends some data to the system, that data will have the basic metadata information shown in table 12.1.

Table 12.1   A PDS label for Cassini

Metadata field	Value
Mission	Cassini–Huygens
Instrument	Cassini Plasma Spectrometer (CAPS); Cosmic Dust Analyzer (CDA); Composite Infrared Spectrometer (CIRS); Ion and Neutral Mass Spectrometer (INMS); Imaging Science Subsystem (ISS); Dual Technique Magnetometer (MAG); Magnetospheric Imaging Instrument (MIMI); Radar, Radio and Plasma Wave Science instrument (RPWS); Radio Science Subsystem (RSS); Ultraviolet Imaging Spectrograph (UVIS); Visible and Infrared Mapping Spectrometer (VIMS)
Target	Saturn

Metadata is made accessible via the *PDS Data Distribution System*, or *PDS-D* for short. Each PDS product has an associated metadata entry available in PDS-D, made available in a variety of formats ranging from the Object Description Language (ODL) to the W3C standard Resource Description Framework (RDF).

Core understanding of the PDS data model is necessary to understand how to improve the search and access the information in the system described by instances of that model. On the surface, most PDS searches are domain-specific, powered by form elements, corresponding to some subset of the model. For the expert user, this is precisely the type of search that still today is useful for finding information in the system. But naive users of PDS were quickly put off by the difficulty of using these domain-specific search utilities, and wanted something as simple as a "Google-box" to input keywords in to, and to receive pointers to PDS data from.

Next, we'll describe the redesign of the PDS search system that we began in 2005. Here's where Tika comes in.

12.1.2 *The PDS search redesign*

In 2005, the PDS team began an effort in response to the growing desire for free-text or Google-like search within the PDS. To construct this capability, the decision was made to dump PDS metadata from PDS-D in the emerging W3C standard RDF format. RDF is an XML-based format, similar to the RSS example[2] we showed you in chapter 8.

Once the RDF files were dumped for datasets in the PDS, the files would be indexed in the Apache Lucene (and eventually Apache Solr) search technology, making them easily searchable and available for the PDS-D website and portal to leverage as shown in figure 12.2.

This sounds eerily familiar to examples from chapter 1, 3, 8, and 9 where similar search pipelines resulted in making content available using the Lucene ecosystem of technologies. In the case of PDS, we ended up writing a parser for PDS metadata outside of the context of Tika (it was only a glimmer in our collective eyes at that point) that was eventually translated into a Tika `Parser` interface implementation. The `PDSRDFParser` extracted PDS dataset metadata and text that we then sent to Solr for indexing.

One nifty portion of this example is that we were able to leverage the PDS and its rich data model to identify facets that you see on the main PDS website at http://pds.nasa.gov, an example of which is shown in figure 12.3. Those facets are extracted by the Tika `PDSRDFParser` class and then sent to Solr, where the field names are specified as facet fields in the Solr schema. This allows the values to be counted and "bucketed," allowing interested PDS users to use a combination of the facets and free-text search to find the PDS data (called *products*) of interest. Once those products are found, a user may click a link to find and download the product from a particular PDS discipline node site.

---

[2] Earlier versions of RSS actually leveraged RDF schema.

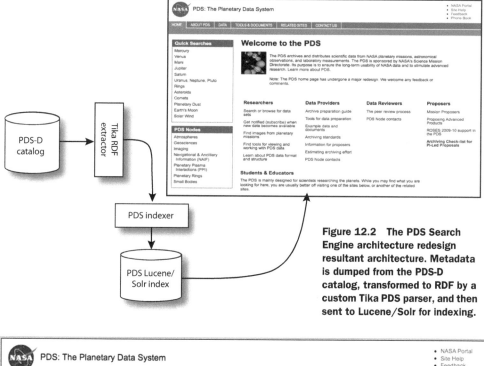

Figure 12.2   The PDS Search Engine architecture redesign resultant architecture. Metadata is dumped from the PDS-D catalog, transformed to RDF by a custom Tika PDS parser, and then sent to Lucene/Solr for indexing.

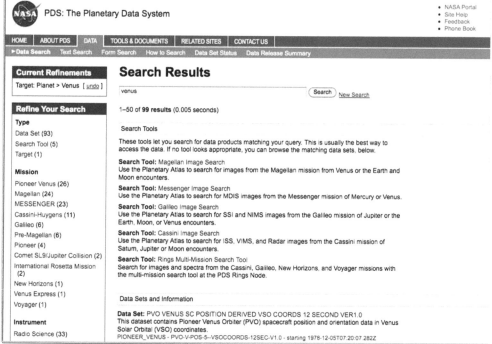

Figure 12.3   The NASA Planetary Data System (PDS) main web page and its drill-down (facet-based) search interface

Porting the original PDS parser to Tika was natural and didn't require any additional overhead. And, like we mentioned in chapter 10, since Tika is one of the load-bearing walls for a number of other Lucene technologies, we were able to easily integrate it into Lucene and Solr to help create the new PDS search architecture.

Now that we've described the planetary use case, let's switch gears and tell you how Tika is used to power data systems focused on *our* planet, rather than our neighbors in the solar system!

NASA Earth science data systems are traditionally more computationally intensive and more focused on data processing rather than data archival, so it represents another important and relevant domain to see where and how Tika is being used. The great thing is that Tika is just as useful in Earth science data processing systems (for file identification, classification, parsing, and more) as it is for extracting text and metadata from planetary data files and images.

12.2   NASA's Earth Science Enterprise

NASA's Earth Science Enterprise is vast, consisting of three major families of software systems, as depicted in figure 12.4.

One of the most tremendous challenges in keeping up with the data volume, new instruments and missions, and sheer pace of scientific discovery in the NASA Earth

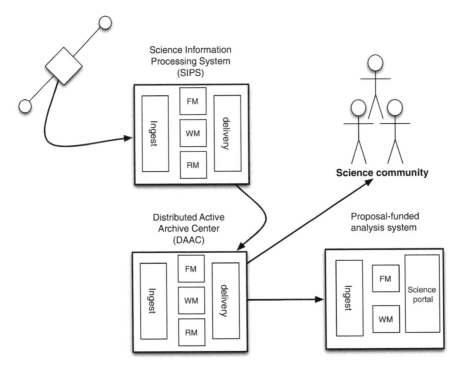

Figure 12.4   NASA's Earth Science Enterprise, consisting of three families of software systems: SIPS takes raw data and process it; DAACs distribute that data to the public; proposal systems do ad hoc analyses.

science Enterprise involves the classification and archival of science information files. Tika is a welcome friend when confronted with this challenge. We'll explain how in this section, but first you'll need some background on NASA jargon to understand what's going on.

Science Information Processing Systems (SIPS) are typically directed by a *principal investigator* (PI), along with a science team, co-located at a particular institution along with the SIPS. The PI and the science team get early access to the data, help to develop the processing system and science algorithms that transform data from raw data records, to geolocated, calibrated, physically meaningful Earth science data files (or products), which are disseminated to the broader community. SIPS typically include components for file management (labeled FM in figure 12.4), workflow management (labeled WM in the figure), and for resource management (labeled RM in the figure). SIPS also include ingestion components and delivery components, which take in raw data records (ingest), and deliver processed science data products to long-term archives and dissemination centers (called DAACs, and discussed next).

Distributed Active Archive Centers (DAACs) are NASA's long-term Earth science data archives, geographically distributed around the United States, co-located with science expertise in oceans, land processes, carbon and atmospheres, to name a few. Each DAAC includes the same basic software stack (FM+WM+RM, ingest and delivery) as SIPS, yet typically has different requirements than that of a SIPS. For example, SIPS aren't expected to *preserve* their data for any long-standing period of time; DAACs are, which uses more disk space and requires more metadata requirements, and more thought in general with respect to software development.[3] DAACs are the recommended NASA dissemination centers for all of the agency's Earth science data.

Rounding out the Earth science enterprise are NASA proposal-funded systems, typically conducting ad hoc analyses or generating value-added data products to distribute to the community. These systems may contain different combinations of the core data system software stack, and may add specific foci, such as science data portals, ad hoc workflows, or data extraction tools. These systems are direct consumers of data made available by DAACs.

12.2.1 Leveraging Tika in NASA Earth Science SIPS

Next we'll explain a few Earth science SIPS systems where Tika has been directly leveraged to help identify files for ingestion, to identify files to pull down from remote sources, and to extract information from those files during pipeline processing.

THE ORBITING CARBON OBSERVATORY
NASA's Orbiting Carbon Observatory (OCO) mission is focused on obtaining high-resolution measurements of carbon dioxide sources and sinks at global scale. OCO is a first-of-its-kind mission, set to produce never-before-seen estimates of carbon throughout the entire world.

---

[3] Imagine if you had to make sure that data produced from a Java algorithm would still be reproducible in 30 years!

The first version of the OCO mission failed to launch in 2009, but is being rapidly reconstructed as OCO2 for a relaunch in the 2013 timeframe. OCO2's SIPS is under construction at NASA's Jet Propulsion Laboratory, heavily leveraging the system developed for launch in the 2009 timeframe.

Next up is the NPP Sounder PEATE mission.

NPOESS PREPARATORY PROJECT (NPP) SOUNDER PEATE

The NPOESS Preparatory Project is a joint NASA, Department of Defense, and National Oceanic and Atmospheric Administration (NOAA) satellite meant to take the United States into the next generation of weather and climate measurements.

NPP Sounder PEATE is one of five Product Evaluation and Testing Environment projects that support the overall NPP mission, assessing the climate quality of several important science data products (vertical temperature, moisture, and pressure).

The last Earth mission that we'll talk about in this case study is the Soil Moisture Active Passive (SMAP) mission.

SOIL MOISTURE ACTIVE PASSIVE (SMAP) MISSION

NASA's Soil Moisture Active Passive (SMAP) mission is one of two current missions identified in the National Research Council's Decadal Survey for Earth Science study that are part of the *Tier 1* objective measurements required to better understand our planet over the next decade (the other Tier 1 mission is ICESAT-2).

> **PRIORITIES FOR THE NEXT DECADE OF EARTH MEASUREMENTS** In 2007, the United States National Research Council produced a study identifying the most important Earth-related measurements that the nation should focus its attention over the next decade. These national priority measurements are proposed as missions that should be flown and tier-based priorities for those missions (Tier 1, Tier 2, and so on). You can read more about the Earth science decadal study report at http://mng.bz/Lj24.

SMAP's main focus is on increasing the accuracy of freeze-thaw measurements, providing necessary information that will improve the overall measurements and predicative capabilities of regional water models.

The good news is that all of the aforementioned Earth science missions are in great shape: Tika's helping out their data systems!

12.2.2 *Using Tika within the ground data systems*

So, where does Tika fit in? All throughout the architecture of each of the aforementioned NASA Earth science missions! File management typically needs to both identify files for ingestion and extract metadata from those files. In addition, ingestion leverages Tika to help identify what files to pull down into the system (based on MIME type). Further, many of the science algorithms that are pipelined together as workflows require the ingestion of pipeline-produced data files and metadata. This information is provided by leveraging Tika to extract metadata and text from these data files, and to either send them for cataloging to a file management component or to marshal the extracted metadata to the next science algorithm, which leverages it to make some sort of decision (how to geolocate the data file, how to calibrate it, and so on).

So what's unique about each of these NASA Earth science missions? Typically the uniqueness comes from the areas shown in figure 12.5.

DIFFERENT DATA FILE TYPES

File types vary from mission to mission. For example, SMAP's data files and OCO's data files, though both formatted using the HDF5 standard, store vastly different data. OCO, stores vertical columns of computed CO_2, and thus stores matrices that represent those columns of data (recall chapter 8 to jog your memory about how information is stored in HDF5 files). On the other hand, data files from SMAP are radar-oriented, and may store data in matrices with different sizes, may use vectors with different names, or may choose some other representation supported by HDF. Tika is a huge help here in normalizing the HDF information extracted into a Tika `Metadata` object instance that can be introspected and transformed (recall chapter 6). This use case is shown in the upper-left portion of figure 12.5.

DIFFERENT PROCESSING ALGORITHMS AND WORKFLOWS

The NPP Sounder PEATE project tests and executes on the order of 5–10 science algorithms with vastly different control and data flow from that of OCO, for example, which uses on the order of 10–20 different science algorithms, arranged into different workflows. To support these differences, Tika helps to send metadata between each workflow task (a step in the overall pipeline) by using a common representation. This is depicted in the lower-/middle-right portion of figure 12.5.

COMPUTING RESOURCES

OCO's projected 100-node cluster and SMAP's similarly sized cluster that will be purchased are five orders of magnitude larger than that of the NPP Sounder PEATE execution environment, which consists of around 20 machines, individually networked and shared between several environments, as opposed to collectively partitioned and clustered together.

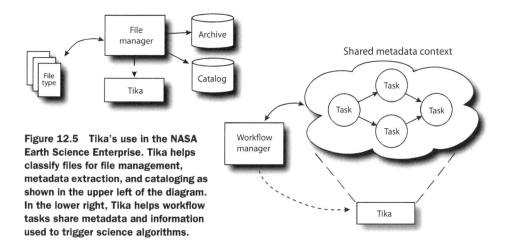

Figure 12.5   Tika's use in the NASA Earth Science Enterprise. Tika helps classify files for file management, metadata extraction, and cataloging as shown in the upper left of the diagram. In the lower right, Tika helps workflow tasks share metadata and information used to trigger science algorithms.

IDENTIFYING FILES FOR INGESTION AND THE OVERALL INGESTION PROCESS

Each mission requires different ancillary datasets and must pull this information from various sources. Tika saves the day here because we've been able to use its MIME identification system to automatically decide which files to pull down remotely, and to then decide how to extract metadata from those files and how to ingest them into the system. This is shown in the upper/middle portion of figure 12.5.

REQUIREMENTS FOR DATA DELIVERY AND DISSEMINATION

The missions all have their own requirements for dissemination to the public, for delivery to an archive such as a DAAC, and for long-term archival. These requirements and functions are supported by Tika, where it's used to augment metadata models that have already been captured by the processing system, add flags for data quality, and decide when the time is right to ship a data product (or set data products) to a DAAC or to the general scientific community. This is shown (partially) in the upper-left/middle portion of figure 12.5.

Tika has infected quite a number of areas within the walls of NASA as you've seen. We'll summarize lessons learned in the next section and get ready for the next case study!

12.3   Summary

We introduced you to two vastly different domains within NASA: the planetary domain, with its rich data model, and its search-focused virtual data system called PDS-D; and the Earth science domain, with its processing-centric family of Earth science data systems.

One of the major lessons learned from our experience using Tika at NASA is that large-scale data archival, processing, and dissemination almost always need the core capabilities that Tika provides along the road. MIME type identification of files was a huge help because we could leverage not just standards provided by organizations like IANA, but also the rigor and detail that NASA itself put into file naming conventions, file type identification, and documentation.

In addition, we've found that NASA data systems are metadata-centric, requiring rich descriptions of datasets as a front line of defense. Since the metadata is at a greatly reduced scale compared to the data (we're talking the difference between hundreds of kilobytes and hundreds of terabytes!), science users appreciate the ability to browse and identify the data they'd like to start crunching on, *before* they have to download it.

We hope that this case study has helped generate ideas in your mind regarding how to leverage Tika within your own data system, and what types of situations and needs arise when using Tika in data ingestion, archival, and dissemination. In the next case study, we'll introduce you another related (but entirely different) usage of Tika's abilities: in the realm of digital content management!

Content management
with Apache Jackrabbit

This chapter covers

- The Apache Jackrabbit Content Repository
- The use of Tika in Jackrabbit
- File detection and parsing for Jackrabbit WebDAV

Apache Jackrabbit, http://jackrabbit.apache.org, is a content repository that provides a rich storage layer on which to build content and document management systems like the ones we discussed earlier in chapter 9. Full-text search and WebDAV integration are two key features of a content repository. In this case study we'll learn how Jackrabbit uses Tika to help implement these features.

We'll start by briefly describing the key features of Apache Jackrabbit and the Content Repository for Java technology (JCR) API (http://www.jcp.org/en/jsr/detail?id=170) that it implements. Armed with this background, we'll then look deeper into how Jackrabbit's search feature uses a pool of Tika threads to achieve the illusion of being able to index arbitrarily large documents nearly in real time. We'll also look at how Tika's type detection feature is used to add smarts to Jackrabbit's WebDAV integration layer. We'll end this case study with a brief summary.

13.1   Introducing Apache Jackrabbit

Apache Jackrabbit is an implementation of a new special kind of a database called a *content repository*. Defined in Java Specification Requests (JSRs) 170 and 283, a content repository is a hierarchically organized storage engine that combines features from advanced file systems and relational databases.

Documents, files, records, and all other kinds of information entities are stored as *nodes* in the content tree inside a repository. Each node consists of any number of *properties* and child nodes. Properties contain numbers, strings, byte streams, or other types of data, including arrays of such values. Figure 13.1 shows how this content model looks in practice.

In addition to storing such hierarchical data, the content repository also makes it searchable, keeps track of past versions of content, sends notifications of changes, and supports a number of other features that make life easier for an application developer. As the reference implementation of JSR 170 and 283, Apache Jackrabbit implements all these features and more.

The most interesting features for this case study are full-text search and WebDAV integration. Jackrabbit uses an integrated Lucene search index to make all repository content, including binary properties, searchable as soon as it has been stored. The WebDAV integration lets users access and modify repository content over the web or to mount a repository as a part of their normal file systems. Tika is an integral part of these features, as we'll see in the next two sections.

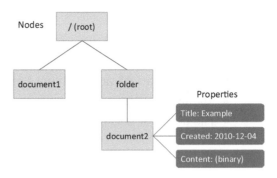

Figure 13.1   Example content in a content repository

13.2   The text extraction pool

One feature that separates a Jackrabbit content repository from a relational database is the ease by which it can handle normal files. You can drop digital documents such as PowerPoint presentations or PDFs into a content repository and have them searchable by content without any custom indexing setup. Let's see how Jackrabbit does this.

Whenever a node is added, modified, or removed in Jackrabbit, the integrated Lucene index is updated to match the change. If the node contains binary properties, the contents of those properties are extracted with Tika and added to the index as text. Since text extraction can be time-consuming for some documents, Jackrabbit uses a set of background threads for this purpose. This allows the index to be updated immediately during a save, and then reupdated as soon as the extracted text becomes available. Together these updates create an illusion of a super-fast index whose accuracy improves incrementally over time.

So how does this work in practice? When an index update is needed, new text extraction tasks are created for all binary properties and scheduled for execution by a pool of background threads. The essential Jackrabbit code for the text extraction task is shown next.

Listing 13.1 Background text extraction task in Jackrabbit

```
try {
    InputStream stream = value.getStream();          Use parse()
    try {                                          ❶ method
        parser.parse(stream, handler, metadata, context);
    } finally {
        stream.close();
    }                                              ❷ Catch
} catch (LinkageError e) {                            linkage errors
    // Capture and ignore                          ❸ Catch other errors
} catch (Throwable t) {                               or STOP event
    if (t != STOP) {
        log.debug("Failed to extract text.", t);
        setExtractedText("TextExtractionError");
        return;
    }
} finally {
    value.discard();
}                                                  ❹ Save
setExtractedText(handler.toString());                 extracted text
```

The code starts in ❶ with a standard use of the parse() method as described in chapter 5. The more interesting bits happen next. The first catch block ❷ takes care of silently ignoring problems caused by a deployment omitting some parser libraries, which is an easy way to customize and streamline an installation. The second block ❸ catches any other problems, including a special STOP exception that's sent by a specially instrumented ContentHandler instance to signal that up to a given maximum number of characters have already been extracted from the binary stream. The extraction process is terminated when the STOP event is received; otherwise an exception is logged and any extracted text is replaced with a TextExtractionError token to make such problems easy to locate within a repository. Finally in ❹ the extracted text is made available for use by the indexer.

Meanwhile, as the extraction task is running, the indexer first waits for a fraction of a second to see whether the extracted text is already available for use in the first index update. If not, the node is first indexed with an empty text extraction result and a new index update is scheduled for when the extraction task is complete. This way a new or updated document is immediately searchable by its nonbinary properties, and by the extracted full-text contents normally within a few seconds from when the changes were saved.

13.3   *Content-aware WebDAV*

WebDAV, or *Web-based Distributed Authoring and Versioning protocol* as it's officially called, is an extension of the Hypertext Transfer Protocol (HTTP) designed for remotely managing files and other resources on web servers. WebDAV makes a web server work like an advanced remote file system, and is thus a great match for a remote access protocol for a Jackrabbit content repository. Most operating systems have a Connect to Server feature that allows a WebDAV server to be mounted as a part of the file system, and many applications ship with integrated WebDAV support for accessing and modifying remote resources. Figure 13.2 shows the WebDAV mount feature in Windows Vista.

Jackrabbit implements WebDAV in two varieties: one focused on integration with traditional WebDAV clients like the ones mentioned here, and another more complicated one that makes nearly all repository functionality available to advanced remote clients. The traditional clients are often fairly simple, and Jackrabbit needs to do some extra work to fill in details that the clients fail to provide. This is where Tika comes in.

A classic use case for WebDAV integration in Jackrabbit is being able to copy files to and from the repository by dragging and dropping them in a normal file explorer window. Another use case is browsing and downloading these files using a web browser. The trouble is that the latter use case needs accurate media type information so that the browser can easily associate a file with the correct application, whereas the WebDAV mount features in operating systems typically don't provide such type information along with added files. The solution is to use Tika to automatically detect the types of incoming files.

If you remember the type detection examples from chapter 4, then the related Jackrabbit code in the following listing will look familiar.

Figure 13.2   Doing a WebDAV mount in Windows Vista

Listing 13.2   Automatic type detection in Jackrabbit

```
Metadata metadata = new Metadata();
if (ctx != null && ctx.getContentType() != null) {          ❶ Type hint
    metadata.set(                                              from client
            Metadata.CONTENT_TYPE, ctx.getContentType());
}
if (systemId != null) {                                     ❷ Name
    metadata.set(                                             of file
            Metadata.RESOURCE_NAME_KEY, systemId);
}
if (stream != null && !stream.markSupported()) {
    stream = new BufferedInputStream(stream);
}                                                           ❸ Detect
type = detector.detect(stream, metadata);                     type
```

The code takes advantage of the possible media type hint ❶ provided by the WebDAV client, the name of the uploaded file ❷, and the contents of the file itself ❸ to automatically detect its type. With this code in place, a user who copies a PDF document to the repository with no associated type information will be able to access it as a properly annotated `application/pdf` resource later on. Small touches like this are essential for a smooth user experience.

13.4   Summary

The purpose of a content repository like Apache Jackrabbit is to make it easy to manage all kinds of content, including collections of digital documents. To do this well, Jackrabbit needs a way to understand and look inside the documents stored in the repository. Tika is the perfect tool for this purpose.

We started this chapter with a brief introduction to Apache Jackrabbit and the content repository model. Then we looked at two ways in which Jackrabbit uses Tika. The first was text extraction for use with the Lucene-based search index in Jackrabbit, and the second was automatic type detection for smooth WebDAV integration.

The Jackrabbit content repository powers many high-end content management systems that are used for purposes ranging from large-scale digital asset management to high-profile web content management. Tika might already be there working behind the scenes when you next visit a large website!

This concludes our discussion of Tika in Apache Jackrabbit. Our next case study is also related to the management of digital assets, but in a different way than in a generic tool like Jackrabbit. Read on to find out how the National Cancer Institute uses Tika to help manage the vast amounts of data it collects.

14

Curating
cancer research data
with Tika

This chapter covers

- The Early Detection Research Network (EDRN) project
- Using Tika within EDRN curation
- Integrating Tika and Apache OODT

For more than 10 years, the goal of the National Cancer Institute's (NCI) Early Detection Research Network (EDRN) program has been to accelerate research into the identification and detection of *cancer biomarkers*, early indicators of disease.

Over the last three years, Tika has been assisting in that fight. Tika helps capture and curate mass spectrometry files, CSV files, PDF files, SAS files, and other data sets produced by lab instruments, analysis programs, and by EDRN investigators for further scientific research and role-based dissemination to the broader community. In this chapter, we'll explain how Tika has been used in EDRN's Catalog and Archive Service, or eCAS. Let's hop to it.

14.1   *The NCI Early Detection Research Network*

The National Cancer Institute's EDRN project has focused on the identification of cancer *biomarkers* for over a decade. Biomarkers are indicators of early onset of disease, and identifying accurate and precise methods for their detection is one of the EDRN's primary goals.

As part of the biomarker discovery process, EDRN collects many different types of data, ranging from information about biomarkers themselves (names, aliases, related organs, and so forth), to instrument-produced raw science data files, study protocols, and specimen information. We'll talk about these types in the next section.

14.1.1   *The EDRN data model*

EDRN's (simplified) data model is shown in figure 14.1. We'll discuss the relationships between each of the major data types and the relationships of these types to Tika. As we'll detail, Tika helps identify, sort, and extract metadata from EDRN's science data sets, shown in the middle of the figure.

In EDRN, research information about biomarkers, science data sets (collections of files produced by an instrument), and specimens (taken during some associated EDRN study), are all guided by common study information called a *protocol*. Protocols are led by principal investigators, potentially from multiple EDRN participating sites.

With that in mind, let's restrict our focus to the science data set portion of the EDRN data model, shown conveniently in the middle portion of figure 14.1. There are myriad science instruments in the EDRN, ranging from high-end mass spectrometers, to biospecimen catalog tools, to low-end microscopes. Each of these instruments produces data associated with some EDRN biomarker, and some EDRN study, and is of interest to the broader program.

This is where Tika comes in. The process of collecting, curating, annotating, and making these data sets available to the rest of the EDRN program is called *scientific data curation*, and we'll explain it in more detail in the next section.

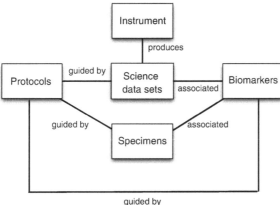

Figure 14.1   Simplified view of the EDRN data model, showing the relationship between protocols, specimens, science data sets, biomarkers, and instruments

14.1.2 Scientific data curation

More and more, the community at large is seeing the importance of data curation. Data curation involves the careful preparation of data for cataloging, archiving, and eventual dissemination to the external community. Just like librarians curate books that codify our collective knowledge, data curators (and the associated tools they use) do the same thing for data.

One of the key goals of the EDRN is to capture rich metadata and data that conforms to the EDRN data model described in figure 14.1. Specifically, EDRN investigators, program managers, and users want to query the system and determine the current state of progress on a particular biomarker or set of biomarkers. This includes answering questions such as the following:

- What publications have been generated for a particular EDRN biomarker?
- What associated science data files are available to help reproduce the experiments and results described in those publications?
- What protocols being studied have produced the most biomarkers?

In order to answer these questions, scientific data curation within the EDRN requires the creation of *linked data*, a term used to reference richly curated and annotated information captured by an information system.

The EDRN curation process is led by the EDRN biocurator, which sits between computer scientists and cancer researchers helping to capture needed information in a way that leverages the underlying technology but is also scientifically meaningful. Biocurators require the ability to perform both "lights-out" ingestion of day-to-day information, as well as carefully review and annotate that data with additional publication information, study and protocol information, and anything else that the biocurator deems useful to link to the existing EDRN datasets.

A key enabling technology in the EDRN curation process is Tika. Let's find out in more detail how Tika enables this functionality.

14.2 Integrating Tika

Within EDRN, we've built a system called *eCAS*, which stands for the *EDRN Catalog and Archive Service*. eCAS provides data curation services for the EDRN and builds upon Apache Tika (along with a number of other technologies, including the Apache OODT framework that we'll mention in an upcoming sidebar), as figure 14.2 and the ensuing discussion will show. The eCAS system is responsible for providing the necessary software to allow rich metadata and information to be extracted and captured, and to be made available to the rest of the EDRN.

> **IT'S NOT JUST FOR CURATING NASA DATA; IT WORKS FOR BIOMARKERS TOO!** Apache OODT (http://oodt.apache.org) is the first NASA project to be contributed to and hosted at the Apache Software Foundation. OODT includes a number of components that deal with file management, workflow management, resource management, and crawling and archiving sets of files and metadata. It's the

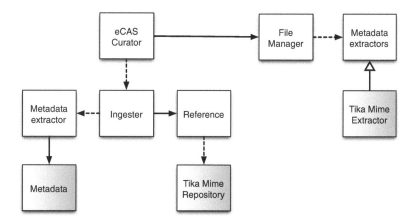

Figure 14.2 EDRN's eCAS architecture. The components on the left side of the diagram use Tika to prepare data for ingestion into a file manager. The components on the right side of the diagram use Tika to classify incoming files. The components that are directly implemented by Tika are shaded in grey.

perfect bootstrapping framework to feed information to Tika. It's a vast framework though, so much so that we can't go into detail on it here. A careful description of OODT in itself is probably the topic of a forthcoming book.

The first step in EDRN data curation is the extraction of metadata before ingestion.

14.2.1 Metadata extraction

EDRN curators need the ability to perform metadata extraction at various stages throughout the data lifecycle. Initially, data files may be delivered in two methodologies: offline or online. Offline methods include hard disks, CD/DVD ROMs, and so forth. Online methods include electronic protocols such as WebDAV and FTP. Once the data arrives at the EDRN, the *eCAS Curator* provides a view into the staging area, as shown in the leftmost portion of figure 14.3.

One of the most important parts about data curation in EDRN is capturing rich metadata that can be used to later discover what information is available on a particular EDRN biomarker. For this purpose, we've constructed a curation system called eCAS Curator, a webapp (we'll show you what it looks like later in the chapter) that orchestrates the curation process as shown in figure 14.2. eCAS Curator invokes an *Ingester* component that's responsible for extraction of metadata from incoming EDRN files delivered from external sites and investigators. The Ingester is also responsible for generation of file location information, called *references*.

Tika assists in the eCAS curation process in two ways. First, Tika helps extract additional client-side metadata on a per-file basis, including file naming convention metadata (recall chapter 8) and other information that becomes useful later during the curation process. This is depicted in the left side of figures 14.2 and 14.3 with the `Metadata` class, extracted from files by Tika. After assisting with metadata extraction,

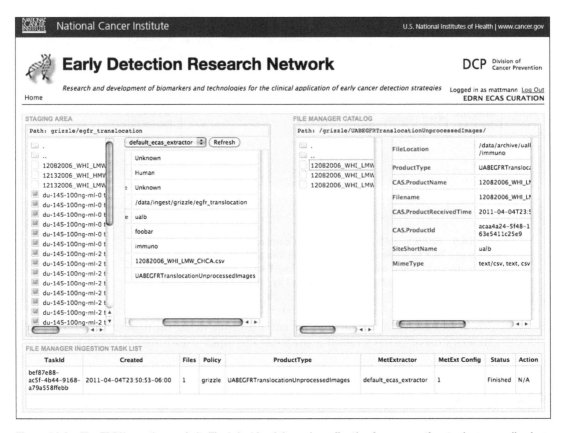

Figure 14.3   The EDRN curation cockpit. The left side of the web application focuses on the staging area, allowing a curator to perform metadata extraction and manipulation. The right side of the webapp deals with data curation and ingestion in the File Manager component, allowing for classification of different file types. Most of the underlying extraction and classification functionality is driven by Tika.

Tika is also used to classify files to be ingested. This is performed using the `Tika Mime Repository` shown in the middle of figure 14.2. The `Reference` class uses Tika to determine the underlying MIME type classification for files collected during the curation process. A snippet of code extracted from Apache OODT's `Reference` class (part of the File Manager module) is shown next.

Listing 14.1   Detecting file types prior to ingestion in the eCAS system

```
public class Reference {
    private String origReference = null;
     private String dataStoreReference = null;
    private long fileSize = 0L;
    private MimeType mimeType = null;
    private static MimeTypes mimeTypeRepository;

    static {
        try {
```

❶ **Properties describing reference**

```
        mimeTypeRepository = MimeTypesFactory.create(
        new FileInputStream(new File(PathUtils
                .replaceEnvVariables(System.
                    getProperty(
     "org.apache.oodt.cas.filemgr.mime.type.repository",
                        "mime-types.xml"))))));
      } catch (Exception e){
        mimeTypeRepository = TikaConfig.
        getDefaultConfig().
        getMimeRepository();
      }
  }

  public Reference(String origRef, String dataRef, long size) {
      origReference = origRef;
      dataStoreReference = dataRef;
      fileSize = size;
      try {
          this.mimeType = mimeTypeRepository
                  .getMimeType(new URL(origRef));
       } catch (MalformedURLException e) {
         e.printStackTrace();
      }

   }
}
```

❷ **Statically initialize Tika**

❸ **Detect file type**

The code in listing 14.1 illustrates that all eCAS `Reference` class implementations store a Tika `MimeType` used to capture the MIME type, along with its fully qualified name (recall chapter 4), illustrated in ❶. This information is detected when the `Reference` class constructor is called in ❸. The `Reference` class tries to load a user-specified Tika MIME type configuration file in ❷ and if it can't be found for whatever reason, then Tika's default MIME type repo is utilized. Though OODT provides other constructors for the `Reference` class, this auto-detect constructor is leveraged during the EDRN ingestion process.

The middle of figure 14.2 depicts the `File Manager` component, responsible for taking the extracted `Metadata` and `Reference` information and cataloging and archiving it. Part of this process involves the creation of derived metadata (final file locations, data versions, file received time, and so on) that's best generated on the server side. Another part of this process involves determining and classifying data sets, a process that involves Tika and that we'll describe in the next section.

14.2.2 *MIME type identification and classification*

Tika helps the EDRN eCAS system classify and organize collected data files based on more granular MIME types as well as file collection types called *data sets* in EDRN terminology.

To compute server-side `Metadata`, Tika is also leveraged as shown in the right side of figure 14.2 with the `Tika Mime Extractor` component. This server-side metadata extractor makes the extracted MIME type information searchable in the underlying

File Manager catalog, breaking the MIME type down into its primary (text in text/html) and subtype (html in text/html) in addition to cataloging its full form (text/html). This functionality is shown in the following listing.

Listing 14.2   **Making extracted MIME information available for search and retrieval**

```
public class MimeTypeExtractor extends AbstractFilemgrMetExtractor {

    public Metadata doExtract(Product product, Metadata met)
            throws MetExtractionException {
        Metadata extractMet = new Metadata();
        merge(met, extractMet);

        if (product.getProductStructure().equals
        (Product.STRUCTURE_FLAT)) {
            Reference prodRef = (Reference) product.
            getProductReferences().get(                      ❶ Gets first
                    0);                                          product reference

            extractMet.addMetadata(MIME_TYPE, prodRef.
            getMimeType().getName());
            extractMet.addMetadata(MIME_TYPE, prodRef.
            getMimeType()
                                                            ❷ Add full, primary, and
                .getType().getType());                         subtypes to catalog

            extractMet.addMetadata(MIME_TYPE, prodRef.
            getMimeType()
                    .getType().getSubtype());
        }

        return extractMet;
    }
}
```

Appending the full, primary, and subtypes to the extractMet variable as shown in listing 14.2 allows this information to flow through to the underlying File Manager catalog used by eCAS. Also, allowing the MIME type to be broken up into subparts allows EDRN users to search for specific kinds of primary files. For example, you could search for all text files associated with a particular biomarker, while retaining the flexibility to drill down into specifics such as subfile categories and data set types. To perform this functionality, during extraction, the Product class and its first Reference instance are looked up as shown in ❶. After locating the first ProductReference instance, the MIME type information is added as shown in ❷.

Besides driving search and display of metadata, the MIME information extracted by Tika is also used to display download links to EDRN data files, and to determine whether the underlying file is capable of being displayed by the browser (in case the primary type is image), versus directly streaming the data file back to the user from the browser link.

At this point, we've covered all of the primary areas where Tika has helped out in the EDRN. Let's review the chapter.

14.3 *Summary*

We explained the US National Cancer Institute's Early Detection Research Network (EDRN) project, and how the goal of the project is to develop accurate and precise means of identifying cancer biomarkers, early indicators of disease.

Part of the identification process involves understanding the types of data made available within the EDRN, ranging from specimens collected during a protocol or study, data sets associated with instruments that operate on those specimens, biomarker information providing an up-to-date look into the research progress within EDRN, and PI (principal investigator) and investigator information used to track who's researching what and how far they are.

The system within EDRN that allows for the capture, preparation, and dissemination of EDRN science data files is the EDRN Catalog and Archive Service. eCAS heavily leverages Tika to provide needed functionality, including file type classification, metadata extraction (both client- and server-side), search, and data download.

We explained each of these areas of eCAS in detail and described where and how Tika was used to implement key eCAS functionality.

We've made it to the top of the hill. Only one more chapter to go, and it's fitting that it begins where the book itself began—with a classic search engine example!

IG 978 5379

15
The classic search engine example

This chapter covers

- Bixo Labs and the Public Terabyte Dataset Project
- Bixo's crawler that uses Tika
- Charset detection and language identification with Tika

What better way to close out the book then the way we started it—with a classic search engine example?

You're in for a treat. We interviewed Ken Krugler and his team from Bixo labs about their recent *Public Terabyte Dataset Project*, http://mng.bz/gYOt, and how Tika was a core component of a large-scale series of tests that helped shed some light on variations between languages, charsets, and other content available on the internet.

This chapter will show you even more of Tika in action, especially how you can leverage Tika inside of a workflow system such as Cascading, which is built on top of Hadoop to analyze a representative (by today's standards) data set that many other internet researchers are also exploring. The tests run by Bixo labs that we'll describe in the rest of the chapter should identify areas of further refinement in Tika, particularly in charset detection and language identification (recall chapter 7). Heck, they may even motivate you to get involved in improving Tika and working within the community.

Let's hear more about it!

15.1 The Public Terabyte Dataset Project

The web contains a staggering amount of useful source data for a variety of interesting programming projects (for example, analyzing the geographical distribution of Chinese restaurants in the United States, as shown in figure 15.1). In order to make use of that data, you must enumerate a target set of URLs, make connections to each web server, and then individually download each page of content. Web crawlers are employed to automate this web mining process, but the complexity of developing a web crawler or even using an existing web crawling tool requires a large time investment before any work can be done to process the data collected.

In 2010, Bixo Labs, Inc., Amazon Web Services, and Concurrent, Inc., decided to sponsor a large-scale crawl of the top 1–2 million web domains, based on traffic from clients in the United States. The goal was to fetch approximately 100–500 million pages from these domains and then put the content into the public domain on Amazon's S3, in a format that would be easy to import into other applications, particularly those using Hadoop for scalability. This Public Terabyte Dataset would therefore constitute a very large corpus of both high value and relatively easily accessible web content.

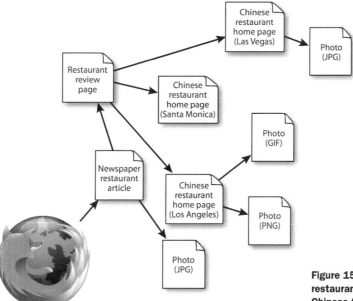

Figure 15.1 Searching the web for restaurant reviews discussing Chinese food by geographic location

Although most web content is delivered in HTML, a great deal of potentially useful content is available in other formats such as Microsoft Word, Adobe Portable Document Format (PDF), and so on. Parsing this web content to extract the text (and graphics) after it's fetched makes the resulting data set much more useful than it would be in its raw form. Tika provides an attractive architecture for parsing arbitrary web content because its `AutoDetectParser` feature (recall chapter 5) automates the process of selecting an appropriate parser for each fetched document.

In addition, an essential part of any web crawler is its ability to collect outbound links from each fetched page and then add the target URLs to a database that it'll use for subsequent content fetching. The Tika `HtmlParser` (recall the discussion of customizing parts of this component in chapter 8) also provides excellent support for link extraction while each page is being processed.

Now that we have some background on the Public Terabyte Dataset Project, we'll explain a bit about Bixo, a company building software focused on exploiting such a corpus.

15.2 *The Bixo web crawler*

Bixo (see http://openbixo.org/) is an open source web mining toolkit based on Hadoop, the dominant open source implementation of the MapReduce algorithm. Bixo uses the *Cascading* open source project (see http://www.cascading.org/) to define the web crawling workflow. The use of Cascading allows Bixo to focus on the mechanics of web crawling and the associated data flow rather than Hadoop/ MapReduce implementation details.

Cascading provides a rich API for defining and implementing scale-free and fault-tolerant data processing workflows on a Hadoop cluster. The Cascading workflow model is one of operations that are connected via "pipes," much like classic Unix tools. Bixo consists of a number of Cascading operations and subassemblies, which can be combined to form a data processing workflow that (typically) starts with a set of URLs to be fetched and ends with some results extracted from parsed HTML pages. The entire Bixo workflow is shown in figure 15.2.

The `Fetch` subassembly is the component where the heavy lifting is done. URLs enter via the input data pipe, and its two tail (results) pipes emit the raw fetched content and status information (such as whether the fetch was successful or failed due to a particular transient or permanent error condition).

The `Parse` subassembly is used to process the raw fetched content. As mentioned, it uses Tika to handle the details of extracting text from various formats and to help extract outbound links.

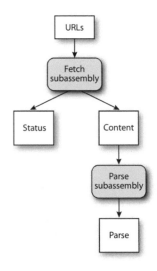

Figure 15.2 Bixo data flow

Bixo also takes care to crawl in a "polite" manner, honoring the directives in each web server's `robots.txt` file (a file specifying areas of the website to be excluded from crawling, how long to wait after completing a small set of requests to the web server, and so forth). Pages with `noarchive` HTML meta tags are also automatically excluded from the data set.

15.2.1 *Parsing fetched documents*

When Bixo was first developed, the team considered incorporating Nutch's complete parsing architecture. But they were pleased to discover that Tika provided most of the required support, eliminating the hassle of maintaining such a large, complex body of code and keeping it synchronized with the Nutch project. Since then, the folks at Bixo have been encouraged to see Tika adopted by both Nutch and Apache Droids, as this can only help to improve Tika's stability and performance, as well as support for features of particular interest to crawler developers (such as language detection, which you read about in chapter 7).

> **SPREADING THE WEALTH** Apache Nutch was the progenitor of many of the modern popular open source web and big data technologies, including most notably Apache Hadoop, Droids, and Tika. The ability to use these descendants without having to pull in all of the Nutch core has greatly increased not only the individual user bases of Hadoop, Droids, and Tika, but, Nutch's as well.

Most web pages fall short of compliance with any HTML standard, and so web browsers are extremely forgiving when displaying content. Tika's `HTMLParser` makes use of the TagSoup software library to perform the actual parsing, and TagSoup's ability to handle and clean up badly broken HTML documents is essential when parsing web content. Because a web server can also return an arbitrarily long document, Bixo is configured to abort the fetch after a user-configured limit (such as 128 KB of text). Accordingly, TagSoup's forgiving nature is also important in collecting content from such truncated pages.

Bixo uses Tika's `TeeContentHandler` to employ two separate `ContentHandlers` simultaneously: one to extract the content itself and another to extract outbound links, as demonstrated in the following listing. If content language detection is desired, Tika's `ProfilingHandler` that you might recall from chapter 7 can be used simultaneously as well.

Listing 15.1 Linking together link extraction and language detection

```
TeeContentHandler teeContentHdlr;
ProfilingHandler profilingHdlr = null;                    ❶ For language
                                                            detection
if (extractLanguage) {
    profilingHdlr = new ProfilingHandler();

    teeContentHandler = new TeeContentHandler(contentHdlr, linkHdlr,
```

```
        profilingHdlr);

} else {
        teeContentHdlr = new TeeContentHandler(contentHdlr, linkHdlr);
}

parser.parse(input, teeContentHdlr, metadata, makeParseContext());
```

❶ Extract links
❷ and language

❸ Just
    extract links

If language detection is desired, Bixo uses the `ProfilingHandler` as shown in ❶. The `ProfilingHandler` is used to hand off SAX events containing the text extracted by Tika to the language detection mechanism (remember this from chapter 7). Then the `TeeContentHandler` joins the `ProfilingHandler` to the existing `LinkHandler` shown in ❷. If language detection isn't desired, Bixo joins the `LinkHandler` to extract links from the existing content handler stream as shown in ❸.

Although not used directly for the Public Terabyte Dataset Project, Tika's `Boiler-pipeContentHandler` can be useful for focusing on the meat of each HTML page by ignoring banner advertisements and navigation controls that typically appear in the header, footer, and margin areas.

Parsing is always a relatively CPU-intensive operation, especially when compared with other jobs in a Bixo workflow. For example, fetch performance tends to be I/O bound (say, by the bandwidth of the cluster's internet connection and the constraints imposed by polite fetching), so it can be accomplished easily with a small army of relatively inexpensive machines. We found instead that parsing was best accomplished using a cluster of higher-end machines (dual-core CPUs with 7.5 GB of RAM, aka m1.large instances in Amazon's EC2 environment). Despite the best efforts of the Tika development community, arbitrary web content sometimes causes a parser to hang. Accordingly, Bixo runs the Tika parsers in a separate thread via a `TikaCallable` object whose `FutureTask` will attempt to abort the parsing thread after a user-configured time limit has expired (say, 30 seconds). Unfortunately, it's difficult to reliably terminate parsing threads. Note that there's an outstanding JIRA issue (TIKA-456) to further insulate the client application from such zombie threads. Jukka Zitting has also developed a way to perform Tika parsing within a separate child JVM that could be killed off completely if necessary.

In order for TagSoup to successfully parse HTML content, the encoding of the text stream must also be provided. Although the HTML 5 specification states that clients should trust any Content-Encoding response headers returned by the web server, we've found that Tika's "trust but verify" approach is far more robust when faced with arbitrary web content. Bixo puts the Content-Type and Content-Language from the server response headers into the metadata it passes to Tika. Tika first searches the initial 8 KB of the content for <meta> tags with Content-Type and charset attributes. If the charset isn't found in the <meta> tags, it uses its `CharsetDetector` (along with any hints from the server response header) to pick the best charset, using statistical analysis of short character sequences.

Next, we'll hear about an interesting analysis result we arrived at directly as a benefit of using Tika in the Public Terabyte Dataset Project. Yes, this example is more than just cool technology—it's also produced a genuine scientific result that will be used to further improve charset detection mechanisms within the domain of internet-scale web crawling. Read on to find out!

15.2.2 Validating Tika's charset detection

As an interesting dataset use case, we took a sample set of several thousand pages that each provided the charset via <meta> tags, and then examined the accuracy of the Tika CharsetDetector (we assumed that the charset provided in the <meta> tags was correct.) The results are summarized in figure 15.3.

It would be ideal if the most common character sets (particularly UTF-8) also enjoyed the highest detection accuracy, but unfortunately this wasn't the case as indicated in figure 15.3. Instead, there seem to be significant biases in the Tika Charset-Detector toward unusual character sets. For example, many UTF-8 pages were incorrectly classified as gb2312. We hope that future analysis using the full Public Terabyte Dataset will help support efforts to improve Tika's character set detection support. Similar analysis could be performed to diagnose and improve Tika's language detection support, which typically provides even poorer results despite requiring a great deal of extra processing time.

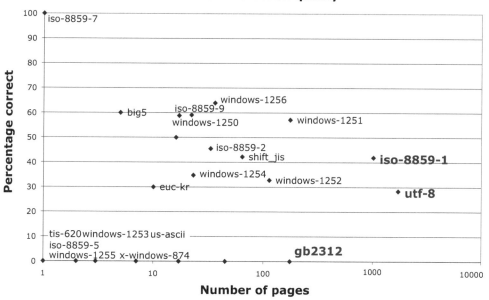

Figure 15.3   Evaluating Tika's charset detection with a web-scale data set

15.3 Summary

We hope you've enjoyed hearing about the way in which Bixo Labs, Inc., Amazon Web Services, and Concurrent, Inc., leveraged Tika to generate the public internet-scale web dataset called the Public Terabyte Dataset Project. To date, they've already produced an interesting scientific result, and we anticipate this result will help further efforts in improving the Tika system, especially in the areas of charset support and language detection.

To summarize, we heard about

1 The goal of the Public Terabyte Dataset Project: to build a semi-processed web-scale dataset where the text and links have been pre-extracted, making the data more easily processed and amenable to analysis.
2 The Bixo web crawler, and its layering on top of technologies like Tika, Hadoop, and Cascading. We heard about the Bixo crawler workflow, and how it separates out the fetching and the parsing steps.
3 How Bixo's web crawler allows link extraction and language detection via Tika.
4 An interesting real-world science result demonstrating the need for improvement in Tika's charset detection mechanism, especially on not-so-common character sets.

We'd also like to acknowledge you for sticking with us to the end. The development of Tika has been a tremendously challenging, intellectually stimulating body of work over the past five years, and describing it here over the past 15 chapters has been a blast. We hope you've had as much fun as we have and that you find Tika truly useful in your own software development. Stop by the Author Online forum or the user@tika.apache.org or dev@tika.apache.org Apache mailing lists and share your experiences with the rest of the community!

appendix A
Tika quick reference

All the key interfaces in Tika were described in detail earlier in this book and their Javadocs are all available online, but it's often useful to have a quick reference for looking up some of the more commonly used functionality. This appendix answers that need by providing a summary of the key parts of the Tika API.

A.1 *Tika facade*

As discussed in chapter 2 and later in this book, the `org.apache.tika.Tika` facade class is designed to make simple Tika use cases as easy to use as possible. The facade class supports the methods shown in table A.1.

Table A.1 Key methods of the Tika facade class

Method	Description
`detect(...)`	Returns the automatically detected media type of the given document. The return value is a string like `application/pdf`.
`parse(...)`	Parses the given document and returns the extracted plain text content. The return value is a `java.io.Reader` instance and the parsing happens in a background thread while the text stream is read.
`parseToString(...)`	Parses the given document and returns the extracted plain text content. The return value is a string whose length is limited by default to avoid memory issues with large documents.
`setMaxStringLength(int)`	Sets the maximum length of the `parseToString` return value.

The type detection and text extraction methods accept the document to be processed in various different ways. Table A.2 lists the most common ways of specifying a document.

Table A.2   Document arguments to the `Tika` facade methods

Argument type	Description
`java.io.InputStream`	The document is read from the given byte stream. You can also optionally specify an explicit `Metadata` instance to be used along with the document stream.
`java.io.File`	The document is read from the given file. The filename and other file metadata are passed along with the document stream.
`java.net.URL`	The document is read from the given URL. The possible filename at the end of the URL and any content type and other metadata hints included in the access protocol are passed along with the document stream.

A.2   Command-line options

The `tika-app` runnable JAR file allows you to use Tika as a command-line tool. To use this jar, start it as follows:

```
java -jar tika-app.jar [options] [file|URL]
```

The most commonly used command-line options are summarized in table A.3.

Table A.3   Tika command-line options

Option	Description
`--xml` or `-x`	Outputs the extracted document content as XHTML. This is the default mode.
`--text` or `-t`	Outputs the extracted document content as plain text.
`--metadata` or `-m`	Outputs the extracted document metadata using a simple `key: value` format.
`--json` or `-j`	Outputs the extracted document metadata as a JSON object.
`--detect` or `-d`	Outputs only the detected document type.
`--gui` or `-g`	Starts the Tika GUI. Useful for quick manual testing or experimentation.
`--help` or `-?`	Prints a detailed listing of all the available command-line options.

A.3   ContentHandler utilities

As discussed in chapter 5, the document content extracted by a parser is returned as XHTML SAX events to the client application. Handling these events can be complicated at times, so Tika provides a number of utility classes in the `org.apache.tika` `.sax` package for various different purposes. Table A.4 summarizes the most commonly used utility classes.

Table A.4   `ContentHandler` utility classes

Class	Description
BodyContentHandler	Captures the contents of the `<body>` tag of the incoming XHTML document and writes it to another `ContentHandler` instance, a character or a byte stream, or to an internal string buffer that can be accessed using the `toString()` method.
LinkContentHandler	Collects all links from the incoming XHTML document. The collected links are available as a list of `Link` records from the `getLinks()` method.
TeeContentHandler	Forwards the incoming XHTML document to any number of `ContentHandler` instances. Useful when you want to, for example, combine link extraction with other types of content processing.
XHTMLContentHandler	Utility class used by `Parser` implementations to make it easier to produce valid and complete XHTML output.

appendix B
Supported metadata keys

Here's a quick reference for the metadata models and keys that are supported in the latest version of Tika, as of 1.0. The models are briefly described, as are the metadata keys associated with them. The keys are found in the Tika code package `org.apache.tika.metadata` and its associated classes.

B.1   Climate Forecast

The Climate Forecast (CF) metadata model is used to describe climate-relevant data stored in NetCDF files. Tika currently supports a subset of the metadata keys:

ACKNOWLEDGEMENT—An acknowledgment that is traditionally added describing the sponsor and contributors to the generation of the associated data file.

COMMAND_LINE—The command line used to generate this data.

COMMENT—Free-text comments from the data provider.

CONTACT—Information such as email, phone, address, and so on for getting more information about this file.

CONVENTIONS—Identifies the specific CF conventions that are applied to this data file.

EXPERIMENT_ID—A unique identifier typically associated with the model experiment that produced this file.

HISTORY—Lineage or processing history for this file.

INSTITUTION—The institution that generated this file.

MODEL_NAME_ENGLISH—An English name describing the climate model that generated this file.

PROGRAM_ID—The funding program or agency that generated this model output file.

PROJECT_ID—The specific project (part of a program) that generated this file.

REALIZATION—Identifies the parameters and variables that this file realizes.

REFERENCES—Any associated references, including URLs, papers, and so forth that describe the science behind this file.

SOURCE—A pointer to the software, the system, the institution, or the contact that generated this file.

TABLE_ID—The identifier of an associated table that this climate file was generated from.

B.2 Creative Commons

A set of basic descriptive elements for software produced using Creative Commons Licenses. You can read more about Creative Commons Metadata at http://wiki .creativecommons.org/Metadata.

LICENSE_LOCATION—The local (non-URL) location of the Creative Commons License that is applied to this content.

LICENSE_URL—The URL location of the Creative Commons License that is applied to this content.

WORK_TYPE—The type of work that the Creative Commons License applies to, one (or more) of Text, Still Image, Moving Image, Interactive Resource, Sound, or Other.

B.3 Dublin Core

A set of 15–20 (depending on the version) metadata elements that are said to describe "any electronic resource." See http://dublincore.org/documents/dcmi-terms/ for more information.

CONTRIBUTOR—An entity responsible for making contributions to the resource.

COVERAGE—The spatial or temporal topic of the resource, the spatial applicability of the resource, or the jurisdiction under which the resource is relevant.

CREATOR—An entity primarily responsible for making the resource.

DATE—A point or period of time associated with an event in the lifecycle of the resource.

DESCRIPTION—An account of the resource.

FORMAT—The file format, physical medium, or dimensions of the resource.

IDENTIFIER—An unambiguous reference to the resource within a given context.

LANGUAGE—A language of the resource.

MODIFIED—Date on which the resource was changed.

PUBLISHER—An entity responsible for making the resource available.

RELATION—A related resource.

RIGHTS—Information about rights held in and over the resource.

REFERENCES—A related resource that is referenced, cited, or otherwise pointed to by the described resource.

SOURCE—A related resource from which the described resource is derived.

SUBJECT—The topic of the resource.

TITLE—A name given to the resource.

TYPE—The nature or genre of the resource.

B.4 Geographic metadata

A set of basic geographic metadata to describe the spatial extent of content.

ALTITUDE—The altitude, measured in some units (height, millibars, and so on) of this content at the time it was generated.

LATITUDE—The angular distance of a place north or south of the earth's equator, usually expressed in degrees and minutes.

LONGITUDE—The angular distance of a place east or west of the meridian at Greenwich, England, or west of the standard meridian of a celestial object, usually expressed in degrees and minutes.

B.5   HTTP headers

HTTP metadata headers as specified in RFC 2616 (http://mng.bz/vdx0 and http://mng.bz/QWw7).

CONTENT_DISPOSITION—A means for the origin server to suggest a default filename if the user requests that the content be saved to a file.

CONTENT_ENCODING—Defines how to decode an HTTP payload's content, and may affect the underlying media type.

CONTENT_LANGUAGE—Specification of the language of the underlying HTTP content.

CONTENT_LENGTH—A length specified in octets (8-bit bytes) for the underlying HTTP content.

CONTENT_LOCATION—An alternate location for the returned data.

CONTENT_MD5—A Base64-encoded binary MD5 sum of the content of the response.

CONTENT_TYPE—The mime type of this content.

LAST_MODIFIED—The last modified date for the requested object, in RFC 2822 format.

LOCATION—Used in redirection, or when a new resource has been created.

B.6   Microsoft Office

Metadata fields captured in standard Microsoft Office document formats like Word, Excel, and PowerPoint, as specified at http://msdn.microsoft.com/en-us/library/cc313118%28v=office.1.2%29.aspx.

APPLICATION_NAME—The MS Office application that generated this file.

APPLICATION_VERSION—The version identifier of the MS Office application that generated this file.

AUTHOR—The original author of this MS Office file.

CATEGORY—A categorical classification of this MS Office file.

CHARACTER_COUNT—The number of characters present in this MS Office file, without spaces.

CHARACTER_COUNT_WITH_SPACES—The number of characters present in this MS Office file, with spaces.

COMPANY—The company registration information for the MS Office application that generated this file.

CONTENT_STATUS—The status of this content, for example draft, in-review, and so on.

CREATION_DATE—The date on which this file was created.

EDIT_TIME—The last time that this file was edited.

KEYWORDS—Free-text comments about this file, specified by the document creator.

LAST_AUTHOR—The username of the last person or software to modify this file.

LAST_PRINTED—The last date on which this file was printed.

LAST_SAVED—The last date on which this file was saved.

LINE_COUNT—The number of lines in this file.

MANAGER—The manager of the project for which this file was created, as specified by the document author/owner in the particular MS Office application.

NOTES—Free-text comments from the author regarding this file.

PAGE_COUNT—The number of pages for this file.

PARAGRAPH_COUNT—The number of paragraphs present in the text portions of this file.

PRESENTATION_FORMAT—For MS Office Power Point files, the presentation style: slideshow, and so forth.

REVISION_NUMBER—The revision number for this particular file.

SECURITY—Groups, rights, and permissions for modifying, reading and accessing this file.

SLIDE_COUNT—For MS Office PowerPoint files, the number of slides present in this file.

TEMPLATE—Indicates the template (if any) applied to this file.

TOTAL_TIME—Total time spent modifying/editing/creating content for this file.

WORD_COUNT—The number of words present in this file.

B.7 Message (email)

A set of metadata fields related to email messaging content, as specified in http://www.ietf.org/rfc/rfc2822.txt.

MESSAGE_BCC—An email address to blind carbon copy (BCC) this particular email message.

MESSAGE_CC—An email address to carbon copy a recipient of this email content.

MESSAGE_FROM—Specifies the From email address of the sender of this email message.

MESSAGE_RECIPIENT_ADDRESS—The actual recipient of this email message.

MESSAGE_TO—The intended recipient of this email message.

B.8 TIFF (Image)

TIFF image metadata as specified in http://mng.bz/I2kQ and Exchangeable image file format (EXIF) metadata as specified at http://mng.bz/sp5V, http://www.exif.org/Exif2-2.PDF, http://en.wikipedia.org/wiki/F-number and http://mng.bz/xh0I.

BITS_PER_SAMPLE—Number of bits per component.

EQUIPMENT_MAKE—The scanner manufacturer.

EQUIPMENT_MODEL—The scanner model name or number.

EXPOSURE_TIME—Exposure time, given in seconds (sec).

FLASH_FIRED—This tag is recorded when an image is taken using a strobe light (flash).

FOCAL_LENGTH—The actual focal length of the lens, in mm. Conversion is not made to the focal length of a 35 mm film camera.

F_NUMBER—In optics, the f-number (sometimes called focal ratio, f-ratio, f-stop, or relative aperture) of an optical system expresses the diameter of the entrance pupil in terms of the focal length of the lens.

IMAGE_LENGTH—The number of rows of image data. In JPEG compressed data, a JPEG marker is used instead of this tag.

IMAGE_WIDTH—The number of columns of image data, equal to the number of pixels per row. In JPEG compressed data, a JPEG marker is used instead of this tag.

ISO_SPEED_RATINGS—Indicates the ISO Speed and ISO Latitude of the camera or input device as specified in ISO 12232.

ORIENTATION—The image orientation viewed in terms of rows and columns.

ORIGINAL_DATE—Original date when the image was taken.

RESOLUTION_HORIZONTAL—The horizontal resolution of the camera focal plane.

RESOLUTION_UNIT—The unit image resolution is measured in (ExifXResolution and ExifYResolution).

RESOLUTION_VERTICAL—The vertical resolution of the image.

SAMPLES_PER_PIXEL—The number of components (channels) in one pixel.

SOFTWARE—The name of the software that created this image.

index

RELATED MANNING TITLES

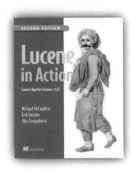

Lucene in Action, Second Edition
by Michael McCandless, Erik Hatcher, and
   Otis Gospodnetić

   ISBN: 978-1-933988-17-7
   532 pages, $49.99
   July 2010

Hadoop in Action
by Chuck Lam

   ISBN: 978-1-935182-19-1
   336 pages, $44.99
   December 2010

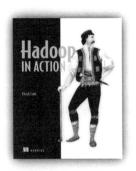

Mahout in Action
by Sean Owen, Robin Anil, Ted Dunning,
   and Ellen Friedman

   ISBN: 978-1-935182-68-9
   416 pages, $44.99
   October 2011

MongoDB in Action
by Kyle Banker

   ISBN: 978-1-935182-87-0
   375 pages, $44.99
   December 2011

For ordering information go to www.manning.com